The summer of 1945 is both the beginning and end of many things for Ellis Carpenter. Ellis, who's somewhere between being a girl and an adult in these last months of World War II, finds herself struggling with her feelings about both the good things and the bad things that happen that year.

A long war is nearly over—all the more reason to celebrate the coming Fourth of July as never before. But Les McConagy, the soldier–hero of Wissining, Pennsylvania, and a special person to Ellis, is reported missing in action, so how can anyone really have fun?

So much did happen that year—or perhaps it just seems that way to Ellis. But somehow she manages to survive everything from the results of the Citizenship Award Contest to a death dare on the rafters of Sibby's father's barn. And when her best friends, Jules and Sam, go to a dance with her but act different around the girls who wear sweet-smelling cologne and fancy dresses and who lets boys dance close, Ellis survives that, too!

As Ellis' courage and maturity are put to the test, she learns to lock away her love and memories of things ended as a way of opening up more love for beginnings. *Don't Sit Under the Apple Tree* is a nostalgic and moving story which will say many different things to many readers.

Don't Sit Under the Apple Tree

ROBIN F. BRANCATO

Alfred A. Knopf   *New York*

For John, Chris and Greg

Don't Sit Under
the Apple Tree

One

"Hey, Ellis! Hey—Ellie-Belly," Sam shouted, "you can't *prove* Hitler's dead!"

"He *is*," I said. "It was in the newspapers!" Sam might be right, though, I had to admit. Some people were saying that maybe Hitler, the German dictator, had gotten away.

The weather was clearing as we walked to school past the wide lawns of the Barth mansion and on toward the playground. There was something special in the air— maybe it was the excitement of V-E Day, or maybe it was just the perfume of lilac bushes. The morning rain had washed earthworms onto the sidewalk and I walked on tiptoe so I wouldn't step on any.

"Hey, Ellis!" Sam cried. Jumping out from behind a hedge, he picked up an earthworm and dangled it in my direction. "Ellis," he snorted, "where'd you get your dumb name, anyway? That's no girl's name!"

"I got it from Miss Mary Ellis," I said. "She was a good friend of my family, and my grandmother says Mary Ellis was a courageous person."

"They gave her name to the wrong kid, then," Sam

laughed. He danced along next to me, waving the earth-worm in my face. Sam Goff was a pain. The gang of us from Milford Square—Sam and Jules and the little kids and I—always walked to school together, but sometimes I wished Sam the Monkeyface would get lost.

"Spit, spit, right in the Führer's face!" Sam was yelling. He ran beside us and sent spit flying as close to Jules and me as he could come without hitting us.

"Hitler's dead, stupid," I said. "It's V-E Day, Victory in Europe—the Nazis surrendered yesterday," I told him. "Miss Fenster says May 7, 1945, will go down in history. If you don't stop it we'll be late for school, and Miss Fenster won't let us hear the announcement on the radio!"

I took a step toward him and gave Sam a sudden push into the hedges that wound around the lawn of the Barths, the richest people in Wissining.

"Ow! I'll get you for that, Ellis Carpenter!" Sam yelled. I dodged him and looked for help from Jules. But Jules McConagy, my best friend, was walking along not paying the least bit of attention to Sam and me. And that didn't surprise me. In the last month or so Jules had gotten very quiet, ever since the telegram had come about his brother Les. Les McConagy had gone off to war. The telegram from the War Department had said that Les was missing in action.

"Maybe Hitler escaped and came in a submarine to America," Sam said, not letting up. His eyes narrowed. "Maybe he's going to hide out here until he can start another war." Sam was always looking for ways to get everybody scared and angry. I tried to understand him as much as I could because his mother had died when he was born. His stepmother was pretty nice, but she was away a lot, working at her job to help the war effort. Still, it was pretty hard to put up with him.

"Hitler's going to hide out with your grandmother," Sam said. "She'll let him, because she's a *German*."

"She used to be a German," I said. "She's American now." I ran ahead, partly to get away from Sam and partly because I didn't want to be late. Miss Fenster was going to tune in President Harry S Truman on the radio, and we were going to paste more pictures in our World War II scrapbook.

"Your grandmother was born in Germany, wasn't she?" Sam asked. He took long leaps to catch up with me.

"Yes." It bothered me to admit it, but I had to.

"Well, if you're born in Germany you're a German!" Sam shouted in my ear. "And if you're related to her *you're* a Nazi too!"

"You're crazy!" I told him. "I'm an American, and if a person lives here long enough they become an American." I was pretty sure about that. My Grossie— that was the nickname my little brother Mick and I used for our *Grossmutter*, or grandmother—had come to America from Germany when she was sixteen. Of all the people in the world, my Grossie was the last one I could picture walking with a goose step, and saluting and shouting "Heil, Hitler!" like the Germans in the movies.

"Germans all love Hitler," Sam said, screwing up his face. "You'll wait, she'll hide him!"

I hoped not, but if Hitler ever came around badly wounded or something Grossie might take him in, I thought, just because she was so kind. Still, I couldn't believe Grossie *liked* Hitler. Probably she had left Germany just to get away from him.

"Hitler's dead," I said again uncertainly. Our teacher Miss Fenster was always showing us gory newspaper photographs of dead war criminals hanging upside down, but so far there weren't any such pictures of Hitler.

All of a sudden Jules stepped quietly between Sam and me. "V-E Day is the best day of my life so far," he said out of the blue as if he hadn't heard one word about Hitler. His face looked serious as usual. Jules' straight reddish blond hair hung down to his eyes. He wore glasses, and even though glasses made some kids look like dopes, they made Jules look good.

"This is your best day?" I was surprised. My best days were Christmas and the Fourth of July.

"My best day *so far*," he repeated. "The very best will be the day Les comes back."

I nodded. That would be my best day too. Everybody on Milford Square loved Jules' big brother Les. All the kids looked up to him, especially me. When I was little I often used to sit in our rose arbor, and if Les came by he would stop and look up at me and say, "Hi, Ellis, Ellis, sitting on the trellis!"

Before he had gone off to war I used to lie in bed at

night and pretend that Les was my older brother. And when he went away on the very next day after high school graduation I clipped his picture out of the newspaper, pasted it in a notebook and started to write a story about him. I used to add a little bit to the story of Les every night until we heard that he was missing in action. Then I stopped. I was afraid to write the ending.

Sam finally let off teasing me as the three of us walked side by side. Probably he felt ashamed when he heard us talking about Les. Even Sam admired Les McConagy.

"Do you think your brother'll ever come back?" Sam asked Jules. Sam always asked about personal things that other people were too polite to mention.

Jules nodded.

"How do you think you'll find out that he's alive?" Sam went on. "Will your mother get another telegram?"

Jules looked straight ahead. "I just have a feeling he'll come back," he said.

In the school yard I waited up for my brother Mick, to make sure he was all together. He and Sam's half sister Ruthie were always tagging behind the rest of us. Ruthie's underpants were showing as usual, so I gave them a tug before we went along into school.

By the time I got inside Miss Fenster's room the day had turned out to be sunny. It was warm enough to open the windows at the top with a long window pole. I stood looking out over the school yard and beyond, past the playground, to where Wissining Creek wound through the woods. Wissining is a little town on the outskirts of Windsor, Pennsylvania. A lot of Pennsylvania Dutch—really Pennsylvania Germans—had settled here, but most people thought of themselves as just plain Americans. There were some very rich people like the Barths, and some medium rich like the Lanes, but most were average.

"Come, boys and girls, gather around my desk," Miss Fenster said when the late bell rang. "History is in the making!" If history was in the making as often as she said it was, our social studies books would have weighed a ton. The things Miss Fenster loved the most were stories about American prisoners of war who survived in jungles and about women spies like one named Tokyo Rose. Miss Fenster was really in her glory because it was V-E Day. I wondered what she would do with herself after the war was over and there were no more war bulletins on the radio and no more sickening clippings for us to paste in the class scrapbook.

Miss Fenster fiddled around with the dial of the radio she had brought from home. When she found the right station we all pressed our ears as close as we could to hear the voice of President Harry S Truman. Half the war was over, Truman said.

When the broadcast ended Miss Fenster motioned for us to bow our heads in silence. "Let's pray for the capture of Emperor Hirohito," she said, "so that we will have peace at last." At the end of one minute she raised her head.

"There are two very important items of business for

us to take care of today," she said. "First, we have a special activity for tomorrow. As you know, there is still much more work to do for the war. And luckily for us the mother of someone in this class has made a very generous offer." We all looked at each other. Miss Fenster went on, "Mrs. Lane has invited the whole class to the Lane farm tomorrow to gather milkweed pods for the war effort."

Sibby Lane beamed until I thought her face would crack. She annoyed me. Her nose was always running, and she tried too hard to be friends. Sibby the Simp, we called her.

"We'll leave for the farm at ten o'clock tomorrow," said Miss Fenster. "Mr. Lane will send his truck to transport us." Everybody cheered. That meant all twenty of us would be piling into the truck for the trip out to the farm. The Lanes must have been pretty rich. Mr. Lane wasn't really a farmer—he had a big business in Windsor and owned the truck and the barn and the farmhouse just for fun. The Lane's farm was a wonderful place. I had been invited there lots of times because Sibby the Simp was always trying to get me to be her best friend.

"Everyone is to bring lunch," said Miss Fenster. "The purpose of the trip will be to look for milkweed and to collect the pods in sacks for the soldiers."

"Soldiers eat *that?*" Sam asked.

"Of course not," Miss Fenster sighed. "The fluffy insides of the pods are used for filling soldiers' life jackets. Things are scarce during a war. We must make use of whatever we can." The whole class started buzzing about the trip.

"Quickly now, boys and girls," Miss Fenster held up her hand to stop the racket. "Our second item of business is even more important. Each year at this time we nominate a student from this grade for the annual Citizenship Award. The winner will be announced at our end-of-the-year ceremonies."

Suddenly I got a funny feeling. I was in the oldest class—the leaders of the school. The Citizenship Award was the biggest honor there was. Les McConagy had won it when he was in our grade.

"I nominate myself!" Sam called out.

Miss Fenster shook her head sadly. "All of you have a responsibility," she said, looking at Sam. "If we should choose the wrong person, we will be letting our country down." She picked up a piece of chalk and stood by the blackboard. "Are there any nominations?"

When I saw Sibby Lane's hand go up I knew what it meant for sure.

"Sybil?"

"I nominate Ellis Carpenter," Sibby said. Sibby always hung around me and nominated me for things. Miss Fenster wrote my name on the board. Then John Elting nominated his best friend, Bruce Brown, and somebody else nominated John Elting.

When Miss Fenster turned around one hand was still up. Philip Helmuth, who loved girls, had his arm stretched out so that he was just about touching Sally's hair.

Philip stood up. "I nominate Sally Cabeen," he said. I knew Sally would get nominated. She was prettiest in the class, and her father was a major in the Army. When she heard her name Sally tossed her blond hair and smiled at Philip. Philip Helmuth was okay, but I preferred boys like Jules who didn't love girls.

"Any more nominations?" asked Miss Fenster, but there was no chance to answer because at that moment bells started ringing. Bells rang everywhere! The school bell clanged and church bells sounded outside. Miss Fenster looked at us in openmouthed surprise. "Oh, my stars!" she said.

There was a knock at the door. Miss Fenster opened it, and we could see her standing in the hallway talking to Mrs. Rice, the principal.

"Good news, boys and girls," Miss Fenster said to us, when Mrs. Rice had waved and walked away. "In honor of V-E Day, school is dismissed early!" Everyone shouted and whistled. "Now, now," Miss Fenster reminded us, putting up her hand for silence, "remember your lunches tomorrow, and remember your manners—we're going to the Lane's farm!"

Two

It was so crowded in the truck the next morning that I thought we weren't all going to be allowed to ride together on the trip to the farm. Mrs. Lane finally agreed that we could all pile in, if we promised not to make noise. Mrs. Lane and Miss Fenster led the way in Lane's old station wagon. Some of us stood and some of us sat on the floor of the truck as we bounced along on the milkweed expedition. The morning heat made all the lunches blend together, so that the whole inside of the truck ended up smelling like bananas and peanut butter.

Once we got on the open road we forgot our promise to Mrs. Lane, and we sang loud songs like, "Off we go, into the wild, blue yonder," and "Would you like to swing on a star, carry moonbeams home in a jar?" I was squashed between Jules and Philip Helmuth.

"Hey, Jules," I whispered, leaning toward him. There was something I had been wanting to ask him. "What did you mean yesterday when you told Sam you had a 'feeling' Les was safe? What kind of a feeling?"

"Shhhh." Jules gave me a signal. "I'll tell you later," he said.

The minute we got to the Lane's farm Miss Fenster put us to work, as if the faster we pulled milkweed, the sooner Hirohito would be falling on his sword. One of her favorite subjects was hari-kari, the Japanese soldier's method of killing himself with honor. I figured that the day that would really go down in history for Miss Fenster would be the one when Hirohito finally did it.

The milkweed was plentiful. Miss Fenster and Mrs. Lane handed out cloth sacks, and in groups of two or three we worked to fill them with pods. The sun blazed down on the field, and the juice from the stems made us sticky. I held the bag open as Jules, perspiration steaming up his glasses, reached up to pull the pods off the stalks.

"Do you really get silent messages?" I asked Jules when we were all by ourselves.

"Yes, sometimes." He brushed the hair out of his eyes and looked around. "But don't tell anyone."

"What are they about—the messages?" I whispered.

"About what's going to happen," he said. "About whether people are safe or in danger."

"Are the messages always right?" I let the sack fall to the ground.

"Most of the time."

"I wouldn't like it," I said. "Say you got a bad message. You'd know it before it happened, and you'd be sad all that much longer." He nodded as if I were right. "Did you . . ." I looked at Jules with hesitation, "did you ever get a secret message about Les before the telegram came?"

"Yes," he said quietly. "But *don't tell anyone*," he said.

I looked into his eyes. "I swear I won't."

By lunchtime more than thirty sacks of milkweed pods lined the road. Lane's hired man came by in the truck and loaded the pods so that he could take them into Windsor. The field next to the Lane's house was steamy in the heat. A few kids who were always weak and tired flung themselves down in the prickly grass. Phil Helmuth sat close to Sally Cabeen, who giggled every time he tried to whisper something in her ear. Bruce Brown was catching grasshoppers and trying to stuff them down the necks of all the girls when Mrs. Lane called us to the edge of the road.

"What hard workers!" she said. Mrs. Lane was very tall and straight-backed. She looked strong like a pioneer woman, which made me wonder how she happened to have a daughter who was so silly and babyish. "I invite you all to rest now," she said. "Come to the barn where it's cool." Mrs. Lane walked behind with Miss Fenster while we ran to the barn.

"Come on, Jules," I said. "Last one there's a monkey's uncle—Sam's uncle!" I had played in Sibby's barn before, and I wanted to show Jules how to walk on the rafters.

The idea caught on quickly. Bruce hoisted himself up right after me, and soon all but the sissy kids had crawled high up in the rafters and were perched in the air, looking down on blocks of clean, strong-smelling hay that were stacked far below around the edges of the barn. Through the loft window I saw Mrs. Lane and Miss Fenster go into the house. The barn rafters were wooden beams just as wide as a pair of shoes. The only way to move along safely was by gently inching forward with arms stretched out for balance. So long as we moved along the outer edges, there was no danger—the hay would break a fall. Some kids even jumped down into the hay on purpose. But Bruce Brown wasn't satisfied. He had to be a show-off as usual.

"Lookee!" Bruce cried, as he moved along his rafter. "Anybody for the Daredevils' Club, follow me!" Shuffling at top speed, he didn't stop until he was in the very center of the barn. Over his head a ray of sun lighted up a nest of cobwebs. Thirty feet under him lay the cement floor. Everyone down below and everyone on the rafters stopped moving. There was an uneasy murmur.

"Bruce, come down!" Sally pleaded, but he only laughed.

"My father says not to go where there's no hay," Sibby called to him.

"President of the Daredevils' Club!" Bruce shouted. He seemed not to hear. Anyway, he was at a point of no return. Half admiring him and half panicked, I held my breath as I watched Bruce scoot above the cold cement. I looked around for Jules to see if I could read in his face any message about Bruce's danger, but Jules had his back to me.

Two-thirds of the way across the open space, Bruce stopped. "Who's going to follow me?" he shouted.

"John, where are you?" John Elting, smiling weakly, stood on top of the hay, clinging hard to the end of Bruce's rafter. His face was pale.

"John, where are you?" Bruce called again. "You gonna make me turn around and look?"

"Bruce, *please* don't turn around," Sally screamed.

"I'm going to turn around," Bruce threatened, as he moved slightly forward.

"I'll tell my father!" Sibby cried. We all knew her father wasn't home. Suddenly it struck me that the whole thing was my fault. I had started the rafter walking in the first place. How did I know that Bruce would be such a show-off? Still, I was the one who had gotten him into it. If he fell I'd never forgive myself.

"I'm turning around," Bruce teased again in a singsong voice.

"Wait, Bruce, don't." John had pulled himself up onto the end of the same rafter. Pale and shaking, he inched forward.

"He answered you, Bruce, don't turn around," Sally called.

"I'm coming, Bruce." John's voice sounded strange. Probably even Bruce noticed that. Everyone stood like statues, watching first Bruce with his arms outstretched and then John, who was now just over the point where the hay ended.

"Don't bother," Bruce shouted. "Don't bother coming," and as he said it, he waved his hand in a way that showed he had forgotten where he was. The movement of his hand was just enough to upset his balance. There was a horrible second or two when the eyes of everyone focused on Bruce as he wobbled back and forth. Then, like a person grabbing the back of a train as it pulls out of the station, he took great steps forward, his feet by some miracle touching the rafter, until at a certain point he completely lost his balance. Just over the place where the hay began, he leaped, threw himself forward with a racing dive, and landed with a dull thump on his stomach in the hay.

"Oh, Bruce," Sally sobbed. John let himself down gently from the rafter on the opposite side of the barn. Sam Goff, who was nearest Bruce, put his face near Bruce's.

"Y' okay, Bruce?" Bruce lay still, so that some of the others close by started gathering around him. I held my breath. "Bruce?" Sam repeated. Sam lay his hand on Bruce's shirt. "Bruce?" Then all of a sudden Sam jumped back. Bruce leaped up on both feet like a man shot out of a cannon at a carnival.

"President of the Daredevils' Club!" Bruce shouted, grinning. I laughed along with everybody else, but when it came time to eat lunch I wasn't very hungry.

Miss Fenster joined us while we were eating lunch, and afterward as we cleaned up our leftovers, she said to the whole group, "I'm happy that while I was inside the house I didn't have to worry about loud noise and disturbance from over here in the barn. I'm glad you've all been so mature in your behavior today. Until the truck comes back for us Mrs. Lane says you may play freely in and around the barn. But please don't climb up on the hay," Miss Fenster warned us. "Someone might slip, and others of you might be susceptible to hay fever. And please remember," she whispered out loud, "to say thank you to the Lanes when we leave."

I felt bad. I always felt guilty when someone said we were good and we really weren't. I wanted to tell Miss Fenster about Bruce on the rafters just to be honest, but it would have sounded like tattling. Besides, I didn't want Miss Fenster to have a heart attack. Whenever upsetting things happened she was always saying, "Oh, my heart!"

After Miss Fenster had complimented us, Jules, Sally and a few others headed for the swings in the yard— swings made of old rubber tires suspended from a tree. They must have been very old tires, because you couldn't get rubber at all during the war. I felt like going with them, but just then Sibby asked me if I would come inside the house with her, and I said I would just to see what she wanted.

The house was dark and quiet. The kitchen, looking practically like one in colonial days, had a rag rug on the floor, pots hanging from the walls, and besides the regular stove for cooking, there was an old potbellied stove that people used for keeping warm in the old days. Sibby stopped to blow her nose, as usual. Maybe she had hay fever, I thought.

"What do you want?" I asked her.

"Come with me," she said. "My mother wants to see you." She pulled me through the kitchen and up the stairs toward the second-floor sitting room.

"Wants to see *me?* What for?"

"My mother likes you." I figured she did, since she was always having Sibby invite me, but it didn't make sense that she would want to see just me, when the whole class was running around outside.

Mrs. Lane was standing straight as a board in the sitting room, a cheerful place with flowered chintz curtains and slipcovers.

"Here she is," Sibby said, and before I knew it she had disappeared and left me alone with her mother. I looked at her in confusion.

"Hello, Ellis," she smiled, taking my hands and leading me over to the chintz-covered couch. It was the first time I had ever seen her close up. She had very rosy cheeks, something like a painted wooden doll's. "Have you had a good time today?" she asked.

"Oh, yes," I said.

"You know, Ellis, of all Sibby's friends, *you* are the one I like best."

I felt myself getting flushed in the face.

"Are you aware, Ellis, of how much Sibby admires and respects you?" Mrs. Lane didn't wait for an answer. "You are her favorite friend," she smiled. "Is it true, Ellis," she turned sharply toward me, "that there is an election in class tomorrow for the Citizenship Award?"

"Yes," I said. Mrs. Lane paused and picked her words carefully.

"You were nominated for the award, weren't you?"

"Yes . . ." I couldn't imagine what it had to do with her.

"Who nominated you?"

"Sibby did."

She nodded. "Just as I thought. Sibby often shows her friendship for you, doesn't she?"

"Yes, I guess so." Sibby was always trying to get in good with people.

"Ellis," she put her hand on my arm, "has it ever occurred to you to show *your* friendship for *Sibby*?" What did she mean? I tried to show friendship by coming to her house even though I didn't like to play with her that much.

"I try to be friends . . ." I said.

"Ellis, if you think about how much Sibby likes you and how much *she's* helped *you,* maybe you'll see what I mean." I didn't see anything except her rosy cheeks, which seemed to have become redder since the beginning of our conversation.

"Am I correct that there could be another nomination for the Citizenship Award tomorrow?" she asked.

"I guess so . . ."

"Could you make that nomination?" she whispered. I must have looked like an imbecile. I had thought of nominating Jules, but I knew that wasn't what Mrs. Lane was talking about.

"Who?" I asked.

"Wouldn't it be a good way to show friendship to Sibby if you nominated her for the Citizenship Award?" Mrs. Lane's eyes filled up, almost as if she were going to cry.

"But . . ." I couldn't believe my ears. Mrs. Lane was

telling me to nominate Sibby. "I guess so," I mumbled. It seemed impossible for me to tell somebody's mother, especially Mrs. Lane, "No, I won't do it." Mrs. Lane made it sound as if it were so important to her. Well, maybe it wouldn't hurt me to put up Sibby's name, just to make them both feel good. She would never win—I wouldn't have to worry about that. Still, I felt my face burning, and I wanted to be out of that room more than anything else in the world.

"Then you'll do it?" she asked. My head swam. I couldn't make any words come out. Suddenly, though, the answer hit me like a flash. It was so simple.

"I'd like to, Mrs. Lane," I said with relief, "but I can't. Sibby nominated me, and we aren't allowed to nominate back."

"What do you mean 'back'?"

"I can't put up the person who put me up," I explained. "We have a rule."

"Oh, I see," she said. "Well, there's no reason why you couldn't find someone else to do it, is there? All the children have such respect for you."

"I don't know," I swallowed hard. "I guess I could try."

"Sibby'd appreciate that." Then she added, "And so would I. Remember, Ellis, Sibby doesn't make friends as easily as you do, and you're her best friend."

"I know," I said stupidly. The light had faded in the sitting room, and even Mrs. Lane's cheeks looked paler. She got up and took me by the hand. I didn't feel like touching her, but I had no choice.

"Thank you, dear," she said, leading me to the door. "I'm glad that Sibby has such a good friend. Please come again soon, Ellis." We started down the stairs. "There's the truck now—I see it coming around the bend." At the bottom of the steps she stooped and kissed me on the forehead.

"Good-bye, dear," she said. "I'm so glad we had our little talk, and do remember . . ." As her words trailed off she turned away from me and burst through the kitchen door into the yard. The next minute she was swarmed by everyone who had come to say thank you. I felt strange, as if I had dreamed the conversation with Mrs. Lane.

We got into the truck, and everyone but me waved good-bye to Sibby and her mother until at the end of the road we couldn't see them any longer. On the way home I didn't talk much. I couldn't exactly say why I felt so awful, so embarrassed, except that I knew Mrs. Lane had done something silly. Mrs. Lane was a grown-up, and a grown-up should have known better.

"How was the trip?" my father asked at supper.

"Okay." I still didn't feel like talking.

"Did you eat all kinds of junk?" My mother shot me an accusing look.

"Practically none."

"Then why are you just twiddling with your noodles?"

"Not hungry," I said.

"Why not?" she asked. Suddenly I burst into tears. I

admit it wasn't a very courageous Citizenship Award thing to do, but I couldn't help it.

"For heaven's sake, what is it?" my mother asked. My brother Mick dropped his fork and stared at me.

"Mrs. Lane . . ." I was gasping from the effort of trying not to cry.

"What about her?" My father leaned over and handed me his napkin to catch the tears.

"She's making me . . . nominate Sibby for the Citizenship Award!"

"She can't *make* you, can she?" he asked. I explained what had happened at the Lane's while all three listened.

"That's too bad," my mother said, shaking her head. "Mrs. Lane shouldn't have done that." But I could tell that none of them understood how bad I felt.

"I know what I'll do," I said. "I'll get Jules to nominate her as a favor, but neither of us will vote for her."

"That sounds peculiar to me," said my father. "You'd be forcing Jules just as Mrs. Lane is trying to force you. You'd be doing the same thing she did." I saw that, but I was afraid not to do what Mrs. Lane wanted. She scared me. Then while my parents were thinking quietly, Mickey looked up.

"*Is* Sibby a good citizen?" he asked.

"No!" I burst out, half crying and half laughing. "She's a terrible citizen!" That evening I told myself I would put off deciding what to do until the next day, but Mickey's question had gotten through to me.

*T*hree

When Miss Fenster reminded us in the morning that the Citizenship Award election would be held in the afternoon, I could see that Sibby's eyes were on me. I had avoided looking at her and talking to her. Fortunately we were kept very busy drawing pictures of milkweed pods and writing thank-you notes to Mr. and Mrs. Lane. As we were walking back to school after lunch, I was still debating what to do.

"Jules," I said, "would you do anything I asked you?"

"I wouldn't jump in the middle of the mine hole," he said. The mine hole was a small lake near our house. Everybody claimed that once, while miners were at work, water had suddenly sprung up from the bottom. The miners had run for their lives. The middle was supposed to be very deep and still full of huge machinery.

"Would you do something that was just words—not hurting anybody?"

"Depends. What?"

"Would you nominate somebody if I wanted you to?"

"For what? Who?"

"Sibby for Good Citizen?"

"No." He didn't even have to think about it.

"Why not?"

"Because she's a terrible citizen." It was no use. I knew I wouldn't get anywhere with Jules when he had his mind made up.

"It's time now to complete our unfinished business," said Miss Fenster when the afternoon session started. "At the end of today I must submit the name of the person you elect for the Good Citizenship Award. The teachers and the principal, Mrs. Rice, must also agree on this person. They have a vote too. The award will be presented at the end-of-the-year ceremonies on the evening of June 8, when all your parents will be there.

"Now," she said, "you see the names of our four fine nominees." She had already written my name, Bruce's, John's and Sally's on the board. "Are there any further nominations?"

The room was silent. I could feel Sibby's eyes boring into me. What I really wanted to do was to nominate Jules, but I decided not to. Everyone knew that Jules and I were friends, and they would think I was doing it just for friendship. They might even think I did it because I *loved* Jules, which would be even worse. So I didn't raise my hand.

Miss Fenster cleared her throat. "Am I correct that there are no further nominations?" I could hear Sibby sighing loudly. I pictured her mother's face when she found out that Sibby wasn't on the list, and I moved my arm slightly. Just then Jimmy Henninger's hand went up, and Miss Fenster called on him.

"I move that the nominations be closed." Bruce Brown seconded it, and before I could do anything, the motion was passed.

"I'm glad we have such fine nominees," said Miss Fenster. "James, will you please distribute the ballots?" As the slips of paper were passed back, Sibby raised her hand.

"May I go to the lavatory, Miss Fenster?" Miss Fenster nodded, and Sibby got up. As she walked past me, she purposely stepped on my foot, but I didn't make a sound even though it hurt. I couldn't tell for sure if she was crying, but I think she was.

"Tough luck," I tried to say to myself. But I couldn't stop imagining her mother doing something awful— coming to school maybe, to tell Miss Fenster that I didn't keep my word; or maybe Sibby herself would tell Mrs. Rice, the principal, that I was the one who had started walking on the rafters.

It was hard to concentrate on who to vote for. I never voted for myself; that would be conceited. Second I eliminated Sally, not because all the boys thought she was beautiful, but because she was always trying too hard to get in good with teachers. Next I decided not to vote for Bruce because he was such a show-off. That left John Elting, who was a pretty good citizen. Not as good as Jules, but the best on the list. Sibby came back, we voted and the ballots were collected and Miss Fenster erased the names from the board.

"You'll find out who won," she said, "on the evening of June 8."

"*You* can't get the Citizenship Award," said a voice. I jumped so hard I bumped Jules and knocked him off the curb, as we walked home past the Barth's mansion. Behind the hedge I saw Sam's face. Sam must have planned to run ahead and scare us.

"Who says I can't?"

"I do," Sam said. "You can't get the award because of your grandmother."

"They aren't giving it to her."

"They do a check on everyone," Sam sneered. "If somebody has a relative who hides the enemy—or who *might* hide the enemy—the person's out. No Citizenship Award."

"You're crazy."

"My father said so, and he's an air raid warden." It was true that Sam's father had a metal helmet and came around during air raid drills to make sure the lights were out, but the business about checking up on my grandmother still sounded fishy to me.

"Let's start a club," Jules said. Sometimes when I was sure Jules was listening quietly, he was really off in another world thinking up some idea.

"What club?" I asked.

"Model airplane?" Jules suggested.

"Well . . ." I hesitated. That didn't sound like much of a club to me.

"A war club, us against Tim Feeney!" Sam said.

"No," I told him. Sam always wanted to be against Tim Feeney, who lived on Milford Square but went to St. Agatha's, a Catholic school. "No fighting club," I said. "Let's do good." I admit it. Having my name up for the Citizenship Award had started the old halo glowing and wings sprouting.

"Let's make model airplanes," Jules said, "and sell them, and give magic shows, and use all the money for war bonds."

"Okay," I agreed. "We can make the models out of toothpicks and tissue paper, like Les used to. Meet on my porch," I said. "I'll be president."

Jules looked up. "I suggested the club," he mentioned politely. "Meet in my cellar," Jules said. "*I'll* be president."

The McConagy's cellar was dark and musty in a pleasant, peaceful way. It was filled with more games than any other place I had ever seen. Even though most of the games were from when Les was little, they were all stacked neatly on wooden shelves, and none of the pieces were missing. Most had been in the cellar so long that they carried a cellar smell along with them even when we took them upstairs so we could play by the big radio.

I was the first one at the meeting. "Go get the other kids," Jules whispered. Since the day when the telegram had come saying that Les was missing, we were very careful not to make noise in Jules's house. It was as if news of Les might arrive at any minute, and we wanted to be ready to hear it. Jules spread out white tissue paper and poured out a box of flat toothpicks on the cement floor, while I ran up the cellar steps and out the front door.

"Hey, Mick!" I shouted. "Yo, Ruthie!" Sam and Tim were chasing the two little kids around the grassy mall in the middle of Milford Square. The square was a quiet street shaped like a U, so that everybody lived close to everybody else. Right in the middle of the mall was a sign that said:

KEEP OFF THE GRASS
BY ORDER OF THE WISSINING POLICE DEPT.

"Sam, Tim, come on!" I called. "The club's starting!" But they didn't pay any attention. Sam leaped over the KEEP OFF THE GRASS sign and knocked it flat.

"Sam, get off of there," I warned him. But it was too late. Old Mrs. Lukesh, who lived at the end of the Square, was already out on her front porch. Mrs. Lukesh loved grass. Whenever she saw kids playing on the mall, she dropped whatever she was doing in her creepy house and came out to waggle her finger at us.

"You children!" she called now to Sam and Tim in a shaky voice. "Get off that grass! Get off that grass right this minute, or I'll call the police!"

Sam jumped over the fallen sign a few times, just to get her mad enough so that she would go in to telephone the cops. As soon as she had disappeared inside, Sam, Tim, Mick and Ruthie came running.

"The cops are coming! The cops are coming!" Sam shouted so loudly that Mick and Ruthie ran screaming into the McConagy's house. When I had shushed them we went down to the cellar where Jules was already working on a model airplane.

"That's nice, Jules," I said. Sticking the tiny toothpicks together with glue was hard, and I could tell right away that the little kids weren't going to be any good at making airplanes. "Go to our house and get a flat box to put the planes in," I told Mick, just to get rid of him. "You and Ruthie can carry the box when we go around trying to sell the models."

I wished there were more kids in the neighborhood to join the club and help us make money, but the only person we could have gotten was that sissy Willie Pflug from the next street, and his fingers were too fat to make toothpick airplanes. Sibby would have joined even though she lived far away. Her father's truck probably would have brought her specially. But I didn't feel like putting up with Sibby. I didn't want a simp in our club.

By the time Mick and Ruthie had come back with the carton, Jules, Sam, Tim and I had each finished a model airplane. The tissue paper on Sam's was half hanging off, and mine had blobs of glue all over it, but Jules had made a P-39 that really looked like a plane.

"Let's charge fifty cents for Jules'," I said, "and ten

cents for the others." We let Mick and Ruthie carry the box between them as we went around to the houses of Milford Square.

"Let's go to your house first," Sam said to me.

"No, my mother'll buy one for sure," I told him. "Let's go other places and let them get first pick. My mother'll buy one even if it's crummy."

"No one's home at my house," Sam said. His step-mother worked in a defense plant. She was never home. At the Shoppe's house, next to Sam's, the grown-up daughter admired Jules' plane and bought it right away for fifty cents.

"She must have bought it just to be nice," Jules said, as we walked away. What I liked about Jules was that he never bragged.

"No, it was really good looking," I told him. "She admired it."

After my mother and Mrs. McConagy had each bought a plane, our luck ran out. At the other houses we tried, either nobody was home or nobody wanted to buy the plane that Sam had made.

"Let's float it in the mine hole," Sam suggested.

"No." Jules shook his head. "We'll make one more sale."

"Where?" I couldn't imagine what Jules was thinking of. He walked ahead of the rest of us with the model airplane in the palm of his hand.

"Hey, Jules, where are you going?" Sam asked. "Jules, you're nuts!" Jules had led us to the end of the Square straight to the door of Mrs. Lukesh, who loved grass.

"I'm leaving!" Sam said. "She'll call the cops!" Mick and Ruthie hid in the bushes.

"Jules," I pleaded. "What does Mrs. Lukesh want with a toy airplane?" He ignored me and knocked sharply on the knocker. Mrs. Lukesh didn't have a doorbell.

"Who's there?" said a feeble voice.

Jules knocked again. The door opened a tiny crack, and a smell like leftover lamb stew seeped out.

"What do you want?" Close up, Mrs. Lukesh was even smaller and skinnier than I remembered.

Jules cleared his throat. "The Milford Square Good Citizens' Model Airplane Club is selling this model airplane to raise money for war bonds. It's our last one. Would you care to buy it? It's only ten cents."

"Heh?" Mrs. Lukesh opened the door a crack wider. Even though Tim and Sam were giggling, Jules repeated his speech and I held out the money we had made to show her.

"No, no. I don't believe so," she croaked, when Jules was finished for the second time. "Don't believe so. Not today," and she shut the door without another word.

"The old crow!" Sam snorted. He pulled a piece of chalk out of his pocket and started drawing a swastika on the front steps, but Jules stopped him.

"She's deaf," Jules said. "Maybe she didn't understand."

"She hears us pretty good when we're playing on the mall," Sam grumbled.

"Let's leave the plane on her step." Jules put it down.

"That's dumb, Jules," I said. "What a waste of ten cents! At least we could keep it as a souvenir for the club."

"Let's leave it," he repeated. I could tell he really felt like leaving it, so I didn't argue. When Jules made up his mind, there was no sense trying to change him.

Very early the next morning as I was getting ready for school, the doorbell rang.

"Answer the door, please," my mother called. It couldn't be Jules or Sam, I thought. They always hollered for me and I hollered for them in our special way: both hands cupped to the mouth, very loud, like a song —"Yo, El-leee!" Jules and Sam would never ring the bell. And it was too early for visitors or salesmen.

When I opened the door I had to blink my eyes to make sure I was awake. No one was there. Then I looked all around, and suddenly I noticed a small white envelope sticking out of the mailbox. I opened it. Inside there was no note, no name—just a dime. Who could have left a dime?

I stepped out onto the porch and looked around the Square. It was a wonderful sunny morning. Birds were hopping around the mall. It was so early that no one was stirring yet—no one, that is, except Mrs. Lukesh, all by herself, going into her house and closing the door behind her.

Four

"I *knew* Mrs. Lukesh would appreciate the airplane!" Jules whispered to me for the third time later that morning when we sat at our desks in school. "I just had a feeling she would."

"You were right, Jules," I told him. "And that's ten cents more for the club." I folded up the envelope with the dime in it and put it in my desk as Miss Fenster began handing out our brown music books.

"We have just enough time to run through our song before we go down to the auditorium to rehearse with Miss Swan," said Miss Fenster. Miss Swan was the special person who came to teach music once a week. She had twinkling eyes and a graceful way of moving her hands. Singing lessons were fun, even though we did have to do some pretty strange things.

"Let's warm up with a few sequentials," Miss Fenster said. Sequentials were exercises that were supposed to warm up your voice. I never understood why we couldn't just get right down to business.

"As you know," Miss Fenster went on, "we are to appear first on the program on June 8, when the awards are presented. Miss Swan wants us to sing 'Watchman, What of the Night?' " Everybody was happy because "Watchman, What of the Night?" was our favorite song in the whole brown music book.

"What does it mean?" Sam wanted to know. " 'What of the night?' "

"It's a poetic way of asking the watchman what the weather is," Miss Fenster said. She usually tried to answer Sam's questions patiently. Maybe she felt sorry for him the way I did.

"Open your books to page 52," Miss Fenster said, "but first let's hear the second sequential." She blew on her pitch pipe. "Do-mi-sol, re-fa-la, mi-sol-ti, do!" Miss Fenster's voice sounded like a crow's compared to Miss Swan's, but the kids who still didn't know their sequentials followed her. There were seven sequentials altogether, and when you could sing them all, solo and by heart, you got a gold star on the Sequential Chart.

"All ready now, page 52!" Miss Fenster blew the opening note on the pitch pipe.

> Watchman, what of the night?
> The stars are out in the sky,
> The merry round moon will be rising soon,
> For us to go sailing by . . .

"That sounds a little weak today," Miss Fenster said when we had finished. "I hope you'll sing out for Miss Swan in the auditorium." I figured it didn't matter whether we did or not. Miss Fenster's voice always drowned everybody out anyway.

"Line up, two by two," she told us. "Miss Swan is expecting us now." I lined up with Jules as my partner. But just as we got the sign to go out the door, a siren wailed outside, and the school bell sounded three long and three short rings.

"Oh, my heart!" said Miss Fenster. "This is an air raid drill," she went on calmly, as if she had just received word directly from President Truman. "There is to be absolutely *no talking*. March single file to the basement opposite the gymnasium door. Crouch, facing the wall. Good citizens *do not talk* during air raid drills!" Miss Fenster led us to the basement with its special odor of dampness and peeled paint. In every direction came long lines from the other classes, with no sound but the dull shuffle of hundreds of feet.

"Bzzzzzz, here they come," Sam said, as soon as Miss Fenster rounded a corner. Sam was always doing imitations of dive bombers. I gave him a disgusted look.

"Whooosh . . . vrooom . . . duck! Here comes a Kamikaze! Suicide attack by the Japanese!"

"Shush!" I whispered. I wasn't just being a goody-goody. Kids from other lines were looking at Sam. He was going too far for an air raid drill. I pinched my lips together as a signal to him to be quiet. We passed the boiler room and rounded the corner.

"Rat-tat-tat-tat-tat!" Sam pretended to man the anti-aircraft. "Rat-tat-tat-tat-tat!"

"Sam!" I warned. Mrs. Rice, the principal, was leading the line coming toward us.

Sam turned around and looked at me. "Rat-tat-tat,"

he said deliberately, just to mock me.

"Shut up!" I yelled at him. Somehow the words came out much louder than I expected. In the silence of the gray basement, with students now stopping on both sides of the corridor, my cry rang out. Clapping my hand over my mouth, I knew it was too late. Mrs. Rice, directly opposite me, frowned and stared. I quickly fell into crouch position, but when I looked up over my shoulder, standing behind me was Miss Fenster. She could only look at me and shake her head hopelessly. I turned my face to the wall. Well, that finishes the Citizenship Award for me, I thought.

After the air raid drill and all during the singing rehearsal in the auditorium I was feeling pretty awful. I thought of telling Miss Fenster that I had just meant to keep Sam quiet, but that would have made me a tattletale. I couldn't stand kids who were always telling the teacher, "It was so-and-so's fault!"

Walking by myself on the way back from the rehearsal, I noticed that Sibby was trailing behind me.

"Wait up," she said. I waited. We walked together until we came to the girls' lavatory. Sibby motioned for me to go in, and she followed me, an ugly look on her face.

"How come you didn't nominate me yesterday?" Her hands were on her hips.

"I couldn't nominate back," I said. She was a puny thing, and silly too, but she made me nervous just the way her mother did.

"You could of got Jules to do it."

"I asked him. Jules wouldn't."

"Jules would do whatever you ask. Jules *loves* you."

"He *does not!*" I protested. "I did ask him, and he wouldn't. That proves it."

"If you kissed him he would." Her eyes glimmered. "I know what I'll do," she smirked. "Too bad you lied to my mother, because now I'll have to get back at you."

"What do you mean?" I pictured her telling Miss Fenster about our walking on the rafters.

"I'm going to tell Jules that you love him and you want to kiss him."

"Don't," I said weakly. All this talk about kissing was bothering me more than the idea of Sibby telling lies about me to teachers. Kids were always joking about boys liking girls and vice versa, and most of the time we knew it was joking, but I could see that Sibby might know how to make Jules believe her. He would be embarrassed. Some day I wanted to grow up. I wouldn't even mind looking like some famous movie star—Betty Grable, maybe. I wouldn't mind kissing then. But now I just wanted to be Jules' friend. Sibby could spoil it. She knew she had found my weak spot.

"I'm telling Jules that when you come to my house, you always talk about him. I'm saying that we sit in the barn and whisper about what boys we like, and you say you like him. I'm telling Jules you wish he would kiss you."

"Sibby, if you do, I'll . . ." What could I do to her? Beat her up? That would make me look silly. I couldn't threaten her about boys and kissing—she liked that kind of teasing. Then suddenly I remembered an old saying that my father always recited: "You catch more flies with sugar than with vinegar."

"Sibby," I changed my tone. "If you promise not to, I'll let you in our club."

She took her hands off her hips and looked at me with interest. "What club?"

"It's called the Milford Square Good Citizens' Model Airplane Club, but you can join even if you don't live on Milford Square."

She narrowed her eyes. "Who's in it?"

"Jules, and Sam, and a boy named Tim Feeney who goes to St. Agatha's and some little kids on our street."

"All boys?"

"Well, just about." I hadn't thought of it that way before.

"Okay, I'll join," she answered quickly.

"And you promise not to tell Jules what you said?"

"I promise. When's the next meeting?"

"I'll let you know." She sure was anxious.

"You could have meetings and not tell me. How will I know?" That kid didn't trust anybody.

"It's called the Good Citizens' Club, isn't it? The whole purpose is to do good, not to trick people." Even though I said it quite nastily, it seemed to satisfy her.

"Well, okay. Will the others let me join?" That might be a problem, I was thinking, but I would work it out.

"Yes," I told her. "They like you." I don't know why I said that—it was a lie. Sometimes I just felt like telling lies to make things easier. Anyway, Sibby smiled almost

as much as the day when Miss Fenster had said that
Mrs. Lane was a generous mother.

"Might you be having a meeting today?" Sibby asked.

"Wait for me after school," I told her, "I'll find out."

"Ellis," she hugged my arm, "you're my best friend."

Lucky me, I thought.

Jules and Sam weren't too happy when I told them
about inviting Sibby into the club, but I threatened to
quit if they didn't let her join. I was still burning mad
at Sam for getting me into trouble during the air raid
drill. Besides, I convinced them more members meant
more money, and the whole point of the club was to
get money for the war effort.

"Wait for us in the playground," I told them when
school was out. "Sibby's calling her mother to tell her
about the club meeting."

"Hurry," Jules said. "We're going straight to Windsor Avenue."

"What for?"

"For magic tricks. The club's going to give a show to
make money. We're going to see Mingus."

The Mingus Magic Shop was one of our favorite
places on Windsor Avenue. Going straight from school,
the long way around, took us past Priscilla's Candy
Store, the library, and the Rialto Theater. Naturally on
the telephone Sibby's mother had said she could go to
the club meeting. If somebody had invited Sibby to play
after school in California Mrs. Lane would probably
have been glad to pick her up.

When we passed by the school yard of St. Agatha's, we saw Tim Feeney.

"Want to come to see Mingus?" Jules called.

"Wait a minute." I could see that his school friends were trying to convince him to stay with them. Tim always played with the Catholic school kids separately or with us separately. It was like he lived a double life.

"Okay, wait up," he yelled. One of his school friends thumbed his nose at Tim as he ran to join us.

"What do ya do at that school?" Sam asked, as Tim fell in step next to him. "Do you pray, or what?"

"Well, yeah, sometimes," Tim said. "It's a regular school." He seemed embarrassed. I thought it was rude of Sam to ask questions like that.

"*Our* school is *regular* school," Sam said, making it worse.

Jules looked at Tim. "Isn't it that you believe God is everywhere, so you shouldn't ignore him anywhere, not even in school?"

"Yeah," Tim said. He looked surprised that the explanation was so simple. "What're you going to Mingus for?"

"We're buying tricks for a magic show for the club," I told him. "When school's over, we're going to have a show and charge money. This is Sibby," I pointed to her.

She was smiling as usual, runny nose and all. "Hi," she said.

Tim nodded and looked at Jules. "A girl in the club?" he asked.

"You dope," I sighed, "*I'm* a girl, and I'm treasurer."

"Oh, yeah," Tim said, "but that's different."

We made one stop before Mingus'. At the Wee Nut Shoppe mosey pans were on sale, two for a nickel. Mosey pans were caramel, like the coating of a candy apple, poured into little fluted molds. They were bad for your teeth but delicious.

"That's fifteen cents of club money going for us and not the war," I worried.

"They send soldiers chocolate, don't they?" Jules said. "That's why it's scarce here. Chocolate helps them feel better and fight better." I admired Jules for the way he always explained things so well.

The smell from Van Horn's bakery was tempting, but we didn't stop. We also went right by Weitzel's Five-and-Ten, the one place our parents had told us not to go into. Someone had supposedly once seen Mr. Weitzel, who was an old man, trying to grab a little girl, so our mothers made us promise not to go there.

"He's a Nazi," Sam said as we went by. I felt sort of sorry for Mr. Weitzel. I could see how a person who didn't like him for some reason could just make up stories to get him in trouble.

Mingus' shop was at the opposite end of the block from the Rialto and the Wee Nut Shoppe. It was in a funny, out-of-the-way building below ground level. We walked down a few steps and through a door that said MINGUS—MAGICIAN. The front of the tiny shop was filled up almost completely by a big combination counter and showcase. Inside it the tricks were displayed.

There were red lacquered boxes with hidden compartments, wands with gold tips, multicolored scarves, strange decks of cards and papier-mâché rabbits. It seemed as if nobody but us ever came into Mingus'.

We had to wait and tap on the case and clear our throats a lot before Mingus finally heard us and came from the back of the shop. Mingus didn't need a costume to look like a magician. He was tall and skinny, with black hair slicked straight back, and he had a small moustache like toothbrush bristles.

"Well, well, well, what can I do for you?" he asked, laying his palms on the counter.

"We want a few tricks to put on a show," Jules said. Mingus knew us pretty well and he was especially nice to Jules. I guess he could tell that Jules was really talented at magic.

"How much do you have to spend today?"

"We have $2.30 altogether," I said. Besides our model airplane money we had collected dues.

"We're putting on a show to make money for the war effort," Jules explained.

Mingus nodded. "I have a trick here that's a new acquisition. I'll demonstrate for you, if you like."

That's what we were waiting for. The five of us sat on a wooden bench against the wall, while Mingus disappeared into the back room. When he came out he wore a top hat and black cape that he swirled around.

"Ladies and gentlemen," he said, "to see is to believe. What you see before you is a plain ordinary can of peanut brittle. A can, that is, that *once* contained peanut brittle but is now perfectly empty—devoid of all matter." I loved the way Mingus talked. He took off the lid and showed us the bottom of the can.

"Now then," he replaced the cover and waved his wand over the can, "did I say *perfectly* empty?" His eyes flashed. "Alas," he said, "nobody's perfect." Lifting the lid he pulled out a piece of real peanut brittle. "Who would like a tasty morsel of this delectable confection?" He tossed a lump of peanut brittle to Jules, who broke off a corner for each of us.

"Now that we have disposed of that tasty tidbit . . ." he showed us the inside of the can again, "perhaps I can convince you that we now have a void container. I will cover said container with this lid." Mingus waved his wand again.

"Make more peanut brittle!" Sam shouted.

"What's that you say?" Mingus bowed to Sam and handed the can over the counter to him. "More peanut brittle? Help yourself, my good man." Sam ripped off the lid and bounced back in surprise. Out of the can at full force burst an accordion-like snake—a kind of jack-in-the-box.

"Help!" Sam cried. "I said *peanut brittle!*" Tim tossed the snake back to Mingus, who dropped it to the ground and recovered the empty can.

"Owing to scarcities resulting from the war," Mingus apologized, "it pains me to say that we have a shortage of peanut brittle. Can I offer you a substitute—something to keep up your flagging spirits?" He waved the wand and beckoned to Sibby, who lifted the lid gingerly.

Nothing popped out. All we could see was a corner of red and white silk.

"Pull," ordered Mingus. Sibby pulled the corner of material—and pulled and pulled—until she had pulled out an enormous American flag.

"Is that trick for sale?" I asked.

Mingus smiled. "Tin can complete with peanut brittle, snake, flag and full instructions is for sale."

"How much?"

"Ordinarily I charge five dollars," he said. "However, in these particular circumstances, knowing that the proceeds from a show will be turned over to a worthy cause, I am happy to offer a reduced rate. A rate, shall we say, of two dollars and twenty-five cents?"

I could tell that Jules wanted it even though it would make us broke.

"Let's take it," I said. We all watched while Mingus explained the written instructions to Jules. Then, still wearing his hat and cape, Mingus wrapped up the trick and took our money.

"It's been a pleasure to do business with you," he said. "May I present you with my card." He handed me a calling card that read:

Mingus—Magician
Performer and purveyor of
MAGIC
1309 Windsor Ave. Wissining, Pa.
Available for entertainments,
private parties, etc.
Call Chas. Wertz   WI3-1731

"I'm appearing at the Windsor Fair on July fourth," Mingus said. "Perhaps you'd like to catch my performance."

Jules and Sam said they would but that they would probably be appearing themselves in the Wissining Fourth of July parade. I didn't say anything. I was still trying to get over the disappointment that Mingus' real name was Chas. Wertz.

On the way home, while we were talking about plans for the magic show, we saw McKinley and bought a twin Popsicle from him with our last nickel. McKinley was a very old man—one hundred years old supposedly —who sold ice cream from a homemade wooden cart. It was easy to spot the cart, a big orange box mounted on wheels. Early in the morning, whenever the weather was good, McKinley pushed the cart for five miles across the Windsor Avenue Bridge to Wissining. Kids at all the playgrounds along the way knew what time to expect him. In the evening you could see him, a wrinkled little man with no teeth, pushing his orange cart back toward the bridge. Some people said that his real name wasn't McKinley at all, but that he had taken that name because he was born in the same year as President William McKinley. I looked it up once and found that that would have made him 102 years old.

We shared the Popsicle five ways as we stopped to wait for the train to pass at the corner by the Rialto Theater. Sam and Tim waved to the man on the caboose, and Jules, Sibby and I looked at the Rialto's

Coming Attractions. The next movie was going to be *The Purple Heart,* about an American soldier who had his tongue cut out by the enemy because he wouldn't talk. I wanted to remember to tell Miss Fenster to be sure and see it.

At the top of the hill that led from Windsor Avenue down to Milford Square we all held our breath as we always did. On the corner stood the Gruen Funeral Home. A funny feeling came over me as we passed Gruen's and crossed to the opposite side of the street. Maybe it was thinking about McKinley being 102 years old, or maybe it was seeing the poster for *The Purple Heart,* or maybe it was just the spooky look of Gruen's with the sun going down, but suddenly I got scared. I felt nervous, as if some bad news was about to come. I even looked at Jules' face to see if there were any signs that he had received a message, but Jules, holding on to the new magic trick, looked calm and happy. I let out my breath slowly as we rounded the corner and moved over a little closer to Jules as we walked down the hill.

Just before we got to the McConagy's house I let the others get ahead of us and I took Sibby aside to tell her about Les' being missing in action. I wanted her to understand why we tried to be quiet in the McConagy's house and why Mrs. McConagy might look sad. I might have known, though, that Sibby would get all interested in the details so that I had to shush her at the door.

"Shut up!" I whispered. "Mrs. McConagy might hear you!"

"But what did the telegram *say?*" she kept on.

"I think they say something like, 'The War Department regrets to inform you . . .'—something like that. Now shush!"

Jules, Sam and Tim had already gone inside and down to the basement. Mrs. McConagy stood at the door smiling and wiping her hands on her apron as we came up on the porch.

"Hello, children," she said.

"She doesn't look sad," Sibby whispered to me so that I had to punch her in the arm to be quiet.

"This is Sibby Lane," I said loudly, to make sure I would drown out any other dumb remarks.

"Won't you girls have something to drink before you go down to the basement?" she asked us. "How about some iced tea?" They consumed more iced tea in Jules' house than in a restaurant. Jules' father was always yelling out the door before supper to ask if he wanted iced tea. Even though Jules always said yes, his father kept on asking every night, even if Jules was at the far end of the square.

I would have liked some iced tea, but I was shy about saying yes. I thought it would be more polite to say no first. "No, thanks," I said.

"Well, then," Mrs. McConagy untied her apron and took it off, "run down to the cellar. The boys are already down there."

Sibby jostled my elbow as we went down the cellar steps. "Why did you say no to the iced tea?"

"I thought she'd insist," I said miserably. I had to admit I was thirsty and disappointed.

"You're dumb," she sighed with disgust.

No sooner had we gotten down to the cellar, where Jules was unwrapping the magic trick, than I heard the sound of an automobile horn outside.

"That must be for me," Sibby said. "Come up with me, Ellis."

That simp couldn't even walk to the door by herself. I followed her up the steps and out onto the porch. A car had stopped by my house. It must be her father's handyman, I thought.

"Come on, Ellis," Sibby pulled me by the arm. "When's the next meeting?" Sibby skipped over to the car and opened the door. I stood behind her, peering through the side window.

"Hello, Ellis," said a voice. I felt weak and limp. It was Mrs. Lane. I stayed where I was, unable to move any closer to the car.

"Hello," I said softly. Sibby hopped in, and Mrs. Lane leaned across her to look at me. I stared at Mrs. Lane. What would she say? What would she do to me for not nominating Sibby?

"It was so nice of you," she smiled, "*so* nice of you to invite Sibby to join your club." I tried to stammer something polite, but I couldn't say anything that made sense. I couldn't believe it. Mrs. Lane was acting as if nothing had happened—as if we had never had the discussion about nominating Sibby for the Citizenship

Award. Her face was an explosion of smiles. I had thought that the world would end for her if I didn't nominate Sibby, but it seemed as if to Mrs. Lane the whole thing has been just another conversation. I still felt weak in the knees looking at her—some courageous person *I* was. But in a way I felt sorry for both of them. No wonder Sibby was such a simp.

When the Lane's car had turned out of Milford Square, I went back down to the McConagy's cellar to join Jules, Sam and Tim. They had finished practicing the new trick and had pulled out the *Omega,* Les' high school yearbook and an album of Les' photographs. The four of us sat on the floor looking at them. Les looked so handsome in his graduation picture—the same picture I had in my notebook—that it made me feel sad again.

"Let's see the baseball team." Sam turned the pages. Les had starred at first base for Wissining High.

"Think Les'll try for the major leagues when he comes back?" Tim asked.

"Maybe," Jules said. "He likes the St. Louis Cardinals."

I edged in closer. "Let me see the other one," I said. Farther on in the book there was another shot of Les sitting under a tree with a beautiful girl named Judy. I had seen the picture a lot of times, but I never got tired of looking at it. I wondered whether Judy wrote letters to Les and how she felt now that he was missing in action. Across the bottom of the picture she had written in big round handwriting with circles dotting the i's,

"Dear Les, 'Don't sit under the apple tree with anyone else but me . . .' Always remember our song. All my love, Judy." Sam snorted as he read the inscription and went on to the photograph album, but Jules and I looked for a long time at the picture of Les and Judy.

Five

The final weeks of school passed quickly, as we worked on our World War II scrapbook, took the big *Weekly Reader* test and rehearsed with Miss Swan for the end-of-the-year program.

"June 8—remember," I told my parents. Everybody was coming. I purposely didn't mention that I was up for the Citizenship Award, because I didn't want to sound conceited, and I was sure I wouldn't win anyway, thanks to stupid Sam. I tried not to think about the award at all. I told myself it didn't matter. Still, as much as I tried to put it out of my mind, the award was one of the things that haunted me as I lay in bed at night.

There was another thing that haunted me sometimes too. On certain nights that same feeling that I had had on the way home from Mingus' would come over me while I was waiting to fall asleep—a feeling that something was going to happen, and I had no control over it. When the feeling came I would try to bury my head in the pillow and imagine pleasant things, but soon I would look up in spite of myself and see shadows on the wall, the hulking clothes tree in the corner, and worst of all, the bookcase. The bookcase was a big piece of furniture with glass doors on each shelf. It had belonged to my Grandma Carpenter, who had died when I was a baby. The long shelves, the dark wood and the glass doors made me think of a picture I had seen of Snow White in a glass coffin. In the dark I imagined that someone was inside the bookcase. Then I would start to think about my Grandma Carpenter and my two grandfathers I had never seen, the Gruen Funeral Home up the street and what it must be like to be dead.

Since I was old enough to remember, nobody I knew had ever died. Sam's real mother had died, but I had never known her. Sometime, I figured, death would have to come close to me. Maybe even now Les McConagy was dead. And some day my Grossie would die —she was already pretty old. I couldn't imagine what it would be like if Grossie didn't come to visit us anymore or tell us stories about when she was little. That reminded me that Grossie hadn't come to bring us things from the farmers' market for more than two weeks. Maybe something was wrong. Suddenly everything seemed dark and scary and uncertain. I tried to get my mind off people dying by thinking of McKinley who was still selling ice cream even though he was 102.

On nights when the bad feeling didn't come over me I would start thinking instead about the Citizenship Award. While I was trying to fall asleep I would predict who would win. Sometimes I was sure it would be Sally. All the teachers liked her, and a lot of boys would vote for her. Maybe people would think she must be a good citizen because her father was a major in the Army. Then again, I figured that boys *and* girls would vote for Bruce. He had the highest rank in collecting tin cans. We got badges to sew on our sleeves for bringing in the most flattened tin cans to be melted down for the war. Bruce was a General—he had brought in 2,354 cans. And Bruce would be sure to vote for himself—that would boost his support. John might win if everybody thought the way I did. He never got in trouble and he wasn't stuck up.

When I thought about my winning I got confused. Sometimes I lay in bed picturing the auditorium filled with people, and Mrs. Rice announcing my name as winner, and my mother crying because she was so happy. I had never actually seen my mother cry because she was happy, but that's the way it always was in books. Other times I pictured Mrs. Rice announcing my name and my walking up on the stage with my head lowered. Then just as she handed the plaque to me I would say, "Thank you very much, Mrs. Rice. I'm sorry—but I can't accept the award. I don't feel that I truly exemplify those qualities that you all admire." The audience would be shocked, but they would understand, and they would applaud even louder than if I accepted it, because I was so modest.

The whole Citizenship Award was getting on my nerves. I wished it would be over. Probably *nobody* had voted for me—not even Sibby.

On the evening of the end-of-the-year program the

auditorium was jam-packed by eight o'clock. My mother had wanted me to wear a fancy dress with things on the shoulders that looked like fish fins, but I insisted on wearing a plain pale blue dress that everybody said matched my eyes. Everybody who was singing "Watchman, What of the Night?" was supposed to sit up front, so I sat down in the only empty seat in the first row, and my parents and Mickey went to find seats in the back. The whole town was there: parents, teachers, older brothers and sisters, Pat the policeman and somebody important from the Army. A special ceremony was going to be held in honor of Jack Laubach, a Wissining boy who had been killed in the war. His parents were going to present a flag to the school in honor of Jack. Mr. and Mrs. Laubach were sitting with the Army officer right across the aisle from me. They must have felt sad, while all around them were people laughing and talking as if nothing bad could ever happen.

Just after eight Mrs. Rice, the principal, stood up on the stage and raised her hand for silence. Mrs. Rice was a widow whose two children were students at the school. The Rices were just two regular kids. It was hard for me to picture kids going home and having the principal as their mother.

"Welcome, honored members of the military," she began, "Mr. and Mrs. Laubach, parents, teachers, and last but not least, students. We have come together tonight to crown the school year with this grand finale and to do honor to worthy students, those who are with us, and"—she glanced at the Laubachs—"and those who are not." I thought it was rude of her to remind them about Jack.

"Our program tonight will begin with 'Watchman, What of the Night?'" sung by the older students accompanied by Marybeth Gruen and directed by Miss Amanda Swan." Everyone clapped a lot for Miss Swan, who was very popular. "I don't know if Miss Swan wants me to tell you her little secret or not," said Mrs. Rice, leaning toward the audience as if she were going to whisper it. Miss Swan looked surprised.

"In a way the news is disappointing, because it means that Miss Swan will not be with us next year." The kids in the audience groaned. "But the children of Walla Walla, Washington will be very happy," Mrs. Rice went on brightly. "Miss Swan will be teaching music next year in Walla Walla, where she will be moving with her husband-to-be, Mr. Warren Fritz." Even though I joined in the applause I was upset. First of all, Wissining would probably get a much worse music teacher, and second, I felt sorry for her that she had to change a beautiful name like Swan to Fritz. I was in a pretty nervous condition anyway, just from thinking about the Citizenship Award.

"Watchman, What of the Night?" sounded wonderful, and when Miss Swan blew the pitch pipe at the end, we were on the exact note we were supposed to be. Next, a girl from fourth grade played "Nola" on the piano, and then Mr. and Mrs. Laubach and the officer came up on the stage. There were tears in Mrs. Laubach's eyes when Lieutenant Frazier, the officer, made a speech about how brave Jack had been. After she presented the new flag to the school we all saluted and observed a moment of silence for Jack. The whole ceremony made me think about Les. Maybe someday the McConagys would be giving a present to the school in honor of Les. I had never known Jack Laubach personally, but I felt like crying anyway.

My stomach started feeling strange as soon as the awards part of the program began. My whole insides felt as if they had melted and as if heat rays were going out to my arms and legs and making them numb. I strained to try to see my parents, but the auditorium was too crowded.

"The first award," said Mrs. Rice, "goes to a girl who is well known and liked. In this case the prize is for her penmanship. Miss Mienig will present the Good Writer's Medal." There was some clapping. Meany—that was our nickname for Miss Mienig, who taught art and hand-writing—had taught in Wissining so long that the audience gave her a hand just for still being alive.

"It gives me great pleasure," Meany said, "to present this year's Good Writer's Medal to a young lady who writes in a clear, legible hand. She has truly mastered the fine points of the Palmer Method. A member of the Good Writers' Club for some weeks now, she is Miss Sally Cabeen." The audience cheered. I wondered if the evening would start and end with Sally. The Citizenship Award, I knew, would be last.

There were lots of other awards—for growing the best victory garden, drawing the best fire prevention poster, writing the best composition on "Why We Are in the War," and things like that. Bruce won an award for his 2,354 tin cans. Jules got a blue ribbon in a model airplane contest. And then came the Good Citizenship Award.

My teeth were chattering. I saw Mr. and Mrs. McConagy, but I still couldn't catch a glimpse of my parents. From the row behind, Sibby leaned over and pinched me. "Good luck," she said.

"The winner is . . ." Sam was horsing around, "the winner *is*—Sam Goff!" he whispered.

Mrs. Rice closed her eyes and waited for complete silence. "This is the high point of our evening. The older students have selected from among their number the one whom they think is the best citizen." Please don't talk long, I thought. She mentioned all the good points the winner was supposed to have—leadership, patriotism, and courage. Sally Cabeen, at the end of the row, was calm and smiling.

"And so, without further ado," said Mrs. Rice, "I present to you the winner of the 1944–45 Citizenship Award—Ellis Carpenter!" Even though I had pictured various scenes in my mind while lying in bed, my reactions were slow now that the moment had finally come. I sat motionless in my seat.

"Ellis!" Sibby shouted as the clapping started. Everyone in the row was staring at me. Sibby poked me furiously in the back. "Ellis, get up there!"

Dazed, I stumbled up the steps of the stage as the applause grew louder. Had I dreamed of making a speech to turn down the award? Impossible—I couldn't have gotten out one word. Mrs. Rice held out the plaque in one hand and put her other arm around my shoulders. While she read the inscription aloud she patted me warmly. Had Mrs. Rice forgiven me for making noise during the air raid drill? Or had she been outvoted by the other teachers and was just being a good sport about it? Probably she was still mad at me and didn't think the award meant anything now that I had won.

My head was spinning with all the selfish, cowardly, and unpatriotic things I'd ever done—the incident in the barn, being afraid of Mrs. Lane and Mrs. Rice, spending war stamp money for Popsicles and candy, yelling "shut up" during an air raid drill—and I felt as if a very heavy weight were on me. Whether or not I *was* all those things, now I'd have to try to be them. The winner, Miss Fenster had said, was supposed to be a model. Could you be a model and still be a regular person that people liked? As I walked off the stage, and parents and friends began to congratulate me and hug me, I was glad I had won, but I wasn't completely happy.

In the pit below the stage the school orchestra started up its concluding number, "Don't Sit Under the Apple Tree," one of the most popular songs of the war—the song title, in fact, that was written under the picture of Judy and Les in the yearbook. As I scanned the auditorium for the faces of my mother and father the words kept going through my head. *Don't sit under. Don't sit. Don't.* I guessed there would be a lot of don'ts for a person who was trying to live up to the Citizenship Award.

I hurried toward the back of the audience to find my parents and Mick. Seeing me coming, my father smiled.

"Wonderful!" he said as he hugged me.

"Where's Mother?" The expression on his face changed. "Where's Mom?" I repeated.

He drew me aside, away from the people who were pushing their way out. "She left early. Grossie is sick."

"Sick? Sick with what? Who called her? Who knew Mom was here?" I couldn't understand what illness was so bad that my mother would have to run off suddenly.

"Don't worry, don't worry." My father held my shoulders. "Grossie's in the hospital, but she'll be coming home. Mother knew today that she would have to leave early, but she didn't want to spoil your evening. She was awfully sorry to miss the awards. She knows you won. Miss Fenster called her this afternoon."

"But what's the matter with Grossie?"

"She's had an operation. We'll know more about it after Mother talks to the doctor. Uncle Frank picked her up and took her to the hospital." My father took my free hand and with his other hand grabbed Mickey as he ran by. "I mean it now." He fixed his eyes on me. "Don't worry. Let's celebrate the award on the way home with an ice cream sundae." Sundaes were a special treat. We wouldn't be celebrating with a sundae unless everything was going to be all right.

"What a fine daughter you have," someone said to my father. When I turned around I saw that it was Mrs. Laubach and the lieutenant.

"That's what I think too," my father said.

"Thank you," I said, blushing. The evening had been so exciting and confusing. I hadn't seen Jules since before the award. I wondered if *he* thought I deserved it. Even though I was scared about a lot of things, there was also a lot to be happy about, I thought. School was over; the vacation was just beginning. There would be club meetings and the Fourth of July parade. And winning the award—that at least *should* be making me happy. I looked again at the inscription on the plaque in my hand. "To a student who exemplifies qualities of leadership, citizenship, and courage—Ellis Carpenter." I sure hope so, I thought.

Six

As my father, Mickey and I walked in the door, I knew right away that my mother wasn't home yet. An empty house sends out signals even before you enter it. I hung the Citizenship plaque next to the bookcase in my bedroom, in a spot where I could see it easily but other people couldn't. I figured that even though I didn't want to show it off, it wouldn't be a bad idea to have it around as a reminder to myself of what it stood for.

"Mother may be home very late," my father said. "I think you'd better get into bed."

I lay in bed thinking of everything that had happened during the day. First I pictured over again in my mind the award presentation. I hoped that I hadn't looked too silly and embarrassed on the stage. That was one thing about Sally Cabeen, she always looked and acted the same, as if she lived her whole life being ready to be called up for an award. I admired that, in a way. How would Sally feel about me now that I had won the award, I wondered. I wouldn't have minded being Sally's friend, but she acted as if she thought I was immature because I played with boys. Well, it didn't matter. Jules and even Sam were much more fun than Sally.

Even though it was late, I couldn't fall asleep. I kept expecting to hear my mother come in the door. What could be wrong with Grossie that could take my mother away so suddenly? And why didn't adults tell kids about serious things like illnesses, I wondered. *Anything* was better than not knowing. I thought of Grossie lying all covered up with a white sheet in the hospital. It was hard to picture. Usually Grossie was so strong and full of life. She was always telling me stories about the things she and her good friend Mary Ellis had done when they were girls . . . things that got them into trouble but were funny when you told about them years later, like playing hooky from school and dressing up to look old enough to get a job. I was close to Grossie, and suddenly the thought that she might be very sick brought on my scared feeling. The reflections on the glass panes of the bookcase didn't help me, either. "It's just a bookcase," I kept telling myself. But the eerie, hollow feeling inside me didn't go away. What would everybody think, I wondered, if they knew that the courageous award winner was lying in bed afraid of a bookcase? Finally, forcing myself to turn my back to it, I dropped off to sleep.

When I woke up the next morning Snow White's coffin had turned back into a piece of furniture. The sunlight streamed through the window, and there stood my mother examining the Citizenship Award.

"Congratulations," she said. "I'm sure sorry I missed it. Miss Fenster telephoned me, you know, and Daddy told me all the details about the program."

"How's Grossie?"

My mother hesitated for a minute and then sat down on the end of my bed. "She's doing all right. She's going to be in the hospital for a few weeks, and then she'll go home to her house."

"What's wrong with her?"

"She's had an operation. It was pretty serious, but the doctor says she's strong."

"But what's *wrong* with her?" I insisted.

"It's . . ." My mother hesitated again. "She's going to get better." I couldn't tell whether or not my mother was keeping anything from me. If Grossie were going to die, would Mom tell me the truth? I felt like asking more questions, but I was afraid I'd upset Mom, and I was afraid of what the answer might be.

"During these next two weeks I'll be visiting Grossie in the hospital every day," she said. "I'm sure I can count on you to take care of yourself and to watch Mick when I go into Windsor, can't I?"

I nodded. "Can I go too?"

"No, they don't allow children in the hospital. But you can see her just as soon as she comes home. She misses you."

"I was wondering why she didn't come to our house for two Fridays."

"She hasn't been feeling well. She went into the hospital two days ago, but I didn't want to worry you, especially before the awards program." Maybe Mom wasn't telling me more now because she didn't want to worry me.

"I think it's wonderful about the award," Mom looked at me seriously. "I'm very proud." Then she laughed and pulled off the sheet. "Now hop out of bed! First day of vacation!"

I had almost forgotten. Jules, Sam and I had agreed to have a club meeting. Before I had finished my breakfast, I heard Jules and Sam on the porch calling me.

"It's great that you got the award, Ellis," Jules said to me right off. He looked as if he meant it.

"Wait'll they find out." Sam paced around me like a detective cornering a criminal. "When they find out your grandmother is a Nazi, they'll come and take the award back."

"My grandmother's sick," I said. "She's in the hospital." Most kids would feel bad if they made mean jokes about a sick person, but Sam didn't care.

"I guess there's lots of places to hide Hitler inside a hospital," he said. "The doctors there could do an operation on his face to disguise him." Even though I gave Sam a dirty look, I had to admit that a trick like that might work, if Hitler were still alive.

"You're stupid," I said. "Germany's not even our enemy anymore. They gave up. They're sorry Hitler started the war."

"You two arguing won't solve anything," Jules interrupted. "I have ideas we can start working on for the club."

I turned my back on Sam. "What ideas do you have, Jules?"

"The whole club should dress up and go together in the Fourth of July parade," Jules said, "and when they hold the money scramble in the swimming pool on the Fourth we should contribute all we get to the club." I nodded.

Jules went on. He was loaded with ideas. "Tomorrow let's go to the creek and pick watercress to sell to people."

"Pfoooeee!" Sam made a face. He hated the taste of the watercress that grew in patches on the banks of Wissining Creek.

"*You* don't have to like it," I told him, "just so long as grown-ups buy it. What'll we do today, Jules?"

"How about a show right here in the neighborhood?"

"I know what," I suggested. "Let's go around when all the neighbors are home tonight and ask them if they want us to sing for a penny."

"Cri-men-ent-lees!" said Sam. That was a favorite word of his when he was disgusted. "Singing for a penny!"

"It'll be easy," I insisted. "We can just sing 'Playmate,' and 'Anchors Aweigh,' and maybe 'Watchman, What of the Night?'"

"The little kids don't even know that one."

"I'll teach it to them," I said. "We'll play school, and I'll teach them."

"Play *school*—ugh. On the first day of vacation?" Sam looked at me as if I were crazy.

"Don't worry," I told him. "We'll just sing for fun. There won't be any sequentials."

In the afternoon while we were sitting on my front steps practicing songs, Willie Pflug came waddling from his house on the next street. Willie was fat and babyish, even though he was practically our age.

"Hey," he puffed. "Hey, you kids. Somebody's moving into the house next door." When we looked, we could see through the backyards that a big van had pulled up next to Willie's house.

"Let's go!" Sam tore across the mall and through the yards to Willie's street. The rest of us followed.

"Do they have any kids?" Jules asked Willie.

"Don't know yet," Willie said. "My mother says they come from New York."

The whole club, including Tim, Ruthie and Mick, watched the movers carry things into the house.

"They've sure got *old* furniture," Sam said, as we watched the men squeeze a fancy cabinet through the front door.

"Those are antiques," Jules said. "Antiques are valuable."

"Hey, look at that!" I pointed to a rolltop desk with flowers on it. "I bet there's a girl!"

"Ugh," Sam said. He turned away in disgust.

That evening at seven o'clock the Milford Square Good Citizens' Model Airplane Club, with everybody present except Sibby Lane, met at the lamppost on the mall. We had invited Sibby, but she had a piano lesson.

"We're going to go around," Jules explained, "and ask the neighbors if they'd like to hear a song. Ellis will hold out the tin can when we finish, and we'll hope that they make a contribution to the war effort."

Following Jules, we made the rounds of the houses with Sam trailing behind. "I'm not singing," he said.

We must have picked a good time because most of the families in the square were sitting out on their porches. At the Shoppe's house they wanted to hear us sing "Playmate," a song about a little girl who couldn't play because her doll was sick. Their grown daughter kept laughing at how cute Ruthie was, and she got her to sing a solo, acting out the words.

The Shoppes appreciated it so much that they gave us a nickel. Ruthie was smiling, and I personally think it was the first time that anybody ever paid attention to her in her life.

"Dumb song," Sam said under his breath as we walked to the next house.

At the Goff's house Sam disappeared completely, but Ruthie sang "Bell-bottom trousers, coat of navy blue," about a little girl who admires a sailor, and when she grows up she falls in love with him. At Tim Feeney's house, his old grandmother who lived with the Feeneys, wanted us to sing "Ave Maria," but we didn't know that, so we sang "Mairzy Doats" instead. Mairzy Doats was a nonsense song, but it made sense if you sang it very slowly.

Grandma Feeney probably didn't understand, but she clapped anyway, and the Feeneys gave us another nickel.

After we had gone to all the other houses I thought Jules might suggest singing for Mrs. Lukesh, but when I pointed to her door, Jules shook his head no.

"Her lights are out," he said. "We might bother her." As far as I could remember, Mrs. Lukesh *never* had lights on. She must have spent every evening alone in her dark, creepy house. I hoped when I got old, I'd turn out to be full of life like Grossie and McKinley, and not a crab like Meany, our writing teacher, or a person who loved only grass, like Mrs. Lukesh.

Lightning bugs suddenly appeared, the street lamp in the middle of the mall went on, and I heard my father calling from the porch, "Time to come in!"

I grabbed Mick by the wrist and started pulling him toward home.

"Don't forget tomorrow," Jules said. "Let's leave early for the creek."

"Let's not take the little kids," Sam called. He tried to get rid of his half sister Ruthie whenever he could.

"I'm going," Mick said.

I felt like saying "No, you're not," but I was pretty sure my mother would expect me to take care of him while she was at the hospital, so I just gave him a mean look. Mick could be a pain. I dragged him the last few feet onto the porch where my father was waiting.

"Okay, you two, up the wooden mountain!" my father said. That's the way he always put it when it was time to go to bed.

Seven

The following day was perfect for the mile-long walk to the creek. Sibby met us at my house. Willie was never allowed to go anywhere out of his mother's sight, and Ruthie stayed home because Sam's stepmother had a day off from her defense plant.

"You'll take Mickey with you, won't you?" my mother asked. I felt as if I didn't have any choice.

"Do I have to?"

"You don't have to, but I wish you would. It won't be much longer that I'll ask this of you." I always wished my mother would just say, "You *have* to." That made things easier than leaving it up to me. Whenever she left a decision up to me I felt terrible if I didn't do the thing she wanted.

"C'mon, dumbbell," I grabbed him by his skinny wrist.

"Now, Ellis," my mother gave me a look, "I'm sure Mickey won't stand in the way of your having fun. Be careful," she said, as I picked up our lunch bags and walked out the door.

Wissining Creek, which curved through the town and

emptied into the Schuyler River, was one of my favorite places. In most spots the creek ran shallow enough to wade in up to the knees. There wasn't any place along the creek that was very deep, which was why we were allowed to go there by ourselves. On one side of the rippling water lay sunny fields of tall grass and daisies. On the other side were woods full of evergreens and pine cones, umbrella plants and jack-in-the-pulpits, rocks and moss.

"Let's head for the springhouse," Jules said, as the six of us—Tim had come too—walked along the path that ran parallel to the creek. The springhouse, a low building made entirely of stone, wasn't in use. Maybe, years before, someone had lived nearby, but now the springhouse was just a decoration in the grassy field. No one could go inside; there was a heavy rusted chain across the door. But the low, rounded shape and the rough stone surface made it perfect for climbing over.

"I'm for eating lunch on top of the springhouse," Sam said. "Right now." Even though it was still early, we all scrambled up on the roof and took out our sandwiches. Mick had been dragging behind us the whole way, just as I had expected. I had to push him up onto the roof from the bottom, while Sibby pulled him from the top.

"You're a pain," I told him, as he let pieces of egg salad fall out of his sandwich onto the rooftop.

"Let's go wading as soon as we eat," Sibby suggested. She wasn't anxious to start working.

"Save the lunch bags," Jules said. "We have to have

something to carry the watercress in. I brought a jar, but it won't all fit in there." Since we had left home Jules had been carefully juggling a Mason jar, the kind our mothers used to preserve homemade things from victory gardens. We finished our lunch.

"Last one down to the creek is a Nazi!" Sam yelled, as he leaped off the roof. Mickey balked at jumping, and we only got him to come down by Sibby's pushing and my catching him in my arms. The two of them took off, leaving me trudging behind. The others, minus their shoes and socks, were already wading in the creek.

"You're last! You're the Nazi!" Mick stood on the bank and giggled at me.

I was annoyed. "Get lost," I said. "You give me a bigger pain than a Nazi." I ignored him and stepped into the creek.

At first the cold water tingled and made our ankles numb, but soon we were all in up to our knees.

The stones in the creek bed were slippery, and it was a trick to keep balance.

"Watch it," I warned Mick. "Two bits you'll fall in and get your pants wet."

Everybody had forgotten about watercress for the time being. Sibby had spotted a cluster of cattails, and Jules was trying to scoop minnows into his Mason jar.

"Hold it, Jules," I shouted. "Let me get you something." I climbed out of the water to the spot where I had put down my lunch bag. Leftover sandwich crusts made perfect minnow bait.

"Good," Jules said, as he held the bread close to the mouth of the jar. "Hey, I got one." The minnow looked lonesome and confused inside.

"Yo, Jul-lee!" Sam yelled just at that moment from downstream. "Yo, El-lee!"

"What do ya want?"

"Come here and see what I see." Sibby, Tim and Mick followed us as we slid over stones to where Sam was perched on a flat rock. "Up there." Sam pointed into the woods. "There's that pipe Bruce Brown was talking about." Some yards up the bank, buried in the hillside—its opening partly camouflaged by roots and branches—was a cement sewer pipe big enough to walk into. Bruce had once bragged to our class that he had walked from one end of it to the other.

"Let's go up and look at it," Jules said. He left his jar on the flat rock, and even though I was annoyed at Mick, I helped him across the sharp stones between us and the bank.

The soft earth crumbled as we picked our way up the incline. There was a bit of a rocky shelf at the opening to the pipe. A thin trickle of water ran over the shelf and down into the creek. The six of us stepped inside. It was like a tunnel with no end. The first few feet were light enough for us to make out the damp cement over our heads, the rusty trickle of water under our feet, and the features of each others' faces. Beyond that was sheer blackness.

"Yooooooo!" shouted Sam suddenly. We all jumped. The echo of Sam's cry rang through the pipe. "There's a pit inside, you know," he said in a hushed voice.

Usually I didn't believe half the things Sam said, but this time I had heard the same story from Bruce Brown. There was supposed to be a great round hole in the floor somewhere in the pipe.

"If you fall in it," Sam's voice sounded hollow, "there's no hope. It's filled with garbage and rats."

"Who says?" I had never heard of that.

"Everybody knows it. That's why it's called a *sewer* pipe."

"Is that true, Jules?" Sibby asked him. "Are there rats?"

"I don't know. Let's walk in a little and see what the pipe is like."

"Jules, I don't want to." I didn't want Jules to think I was scared, but the thought of dropping into a pit of rats was horrible.

"Then don't," he said. "I'm only going to walk with a stick in front of me, so I can tell if there's a pit or not." Jules stepped out of the pipe and picked up the first good-sized stick he could find. It was an inch thick and taller than he was.

"I'm going in," Sam said. He liked to act big. "I'm telling Bruce we found the pit and walked around it."

"I'm going in," Sibby said. She was getting pretty courageous since she had started hanging around with our club.

"I'm *gone!*" Tim stepped in front of all of us and walked forward until we could see only a dim outline.

"Help!" he cried in a fake voice, as if he were disappearing into the pit.

"I'm going," said Mick.

"Well, stay behind me," I told him. "You're too little for this stuff." If everybody else was going into the pipe I had to go too. Otherwise they would think I was a coward.

"Let me go first, Tim." Jules advanced, tapping the ground ahead of him with a stick like a blind man. Tim and Sam inched along behind him. I tried to hang back, but I couldn't let Mick go without me.

"I told you to stay behind me!" I yelled.

"Off we go, into the wild, blue yonder . . ." sang Sam. Usually he hated to sing.

"Ugh, the walls are slimy!" Sibby must have figured that you couldn't get into much trouble walking on the curved part of the pipe. Just like in Sibby's barn, the danger lay in the middle. Tim was making hooting noises up ahead. All the voices bounced off the walls and made the pipe sound like a madhouse.

"Shush, everybody!" Jules shouted all of a sudden. The pipe grew deadly quiet. Over our shoulders we could see the circle of light at the entrance, but we could barely see each other. The only sound was the slight scraping of Jules' stick against the cement. Jules held still, and all was quiet. Then we heard a faint rustling and a drip, drip.

"Help!" screamed Sam, "we're at the pit!" Nobody waited to decide if he was right or not. We all turned and ran back as fast as we could until we breathed the fresh air outside the pipe.

"You scaredy-cats!" Tim said as we caught our breath. "That wasn't anything!" Still, the sunshine felt good. Jules stepped off the rock ledge and put a twig between his teeth.

"Remember why we came to the creek?" he asked.

"For watercress!" I said. Before anybody could suggest going back into the pipe I jumped off the ledge, and clinging to roots and rocks, I led the way to the water below.

"I see some!" Jules cried, and we followed him to a spot where the water ran cold and clear under shade trees. The watercress grew right there in the creek.

I ate my first handful, washing it off in the creek water. It made my tongue burn slightly, in a pleasant way.

"Leave it wet," Jules called, "it stays fresher that way."

We had gathered quite a bit of watercress before I looked around and first noticed that Mick wasn't there. Before I said anything I turned in a complete circle, checking every spot in view.

"Anybody seen Mick?" I tried to ask calmly, but my voice cracked.

"Mick?" Everybody stopped picking and looked up.

Jules paused and thought. "I don't remember seeing him at all since we started gathering watercress."

"Did somebody help him down the hill after we came out of the pipe?" I asked.

"Not me," said Tim. The others shook their heads. Jules calmly waded over to the bank nearest the woods and laid down his watercress.

"You don't think he could still be up there, do you?" I asked him.

"We'd better check," he said. The rest of us came out of the creek.

"The first thing to do," Jules said, "is to call him very loud. No sense chasing in the wrong direction." He cupped his hands in front of his mouth. "Yo, Mick-kee!"

"Yo, Mick-kee!" we shouted in unison. The only answer was the hum of insects in the grass and the cry of one lone mourning dove. I faced the other way and called again.

"Let's check different places," Jules suggested. "Ellis, come with me up to the pipe. Sam, go to the springhouse. Tim and Sibby, walk across the fields to the road. Keep calling his name a lot and meet back here in ten minutes."

It was lucky that Jules took charge because I was in a panic. My imagination started running wild, and I felt weak and sick.

"He wouldn't have gone back into the pipe by himself, do you think, Jules?" I asked him as we climbed the hill. I had trouble keeping up, because suddenly I couldn't breathe right.

"I doubt it. Maybe he's playing around the shelf."

"But then he'd hear us yelling."

"Well, maybe the wind is blowing the other way." I knew Jules was just saying that. There was no wind blowing at all. Making our way up to the pipe seemed like hurrying in a dream. The faster I tried to go, the longer it seemed to take. Every minute or so we heard the cry of "Yo, Mick-kee" but no answer.

"Has Mickey ever gone off before?" Jules gave me a hand up to the next stump.

"Not that I know of. Once he and Ruthie ran away, but they only went to the end of the square, and then they came back for cookies."

"He wouldn't hide for a joke, would he?" We pulled ourselves up on the rock shelf.

"He'd better not!" I said, "I'd kill him!" And then, realizing what I had said, I started to cry. "Call him, Jules, I can't."

Jules stood inside the opening. "Yo, Mick-kee!" All we heard was a faint sound like the last water draining from a bathtub. Jules called again.

"Don't," I sobbed. "It's worse to *not* hear him answer!"

"He couldn't fall in the pit." Jules came over to where I was crouching on the shelf and sat close to me. "There *isn't* any pit," he said softly.

I looked in his eyes. "You said there was. So did Sam and Bruce Brown. There *is so* a pit." But I hoped he was right.

"There are plenty of places around here for a kid to hide or get lost." Jules got up.

"Get lost," I repeated. "I told Mickey to get lost! When I was mad at him before for being so slow and being such a pain. Could he have thought I meant it?"

"Little kids can be dumb," Jules said, shaking his head, "but I don't think so. Everybody knows what 'Get lost' means. Besides, even if he did go off because of what you said, we'll find him. You can't hide out forever in these woods. It's not like some jungle in the Pacific. Let's call again—one, two, three, Yo, Mick-kee . . ."

I turned around and looked below, where I caught a glimpse of Sibby and Tim, by now near the road. Only a corner of the springhouse could be seen through the trees, and I couldn't see Sam at all. Every second that went by made me feel more helpless, frightened and sick to my stomach.

"Maybe there's an empty well or something that he could have fallen into," I said. "Or a trap. Or maybe he got bitten by a snake."

"He'd yell if that happened," Jules said. "Maybe he went *up* the hill here, instead of down. I wonder what's at the top." Above the pipe the incline was sharper. There was no path at all, but by hanging on to saplings and rocks it was possible to climb. "Let's go," Jules grabbed my hand.

"Aren't ten minutes up?" I asked. "You said to meet in ten minutes."

"We'll just check this one place before we go down."

"Mick couldn't climb up here," I said as we made our way up the sheer cliff.

"Jules," I jerked his hand to make him look at me. "Have you gotten any message about Mick?"

"Message?"

"You know, message about whether he's safe."

"Oh, that." He bit his lip and looked away for a second. "Not exactly a message, but a feeling. Let's go up on top."

"Is he safe, Jules?" I gripped his hand hard.

"I'm pretty sure he's safe." He let go of me to reach for a higher rock.

I wasn't sure how I felt about Jules' messages. Even though I trusted him more than anybody, the messages seemed like magic, and I didn't really believe in magic. I didn't object to magic tricks like the ones Mingus sold—they could be explained. But knowing things before they happened was scary, and I didn't like to think it was possible.

On the rest of the way up the cliff I started picturing different terrible scenes: finding Mick badly hurt; suddenly coming upon his body, propped against a tree, maybe; facing my mother and telling her that Mick disappeared because I had said, "Get lost." How would my mother feel if Mick wasn't found? Didn't she have enough worries already, and hadn't she warned me, "Be careful"?

Jules reached the top before I did. "Hey!" He shouted with such surprise that I thought he had found Mick. "It's the street! The top of the cliff is just a regular street!" He pulled me up the last few feet. I didn't know the name of the road, but I recognized it as a spot behind John Elting's house. It was strange that we hadn't thought about the fact that the creek and the woods were, after all, right in Wissining. Even though

Mick wasn't there, it seemed a little less frightening to realize that the pipe and the springhouse weren't so far from civilization.

"Mick-kee!" I shouted. And then, far away, where the street turned down toward the creek and the fields, I saw Sam waving his hands and running in our direction.

"Did you find him? Did you find him?" I called, as I headed to meet Sam. When we were close enough to see each other's faces, we slowed to a walk. I thought I might faint from being out of breath.

"Did you find him?" I panted.

Sam smiled. "Yup. Pat's got him." He threw himself on the grass by the road. "Whew!" he sighed. Pat was one of the town policemen. He was known for being nice to kids.

"Where did *Pat* find him?"

Sam's chest heaved from his running. "Mick must've walked sideways through the woods instead of down to the creek the way we went. Then he got scared 'cause he didn't know where he was. Pat found him on the road near the springhouse. He's sitting in Pat's patrol car."

"That dope," I said. But I laughed and kept on running until I got there. Mick was sitting calmly in the front seat of the car playing tic-tac-toe with Pat.

"Here's the criminal, Ellis," said Pat, who knew the name of everyone in town. "You weren't worried about him, were you?" I laughed and cried at the same time.

"Mick, you jerk!" I stuck my head in the window,

"what did you get us worried for like that? I'm telling mother!"

"Go ahead," he said, drawing an X between two O's. That kid could be a pain.

Pat drove us all home in his patrol car. I guess he could tell we had been pretty upset. The only one who wasn't upset was Mick.

"Why did you go off like that?" I asked him, half relieved and half angry.

"Nobody waited for me," he said. He wasn't at all sorry. He was happy in fact, sitting up front with Pat and fooling around with the two-way radio. I knew I'd have to tell my mother about the incident, especially since she would probably see us arriving in a police car. When we drove up in front of our house, everybody piled out, and we thanked Pat a lot for helping us. As Pat pulled away Jules clapped his hand to his forehead.

"Remember what we went for?"

"Watercress!" We all groaned. By now it must have been all wilted on the bank of the creek. The minnow was probably still there too, stranded in the Mason jar.

"We could go again tomorrow . . ." Tim said hopefully.

"*Count me out!*" I said, grabbing Mick by the wrist and pulling him into the house.

$\mathcal{E}$ight

Before we knew it the early days of vacation had passed
—days spent swimming, and practicing magic tricks
and checking every day to see if the new family had
moved in yet next to Willie's house. Suddenly it was the
Fourth of July. The Fourth of July was a very important holiday in Wissining, almost as important as Christmas. Since gasoline was rationed, it was hard to go away
on vacations, and everybody in the whole town came to
the parade, the contests and the big dance on Fourth of
July night.

About eight o'clock in the morning the club gathered
in front of my house to get dressed in our parade costumes. We had decided that the whole club would go
dressed as marines landing on the Pacific island of Iwo
Jima. I thought I looked pretty good. I was wearing a
pair of Jules' old khaki pants and a work shirt of my
father's that was the same color. I had sewn the patches
I won from collecting tin cans onto my shirt sleeve, so
it looked like a real uniform. Jules had also lent me a
pair of hiking boots that once belonged to Les. When

I tucked my hair under Mick's toy Marine helmet, it was pretty hard to tell I was a girl.

It wasn't easy borrowing the Marine helmet from Mick, who wanted to wear it himself. That kid had done pretty much whatever he liked since the day he had gotten lost at the creek. He had told my mother that we left him, and she had blamed me for going near the sewer pipe. The only way I got the helmet from Mick at all was by sitting on him and tickling him.

Jules and Sam carried the McConagys' flagpole between them, and Tim held the sign we made that read: FROM THE HALLS OF IWO JIMA TO THE SHORES OF WISSIN-ING. Sibby wasn't going to be in the parade because her parents were taking her somewhere on a picnic, and Willie's mother wouldn't let him march in the hot sun.

"Good luck!" My mother said, as the six of us started off. "I'll see you tonight." She was going to be away all day. There was good news: Grossie was coming home from the hospital.

By the time we arrived at the playground where the parade was starting people were already lined up on both sides of the street. Some kids were wearing very fancy costumes. Freddy Barth, the grandson of the richest family in town, wore a beautiful George Washington suit with lace cuffs and a silver wig. Sally Cabeen, I had to admit, looked like a movie star in a dress made out of net material. She was supposed to be the Spirit of Liberty. A lot of bicycles and tricycles had red, white and blue crepe paper woven through the spokes of the wheels and flags attached to the handlebars.

"Hey, Ellis!" called a voice. I saw somebody dressed as an American Indian and I had to look twice to be sure that it was Bruce Brown. "Guess who's going to win the next Citizenship Award!" He pointed to himself and pretended to pat himself on the back. This was the first time I had seen him since the awards program.

The high school band played "Over hill, over dale, we will hit the dusty trail, as those caissons go rolling along!" As we marched through Wissining the whole parade stopped and the band played a patriotic song whenever we passed by a house that had a blue star or a gold star in the window. A blue star meant that they had a son still fighting in the war; a gold star meant that a son had been killed in action. I thought a lot about Les, especially since I was wearing his old boots.

The part of the Fourth of July that I liked best took place after lunch—the money scramble. Someone in Wissining, who kept his name a secret, contributed lots of coins to be thrown into the town swimming pool. It must have been the Barths who gave the money. No one else was that rich. You could keep all the coins you dived for, and Jules, Sam, Tim and I had agreed earlier to hand our money over to the club.

The swimming pool shimmered in the afternoon sun. The bottom was clean and blue, with wide black lines that looked magnified through the water. Wait until I get those coins, I thought.

"All contestants will now line up at the side of the pool for the annual Fourth of July coin dive," said a voice over the loudspeaker. I searched for Jules and Sam, but I couldn't see them anywhere. In fact, I hadn't seen much of them since the parade. Two high school boys, both looking like Tarzan of the Apes, shoved in on either side of me at the edge of the pool. While I tried different stances for getting off a good dive the lifeguards walked behind us, hurling coins—mostly pennies—over our heads into the water. The sky rained money, as if we were in a fairy tale.

"Contestants ready." My chest hurt from taking in so much air. "Take your mark." I covered my ears to dull the sound of the blank shot.

"Go!" The starting gun cracked. The two Tarzans jostled me with their elbows as they sprang out over the water. Flashes of spray glistened, bubbles rose from beneath the surface, blurred forms shot along the black lines under the water. I stood rooted to the matting by the edge of the pool. What am I waiting for! I thought.

Taking in an enormous gulp of air, I jumped in feet first. Stupid me, I thought. Dive down! Even though the water was only neck deep, I had trouble getting to the bottom. Just as I turned myself downward my lungs felt as if they were going to burst, and I had to surface. Finally I touched bottom and saw something round, but it turned out to be a pebble. Bodies bumped and shoved me under the water. Once when I had the tips of my fingers on a penny someone bigger snatched it out from under me.

At last I saw a clear space and something that looked like a coin. Filling my lungs, I did a surface dive. It *was* a coin, and it was *silver*. I shoved hard against some-body coming from the right and gulped for air. Nose-diving, I got my hand on it. A quarter? A dime at least? Oh, no! A penny! One of those 1943 silver-colored pennies that they made because copper was scarce. Not even made of real silver but of some ugly mixture with aluminum in it. As I sucked in air for the next dive, the sound of a whistle rang in my ears. The scramble was over. I had found *one penny*.

"That's too bad," my father said as we sat at the supper table. "But you remember, don't you, what Grossie wrote in your autograph book?" I did remember. It said, "A good name is rather to be chosen than great riches." Well, I guess I was pretty lucky. Ellis was a good name. But when it came to the Fourth of July money scramble, I had hoped for great riches.

Jules, Sam and I walked together to the playground in the evening. I had long since taken off my marine outfit and was wearing my favorite pair of shorts for the dance. Jules was especially quiet. I wondered if something had happened during the day—if maybe he had gotten a message.

"Where's your penny from the scramble?" Sam sneered at me. "Are you splitting it three ways?"

"I'm giving it to the club like we agreed," I said glumly.

"What do you mean," he screwed up his face, "*we agreed?* Who said anything about giving the money to the club?" Sam had ended up with forty-five cents in the scramble.

"We all did. Don't you remember?"

"Nuts, I never agreed."

"Sam, you liar." I felt like punching him.

"Only goody-goodies like *you* agreed. Goody-goodies who win citizenship awards!" He twisted his words so that the award sounded like something terrible.

"Jules, didn't we agree to hand over the money?" Jules had found twelve cents in the pool. "Jules?"

He seemed to be thinking about something else. "I . . . I don't remember," he said. I couldn't believe it. Jules never forgot things and he almost always backed me up.

"I mean the *swimming money*, Jules." I poked him.

"I don't remember." There was a tone to his voice that made me drop the subject.

"You going to play hide-and-seek during the dance, Jules?" I asked. We younger kids usually hung around at dances just to watch and get free refreshments, or to play outside.

"I don't know," he said as if he were annoyed. He looked strange. Maybe he had eaten too many hot dogs and Popsicles.

The dance was held at the playground under a long pavilion with a cement floor. For the Fourth of July all the picnic tables were pushed aside and phonograph music floated through the night air. Most of the high school kids had come with dates. As I looked at them laughing and talking, I wondered what it would be like to wear cute short dresses, hold hands with a boy and comb my hair a lot like the older girls at the dance. For us younger kids the dance was mostly a chance to fool around and drink pink lemonade.

Everyone was there. Bruce Brown was showing off as usual. Suddenly Bruce looked toward the entrance to the pavilion. "Hubba, hubba!" he said. That meant a beautiful girl must be coming. I turned around, and so did Jules and Sam. Sally Cabeen, wearing a white dress, her hair down her back in soft curls, had just walked into the pavilion with Philip Helmuth.

"Hubba, hubba, woo-woo!" Bruce called and wiggled his eyebrows up and down until he caught Sally's attention.

"Hi, Bruce," she smiled. "Hi, Jules."

"Hi, Sam," Sam shouted.

"Oh, Sammy, I didn't see you! Hi! And there's Ellis . . ."

For somebody with everything else in such good shape, she sure had poor eyesight. I was sort of sorry I had worn my shorts. Everybody looked so dressed up.

"Ellis, I meant to tell you," she leaned her head forward, close to Philip, supposedly to see me better, "I'm so glad you won the Citizenship Award."

"I'll bet she is," Sam mumbled under his breath, which was exactly what I was thinking.

"Thanks," I said. Sally and Philip drifted off, and I turned to Jules. "Want to go outside and start hide-and-seek?" I asked him.

"Not now," he said, fading back to sit on a bench at the edge of the pavilion. The dancing had begun. I hoisted myself up on a table near where Jules was. It was fun to watch the older kids jitterbugging to the fast numbers and dancing very close when they played something romantic like "I'll be seeing you in all the old familiar places." At the far end of the pavilion I thought I saw Judy, the girl who was in the yearbook picture with Les. Maybe it wouldn't be so bad to grow up and have boy friends who'd write you letters, and wear your hair long and shiny, and dance close.

Then I saw something that almost knocked me over. Right in the middle of all the high school couples stood Philip Helmuth and Sally Cabeen, swaying with their arms wrapped around each other. We had all been forced to take ballroom dancing lessons in the school gym—lessons that usually ended up in a riot that we called "boys chase girls." But now Philip and Sally were holding each other and looking into each others' eyes in a way that we hadn't learned in school.

I turned to Jules. "Look at that," I scoffed. He nodded solemnly. Sam came and sat down quietly next to him. The two of them stared at the dancers.

"Want lemonade?" I asked. They both shook their heads no. As I walked alone over to the refreshment table I saw Bruce Brown tapping Philip on the shoulder to cut in on the dancing. Philip argued for a second and then let Bruce go off with Sally. I hadn't been very surprised at seeing Philip and Sally on the dance floor— Philip loved girls, and Sally was always going around acting like a pinup girl. But Bruce? Was he going to start loving girls too?

Sipping my lemonade, I walked slowly back to where I had been sitting. The floor was crowded with teen-agers, soldiers in uniform and parents. Philip Helmuth must feel bad, I thought, having Bruce cut in on him like that. And then I saw that I was wrong. Philip wasn't feeling bad at all. Instead he looked as if he was having a great time. He and Marybeth Gruen were swaying back and forth with their eyes closed, while the voice on the record sang:

> I only know that love is grand,
> and the thing that's known as romance is
> wonderful, wonderful in every way, so they say.

Marybeth Gruen, ugh! I thought. I wouldn't want to dance so close to the daughter of an *undertaker.*

When the music stopped there was a lot of clapping, laughing and talking. Bruce, Philip and John Elting came over to Jules and Sam, and I could see the whole bunch of them whispering.

"Go ahead," Sam snickered, "ask her. I dare ya." I couldn't tell what they were talking about. Meanwhile Sally and Marybeth were leaning against a post talking to some older boys. Sally threw back her head and laughed a lot. The two of them, Sally and Marybeth, in their cool summer dresses, with their blond hair flowing, looked like an advertisement for Pepsi-Cola.

As the music started up, there was a rush of activity around Sally and Marybeth. It seemed as if every boy in Wissining had just discovered them. One of the Tarzans who had pushed me at the pool swept Sally away. John Elting, who had never pushed anybody before in his life, danced off with Marybeth. Philip, Bruce, Jules and half a dozen others stood with their mouths open, watching in disappointment. Jules! Sam had dared Jules to dance with Sally!

Suddenly I felt sick. The Fourth of July had started out as such a good day. We had looked so good in the parade. The money scramble had been fun, even if I hadn't gotten a lot of coins. I had been so happy just a little while earlier because of wearing my favorite shorts. But now everything was different. Shorts! Nobody was wearing shorts except me. Everybody else was wearing fairy-tale dresses. Maybe boys didn't mind me in their clubs, but when it was time to act like grown-ups, boys looked at Sally, not me. Maybe it would be that way from now on. Boys weren't interested in girls who won citizenship awards.

Even though Tarzan had taken Sally away, the others didn't give up. One by one a steady flow of boys cut in on Sally. Finally Jules got his turn. It could have been my imagination, but it seemed as if she smiled more and snuggled closer to Jules than to all the rest. I was getting sicker. Maybe it was all the hot dogs, Popsicles and lemonade.

I glanced around to see if anyone was looking at me. I would even dance, I thought, if somebody asked me. But nobody did. Every time another couple went out on the floor and every time Sam or Jules laughed or made a remark I shrank farther back in my corner. The record ended.

"I danced with her!" Sam ran up to Jules and pounded him on the back. "Hey, Julie, you owe me a nickel!" I couldn't believe it. Jules was betting good money so that Sam would dance with Sally.

"Not *yet*, I don't," Jules said. "Remember the other bet." I tried to catch his eye, but Jules walked away toward the refreshment stand where Sally was drinking lemonade. The next thing I knew, I saw Jules and Sally leaving the pavilion together. Outside the sky was black, and the woods beyond the pavilion looked spooky.

"Where are they going?" I motioned to Sam. My curiosity was killing me.

"Outside," he grinned. "I promised Jules my whole forty-five cents if he kissed Sally."

I felt as if the cement floor had dropped away. "Is he going to?"

"Sure!" Sam said. "Jules *loves* Sally." I didn't wait any longer. As soon as Sam looked the other way I hurried out of the pavilion. Just as I set foot on the gravel path at the bottom of the steps I saw again a face I had seen earlier. Even though it was quite dark I could pick out a soldier in uniform with his arm around a girl. While I stood there he stooped and kissed her for a long time like in the movies. I knew now for sure that the girl was Judy, who had once written to Les, "Don't sit under the apple tree with anyone else but me."

Things could change awfully fast in this world, I thought. I turned away from Judy and the soldier and ran in the dark as fast as I could, but I didn't actually cry until I was home in bed.

Nine

The next morning when I woke up it was raining hard. I lay on my back, staring at a big stain on the ceiling and feeling pretty bad. The door opened and my mother came in to see if I was awake.

"I'm sick," I said. She came over and put her hand on my forehead, but I guess it didn't feel very hot.

"Eating too much junk," she muttered. A person could be lying in an ambulance, covered with blood, with broken bones sticking out all over, and my mother would be shaking her head and saying, "Comes from eating too much junk."

"Okay, stay in bed," she said on her way out of the room. Probably she thought I would argue and leap right up, but I fooled her.

"I think I will stay in bed." I nestled down in the sheets and pretended to go back to sleep. She stuck her head back in the door.

"Do you really feel bad?"

"Yes," I said. That was the honest truth.

"I'm sorry." She paused. "Then you'll have to wait until tomorrow to go visit Grossie."

"Oh, she's home!" I felt ashamed that I had forgotten. I had been thinking so much about myself. Maybe I should insist even now that I was well enough to visit Grossie today.

"Yes, she's home," my mother said. "How about going to see her tomorrow. Why don't you rest today?"

That settled it. I leaned back and started thinking about things. First I noticed that the spot on the ceiling was shaped like a man with a beard, and I wondered whether it was true that God knew everything and decided who was good and who was bad. If there was a heaven was it hard to earn, like the Citizenship Award, or could anybody who was around get in, like our Model Airplane Club? If God was as kind as He was supposed to be He probably welcomed everybody in, but on the other hand somebody perfect like God might have pretty high standards.

Then I started thinking about the Fourth of July and about winning and losing. That's all anybody cared about. Bruce, Sally, John and I had cared about winning the Citizenship Award. I had wanted to beat everybody out in the money scramble. Sally was probably trying to win all the boys and make them love her. Even the whole country of America was trying to beat Japan now, the way we had beaten Germany and Italy —because they had been trying to beat us first.

Most games were fun, but lately I was seeing how games could hurt people. I had gotten hurt in Sally's game. But that was nothing, I realized, compared to Les' getting hurt or even killed in the war. I knew that

the war was different from other games. We had to win
the war because the Axis Powers—the enemy—had been
too greedy and were killing innocent people. But I
wished the whole thing could be over and that everybody in the whole world, including myself, could stop
caring so much about winning.

Thinking about all that serious stuff made me feel
like getting my mind on something else, so I lay
around the whole morning reading a Nancy Drew mystery book. It wouldn't be bad, I thought, to grow up to
be a girl detective. Of course Nancy Drew had a head
start because of her father being Carson Drew, well-
known criminal lawyer, but maybe an ordinary person
could also get into that kind of work.

After lunch I tuned in soap operas on the radio. Even
though a lot of sad things were happening on all the
different programs, I still got interested. Somebody, for
instance, was on trial for murder, but he couldn't remember if he'd done it, because he had amnesia. In
another serial Mary Noble, "Backstage Wife," had a
husband who was a matinee idol. Mary kept worrying
that he would fall in love with a beautiful young actress.
Whenever one of the stories got to an exciting place
the announcer would interrupt to try to get you to
send a dollar and a box top for a beautiful simulated
pearl brooch or some other piece of junk. The last soap
opera I listened to was called "When A Girl Marries,"
about a girl named Joan. If getting married brought
you all the trouble Joan had I couldn't see why any-

body would do it. I ended up wondering if Jules would marry Sally. It was a pretty depressing day.

"Here's fifty cents," my mother said the next morning. I was to go by myself on a bus and trolley car to Grossie's house in Windsor. "Ten cents for the bus each way, five for the trolley, and twenty for mad money. Put it in a safe place."

My mother always gave me "mad money," which was supposed to be for an emergency, but which I usually spent on things to eat. I put the change in a coin purse and tucked it in the back pocket of my shorts. I was glad to be going somewhere on my own. I felt a lot better than the day before, but I wasn't in the mood to see anybody from Milford Square or anybody at all who was my age.

"Grossie will be resting," my mother said. "There's a practical nurse there today to take care of anything she needs. You help too. Try not to let her get up."

"Does she look the same?"

My mother hesitated for a second. "Yes, but she's been very sick. She's thinner. Tell her what you've been doing. Tell her about the award." My mother walked me to the front porch. "Be careful now, Little Red Riding Hood. Don't talk to any big bad wolves, and don't forget to telephone me when you get there."

I walked up the hill to the Gruen Funeral Home to wait for the Windsor bus. When it came I paid the driver ten cents and took a seat in the front next to a window. Luckily nobody I knew was on the bus because I didn't feel like talking. It was fun to ride by all the familiar places on Windsor Avenue and look at them in a whole different way—as if I were a stranger seeing them for the first time.

At the corner by the Rialto Theater we stopped for a train. Sometimes when the train stopped there kids would try to cross over the couplings between the train cars. For a second I thought I saw Sam Goff standing on a coupling, but the train moved on before I could tell for sure if it was Sam. When we passed the magic shop I looked for Mingus, but I didn't see anyone. Probably he was still appearing at the Windsor Fair. The only person I did recognize on the whole trip across the bridge was McKinley, who looked almost like a dwarf as he pushed his orange ice-cream cart through the middle of the truck and bus traffic.

Once we had crossed the river the scene was different. Windsor was a city. Shops and office buildings were crammed next to each other for blocks and blocks: the Army-Navy store, drugstores with high stools at their counters, the stamp and coin shop. On the corner by Windsor's largest department store stood a vendor selling hot pretzels. My mouth started watering for a pretzel so badly that I got off the bus at the next corner and walked back to buy one. Willie Pflug's mother wouldn't let him eat soft pretzels because she said the seller's hands were dirty, but I didn't care. I munched slowly on my pretzel and took in all the sights and sounds as I walked toward the trolley stop by the farmers' market.

I hadn't meant to go inside the market, but when I looked through the doorway the bustle and excitement and the delicious odors pulled me in. Since it was Friday all the farmers had come from the country with their vegetables, fresh-killed chickens and home-cured Lebanon bologna. Most of the farmers and their chubby, rosy-cheeked wives spoke Pennsylvania Dutch. Every now and then I caught a word I understood, but mostly I just listened to the singsong of their chatter. I stood for a second in front of a bakery booth.

"Want a *fastnacht*, little girl?" a big woman in an apron asked me. Her voice rose up and ended back down again in the Pennsylvania Dutch way when she asked a question. The homemade doughnuts, called *fastnachts*, looked delicious.

"I'm not sure I have enough money," I said.

"There nah, take one." She handed me a fat, sugar-powdered *fastnacht* wrapped in a napkin and waited until I took a bite. "Iss good, ain't?" I nodded. "No money," she said, shaking her head and waving her finger back and forth at me. "For free it iss today. You tell Mother that Schwenner's *fastnachts* iss best, yah?" I smacked my lips to make sure she knew how much I appreciated the treat. Schwenner's *were* best.

I wiped the powdered sugar off my hands as I walked to the corner to wait for the trolley car. It was more interesting to stand on the street in Windsor than back in Wissining where you knew everybody. At the stop a woman and her little boy were already waiting for the car.

"Does the car stop here for Berk Street?" I asked her.

"Yes," she said. "Where are you going?"

"Out there. Berk Street. To my grandmother's."

"You don't live round here?"

"No, I live in Wissining."

"Oh, that's where the rich folks live!" I nodded. I supposed she meant the Barths. They sure were famous.

Her little boy was hanging on her arm as if it were a swing. "Now you mind!" she shouted, shaking him off.

"Money grows on trees in your backyard?" she winked at me.

"No! Not mine! Only the Barths are rich." She gave me a funny look as if she'd never heard of them after all.

Just then the trolley car rounded the corner and I reached in my back pocket for my coin purse. Suddenly my heart started pounding—the pocket was flat. I reached in the side pocket. Empty. A terrible wave of panic came over me.

"Here comes the car," the little boy said.

"Oh, my gosh . . ." my face must have shown something was wrong.

"What's that?"

"I can't find my coin purse. It was in my back pocket!" I kept feeling my shorts as if some new pocket would appear.

"You mean, you got no money?"

"No! It's lost! I had it! It was right *here*." I patted the pocket. Maybe she didn't even believe me. I felt like crying. I turned around in circles looking at the ground. The trolley screeched to a halt. Its doors swung open while the motor settled into an impatient chug-chug-chug.

"What'll I do?" I said, talking to myself. I pictured myself getting lost trying to walk to Grossie's or walking all day to get home to Wissining.

"You take this now," The woman pushed something into my hand. It was a quarter.

"Oh . . ." I hated to take money from somebody I didn't know, but just then she took her little boy's hand and stepped up into the streetcar.

"You coming?" The conductor called.

"Yes," I whispered, as I stepped on behind them. The conductor took the quarter and gave me twenty cents change. I followed the woman to her seat and held out the twenty cents.

"No, you keep it, honey. You got to get home." She pulled the little boy onto her lap and motioned for me to sit down next to her.

"But my Grossie'll give me money—my grandmother," I insisted, still holding out the change. "Once I get there she'll give it to me."

"Just for safety," she said.

After that I stopped trying to argue. Settling back on the wicker seat that made crisscross marks on your skin, I looked out the window. The trolley went along past rows of attached houses of brownstone and of brick painted red. In front of some of them women were sweeping the sidewalks.

"I must have dropped my coin purse by the pretzel man, or in the market," I said.

"That's a shame. But don't you mind." She patted my hand. I wished that I still had the pretzel or the *fastnacht* to give to her son, but I had finished them both. It was really nice, chugging along next to the woman and her son, passing by playgrounds and unfamiliar corner stores.

"I could send you the quarter back," I said hopefully.

"Don't you mind," she repeated, shaking her head. She stood up then to pull on the cord, and when we reached the next stop, I got up to let them out.

"Thanks a lot," I said. She smiled. When the trolley screeched away again I waved to her through the window.

Once I was sitting all alone on the streetcar I started feeling a little nervous about getting off at the right stop. Things like losing the coin purse made you realize that you could never be sure of anything. I thought back to all the places I had been in Windsor and tried to picture where it might be lying right then. Luckily there was only forty cents in it, but the purse itself was one I had made by hand, and I felt sorry that I would probably never see it again.

"Would you please tell me when we get to Berk Street?" I asked the conductor in a small voice.

"Coming up next," he said.

$\mathcal{T}_{en}$

Grossie's block was a row of brownstone houses that all looked the same. Each one had a porch that gave a clue about who lived there. Some had gliders, or hammocks or wicker furniture with thin cushions covered in flowered material. In the evenings the porches were always full of people sitting outside to enjoy a breeze and to talk to those who passed by. Now, in the late morning, there were just a few children playing on the porches as I walked towards Grossie's house. The Berger girls, next door to Grossie's, were playing paper dolls on a card table.

"Hi," I said.

"Hi, Ellis!" Dorothy, the older one, always acted as if I were her best friend, even though she saw me about three times a year. Claire, the younger one, just grunted. She must have thought her sister would quit playing with her and hang around with me.

"Want to come on up to my room and play paper dolls?" Dorothy asked.

"Sorry, I can't" I said. "My Grossie's sick."

"Why do you call her Grossie?" Claire wanted to

know. She gave me a nasty look even though she knew now that I wasn't going to take her sister away.

"It's short for *Grossmutter*—grandmother in German. My cousins started it so they wouldn't get their two grandmothers mixed up. I gotta go in now," I said.

The screen door was unlocked. First I thought maybe I should ring the bell to let the practical nurse know I was there, but I ended up just walking in. The downstairs of the house was always dark and silent, even when Grossie was well. The living room was filled with heavy carved furniture. I wondered if they were valuable antiques like those the new people next to Willie had. On the walls hung a lot of oil paintings and a number of deer heads and antlers. My grandfather had been a painter. Most of his scenes were of forests, lakes, wrecked castles and brown windmills. Together with the deer heads, they gave you the feeling of being in the middle of the story, "Hansel and Gretel." There was even one place where he had painted ivy right on the wall. Although it was dark, the room wasn't creepy but sort of peaceful.

I would have liked to sit in the living room for a while without anyone knowing I was there, but I didn't want to frighten the nurse in case she suddenly came in and saw me sitting there. Besides, I wanted to see Grossie.

"Grossie," I called, as I ran up the steps. Then I clapped my hand over my mouth. Maybe she was sleeping, I thought.

"Here!" a voice answered from the bedroom. "Ellis?"

The light in the room was dim. I drew in my breath. I had never seen Grossie sick before. Wearing a peach-colored dressing gown, she looked small propped up in her big carved bed. Grossie held out her arms to me. I ran toward her and when I grabbed her hands she squeezed mine hard.

"See how strong I am?" she laughed. Grossie spoke with a slight accent—not like German in the war movies —just a gentle sound in her throat when she said the letter r.

"You look good," I said. She did look pretty good but much thinner and paler than the last time I had seen her. Next to her on the bed lay a box of photographs, old letters and other things from the past. When she pushed aside a little blue book that she must have been reading I noticed that her hands shook. Just then the practical nurse came into the room.

"Mrs. Heard, this is my granddaughter Ellis."

"What a nice big girl!" I wasn't very big at all, but she must have been trying to be pleasant.

"Is that the child who's named for Mary?" she asked Grossie.

"Yes," my grandmother nodded. Then turning to me, "Mrs. Heard knew Mary Ellis too."

"A lovely woman," Mrs. Heard said. "So full of life. I took care of her for a time."

"Was she sick long?" I asked that partly to make conversation and partly because I had never really known what Miss Ellis had died of. I guess adults keep talk about illness and death from kids to protect them, but

I don't think that's so good. *Not* knowing things, I thought again, is almost always worse than knowing them. It was terrible, for instance, for the McConagy's to wake up each day wondering if Les was dead or alive.

"No," Mrs. Heard counted on her fingers, "Mary wasn't sick too long. About a year altogether." I thought a year sounded like forever. *One day* in bed with nothing but Nancy Drew and soap operas had been enough for me.

"I'll just leave you two alone now," Mrs. Heard said, as she picked up an empty glass from the bedside table. "Will you be wanting anything?"

"No, thank you," Grossie said. "I'm getting up in a little while. My one trip downstairs today is going to be to the kitchen with Ellis."

"Mom says you're to stay in bed," I protested.

"Let me bring you what you want," said Mrs. Heard.

"No, ma'am. I'm going to the kitchen." Grossie had a way of letting you know sometimes, as Jules did, that she wasn't about to change her mind. After Mrs. Heard had left the room the two of us settled back and just smiled at each other.

"I've been looking at the old photographs," Grossie pulled the black album toward her lap.

"I love to look at them. Let me see too." I fixed the lamp so that it spotlighted the album. The first picture showed Grossie in 1912 when she was already married with three children but still looked very young. "You were pretty," I said. Some people thought I looked like

Grossie. I hoped I'd look that good when I had children of my own.

"Do you remember these?" Grossie pointed to a series of photographs of my mother in ballet costumes. In every one Mom stood in front of different scenery that my grandfather had painted. Some of the pictures were beautiful and some struck me as being funny. In one of them she wore an Indian outfit like the one Bruce had worn in the Fourth of July parade. She was pulling back an arrow, ready to shoot at something that must have been running across my grandfather's scenery. There was a startled expression on her face that made me laugh.

"Is that how you got the deer heads downstairs?" I asked.

"You're silly!" Grossie said. "Isn't this one lovely?"

It was. Before they were married my mother and father had posed for this picture in front of a real arbor, not a painted one. There were lots of other photographs of family and friends. Some were of the whole family sitting in a semicircle in front of a painted garden with all the little children, even the boys, in embroidered white dresses. One showed all Grossie's children—my mother and my uncles—looking scrawny in itchy wool bathing suits, up to their knees in a swimming hole. There was my Uncle Frank who always gave us a quarter when he came to visit, and my Uncle Hans, who had died when he was a boy. I didn't stay on that photograph too long because I thought maybe it would make Grossie sad to look at it.

"Here's my favorite picture of Mary Ellis!" Grossie said when we turned the page. Mary Ellis stood leaning over a boardwalk railing to look at the ocean. On her head was a tight-fitting felt hat.

"She was so pretty," I said. "Didn't she ever want to get married?"

"Yes. She was engaged to marry a boy who was killed in the First World War."

"Really?" I had heard a lot of Mary Ellis stories, but I hadn't known that before. "Didn't it make her bitter?"

"Sad, yes. But she wasn't a person to feel bitterness. She had many offers of marriage from nice young men after that, but none of them turned her head." I liked Grossie's old-fashioned expressions like "none of them turned her head." I thought for a minute.

"If you lost someone in a war," I asked her, "would you stay by yourself forever?" I was thinking about Judy, Les' girl friend.

"I can't say," Grossie answered. "For Mary Ellis it seemed to be the right thing. For others perhaps not. Mary, after her loss, threw herself into her work and other interests. She was a teacher who loved her students, and they loved her. Your mother and father were her students, and they have told you that many times, I'm sure."

Remembering Judy and the soldier made me think of Fourth of July night. Suddenly, as I pictured again Jules and Sally going off into the woods, I felt a wave of something that was almost a pain. I started to say something about it to Grossie, but I decided I would never tell anyone what had happened or how bad I felt. I hoped I wouldn't see Jules soon—or ever.

"Seeing the pictures reminds me," Grossie said. "I want to give you something." She reached for the book with the blue leather cover that she had been reading when I came in.

"What is it?"

"It's a book of Mary Ellis' that she gave me and I'm giving to you."

"What's it about?"

"It's a book of poems by a woman named Emily Dickinson, who lived in the 1800s. You may like some of them now; others you may appreciate later. Mary wrote some things of her own in it too. I've enjoyed the book so much that I'd like you to have it."

"Won't you miss it?"

Grossie rubbed the cover with her thumb. "A little," she said. When I reached for the book, she took my hand again and held onto it. Her face looked tired.

"I'll lend it back whenever you want," I said.

"Good."

"Do you feel like sleeping now, or anything?"

"No, no. It's nice to talk."

"Tell me about when you were a girl. About Germany, or about when you and Mary Ellis were in high school."

"Well, let's see," she said. I guess it was hard to think of a new story. She had already told me so many. "A short time after I came to America, when we still lived in Philadelphia, Mary and I were invited to a picnic. I was shy then. I didn't speak English so well yet. Mary was already my best friend, and relatives of hers had invited us to go by horse and carriage to a picnic grove down by the river. It was a beautiful day, and all the women at the picnic had brought their own homemade pies and cakes. Each one had tried her hardest to make the most beautiful, best-tasting pastry. There were Bavarian chocolate cakes, and lemon chiffons and cherry pies, but the one I had my eye on was a cake decorated with lovely fresh strawberries. I couldn't wait to be invited to have a piece of that delicious, tempting dessert. But my mother had always told me to be polite, and aside from that, I was, as I say, quite shy." Grossie was still shy, in a way. I could picture how she must have looked at the picnic. Wearing braids, maybe, and a long dress.

"What happened?"

"Most of the other food was on the table so that every person helped himself, but when the cakes were served at the end, the women who baked them went around to each guest asking who wanted a piece. I was so worried that the strawberry cake would be gone before it was my turn! I turned down all the others, though they looked wonderful too. Meanwhile Mary had already sampled several different ones. Finally, when the woman came to me, there were just two pieces of the strawberry cake left. I remembered my mother's talk about politeness, and I didn't want to sound too eager. 'No, thank you,' I whispered to the woman.

"I was sure she would ask me again, because I was the

only one with no cake on my plate. But instead, she said 'Poor girl, no appetite!' and went right on by! I could have cried. The next two men on my left each took a piece, and that was the end of the strawberry cake! I was so shy and angry at myself that I didn't even ask for one of the other kinds, even though there were plenty left. I sat and watched Mary and the others smacking their lips and raving over the taste of this one and that, feeling miserable."

"Poor you!" I said.

"To this day whenever I'm offered cake I say yes— but no piece has ever been as good as I had imagined the one at the picnic would be."

She sighed. "Isn't it funny. We learn something—that politeness can be carried too far, for instance—and then we go right on saying to our own children, 'Mind your manners! Wait until you're offered something before you take it! Make sure you don't take too much!' "

"The same thing happened to me the other day. Mom's always saying, 'Don't make extra trouble for somebody. Be polite!' Mrs. McConagy asked me if I wanted iced tea and I said no, even though I did!"

"Aren't we silly in our family?" Grossie said. "Some people—like Mary—aren't like that. Without being rude or greedy she could take three pieces of cake. She wasn't afraid to say yes right out to what she wanted. I admired that in her, maybe because I found it hard. I'm still a little shy."

"Me too," I said. I was thinking about the award, and how I still felt as if I didn't deserve it.

"We have to try harder to accept the good things that come to us without feeling guilty," Grossie said, as if she were reading my mind. The telephone rang.

"Oh, my gosh!" I said. "I was supposed to call Mom. I'll get it." I went out into the hall and picked up the receiver. It was my mother.

"Yes, she's in bed," I said. "We were just talking, and I forgot to call. I'm sorry." By the time I hung up, Grossie had gotten out of bed by herself. Standing up, she looked very weak.

"Mrs. Heard will help me downstairs," she said. "You run on down to the kitchen."

Grossie's kitchen, in the back of the house, reminded me of a Dutch painting I had seen in art class. Miss Mienig, our art teacher, often gave each of us our own little prints of famous paintings for "picture study." One of my favorite prints was a Dutch kitchen. Grossie's floor was of red tile, and there were blue and white willowware dishes on all the shelves. I loved to look at the little people and trees and pagodas on the dishes and make up my own stories about them. There was a huge window framing the backyard, but it was almost completely covered with vines and hanging plants, so that the kitchen, like the living room, was dark and cool. Sitting at the blue-enameled table I felt like Snow White in the dwarves' cottage—snug in the middle of a forest.

"I declare, she won't listen to a thing I tell her," Mrs. Heard said, as she followed Grossie into the kitchen. "That woman's overdoing it."

"You run off now, Mrs. Heard," Grossie was firm. "We'll just have a snack, and later I'll let you fix lunch." She sat down.

"I forgot to tell you," I said to Grossie, "that I lost my purse on the way here." Then I told her about stopping for the pretzel, about the free *fastnacht* and about the woman who gave me the quarter.

"You were lucky," Grossie smiled.

"I was careless," I said.

After lunch Mrs. Heard helped Grossie upstairs and into her bed again. I brought up some ginger ale, and as we were sipping it I remembered what I wanted to ask.

"Grossie, did you leave Germany because you didn't like Hitler?" I was hoping I could tell Sam that she had.

"No, no," she smiled. "Don't they teach you history in school? Hitler was only *born* at the time I left Germany. My father brought us here to find better work. Hitler came to power much later." I probably should have known that. Miss Fenster wouldn't have been too proud of me.

"Do you think Hitler's dead?" I asked.

"Why, yes, I think so. Of course there was some trouble being sure about his body, but I think most people agree that he's dead."

"If he escaped and came here, would you hide him?"

"Oh, no!" I could tell she thought my question was stupid. I wished that Sam were in the room so he could see what a dumb question it was. "You mean, because I was born in Germany, would I help Germany in this war? Ellis, you know I'm an American. I have many happy memories of my girlhood in Stuttgart, and I speak with a little accent, but . . . everyone sees that Hitler was a monster, including most people in Germany today. Why do you ask these questions?"

"Oh, some kids think all Germans are bad."

"But you know it's not so." I nodded. "Just as you know all Japanese aren't bad, yes?" I nodded again. "But you still feel a little ashamed that your ancestors were German, and Germany, in these years, has caused misery?"

"Yes," I admitted.

"I know how you feel. I felt so even more, when it was the First World War. I carried around a lot of shame. But there was no need for me to. We mustn't think so little of ourselves, Ellis. Now," she said, noticing my empty glass, "I see you have finished your magic drink that will turn you into a princess. Bring me my purse." She took out a dollar bill and stuck it inside my book of poems.

"It's time now. Keep your money safe, and tell Mickey hello." I hated to leave, but I could see that Grossie was tired. "Go straight home so Mother won't worry," she said.

"I'll come back soon." I sat for a second on the edge of the bed, and Grossie patted my hand.

"Good." Her voice sounded sad. "Then we'll talk some more."

"Thanks a lot for the book. I'll read it on the way home."

"Just be sure you don't pass your stop. And something I didn't say before—congratulations for your award! You're being so modest not to tell me about it."

"Oh, it's not much."

"What kind of lesson have you learned today?" Grossie pretended to be shocked. "We *accept* what we're offered and say 'Thank you very much!' "

"Okay, I forgot," I laughed. "Thank you very much."

"Go now," she said very low. As I went out the door she blew me a kiss, and I carried away with me a picture of her leaning back on the pillow and turning out the light.

In the crowded trolley car I had to stand and hang onto a strap. Every time the car screeched around a corner I was afraid the book would go flying out from under my arm. But later, when I got a seat on the bus, I flipped through the book and read some of the poems. They were pretty good. One of them talked about knowing things without proof.

> *I never saw a moor,*
> *I never saw the sea;*
> *Yet know I how the heather looks,*
> *And what a wave must be.*
>
> *I never spoke with God,*
> *Nor visited in heaven;*
> *Yet certain am I of the spot*
> *As if the chart were given.*

I guess it was like Jules feeling certain of his messages even though he couldn't explain them. I envied Emily

Dickinson and Jules for being certain of things without proof. I was usually uncertain. Some of the other poems, especially the ones about death and losing a person you love, had Miss Mary Ellis' writing around them. I was relieved to see that Mary Ellis had made out okay in life even though she didn't write by the Palmer Method.

"Did you have a nice time?" my mother asked when I got home.

"Oh, yes. Very nice. Grossie gave me a book."

"That's good," she said. Then after a second, "Jules was here."

I looked up. "Jules came here?"

"He called for you twice."

"What did he want?" I wondered if my mother knew that anything unusual was going on, but she didn't seem to.

"I don't know. He said he'd come back first thing in the morning. He said it was something very important."

Eleven

During the night I had a weird dream. I dreamed I was on the rafters in Sibby's barn and a crowd of people stood below, daring me to walk all the way across. Mrs. Lane was smiling up at me and calling, "Come now, Ellis, you don't want the children to lose their respect for you, do you?" I inched forward.

"Be careful!" Miss Fenster shouted. "Remember you're susceptible to hay fever!" I never had hay fever in my life, but in dreams people always say strange things like that. About halfway across I panicked and decided to turn back. As I turned I felt myself falling.

They say that if you dream of falling and hit bottom, you're dead. I don't know if that's true or not, but while I was falling I thought to myself, this is only a dream—I'll wake up. And suddenly there was Jules underneath the rafters to catch me. Before I could say anything to Jules I woke up. In my half-asleep, half-awake fuzziness I thought to myself, Jules must have gotten a message that I was falling.

The next morning I was reading in the newspaper about our troops getting close to Japan when Jules called "Yo" for me. I went to the door slowly and a little nervously. Since I had dreamed about him, it seemed as if Jules and I had just seen each other. Still, when I looked at him through the front window I felt as if he were a stranger. What important thing did he have to tell me, I wondered. That he loved Sally and we'd never be friends again? That he liked me better than Sally? Or that some more news had come about Les? Even though I was very curious, I didn't want him to think I was sitting around waiting for him.

"Hi," I said in a flat voice.

"Ellis," he looked at me gravely, "we have to practice the magic show. We're having it Monday." He was acting just the same as always. Was it possible that he would go back to the way things were without even mentioning the dance and kissing Sally?

"What's the important thing you had to tell me?" I asked him.

Jules looked surprised. "That's it—the show. We said we'd hold it right after the Fourth of July, didn't we? Hey, where were you yesterday?"

"Away," I said shortly. I felt like being mean. Could I be so upset about the Fourth of July dance when to Jules it didn't mean anything? I guess one thing you learned in growing up was that even your best friend didn't always know what was going on in your mind.

"Did you go to the Windsor Fair?" Jules asked.

"Yes," I lied. "I saw Mingus." I knew I shouldn't lie —I wasn't even good at it—but at that moment I wanted Jules to be jealous.

"You did? How was he?" His eyes lighted up, so that I was sorry right away that I had made up the story. It always made me sad when I saw a person being fooled.

"Mingus was good. Much better than the tricks he did for us at the shop."

"Oh, yeah? Which tricks did he do?"

"Hard ones. Ones you never saw."

"Like what? Did he say hello to you?"

"Yeah, he recognized me." I was about to make up more lies about the things Mingus had said, but I was afraid I'd get trapped later.

"Wow, you're lucky," Jules said. "Who'd you go with?" I went blank for a second.

"Uh, my Grossie . . ."

"Isn't she sick anymore?"

"My Grossie's . . . next door neighbors, this kid named Dorothy and her . . . brother." I thought it was pretty shrewd of me to get that in about a boy being with us, but Jules didn't seem to notice. "Her brother's two years older. He's nice," I said.

"Well, I wish I could have gone. I was looking for you yesterday. Sam and I decided to have the show on Monday, because they're saying the war'll be over soon, and we have to hurry, if we want our money to do any good."

I still couldn't believe it that Jules was just going on as if nothing had happened, as if there hadn't even been a dance. Had the dance been a dream too? It was all so strange. And here was Jules, talking about the magic show as if it were the most important thing in the world. I guessed there was nothing to do but to go right along with him. Maybe the whole business about kissing Sally had just been a joke. Boys were hard to figure out.

"Hey, Jules," I said feeling better about him, "you didn't hear anything more about Les, did you?"

Jules shook his head. "No, we didn't hear anything," he said, just as Sam Goff sprang over from the next porch. He must have been perched on the divider, waiting to take us by surprise. I didn't care to see him at that moment, but there was no choice.

"She's here," he said, "and is she *ugly!*" Jules and I looked at each other and then at Sam.

"Who?" we asked together.

"That *girl*. The one with the flowers painted on her desk. The girl who moved in next to the Pflugs."

"The new girl?" Suddenly I remembered the moving truck that had come on the first day of vacation. It seemed like a thousand years had gone by.

"Where did you see her?" Jules asked.

"She's sitting on her porch steps with Willie Pflug. They make a good pair. He looks like a circus fat man, and she looks like the skinny lady. She's got yellow hair that sticks out, and big glasses and she talks funny."

"She talk to you?"

" 'Greetings and salutations,' she said. That's how she talks! Honest!"

Jules made a face. "Is she a brain?"

"Probably," Sam said. "She wears big glasses. Comes from New York."

"What's her name?" I asked.

"Betsy. Betsy Harris. Hair sticks out like this!" Sam gave us a demonstration. I laughed. Usually I thought Sam was stupid for making fun of people on account of their looks, but to tell the truth, this time I was glad to hear that the new girl wasn't beautiful.

"Let's get on with the magic show," Jules said.

"Aw, come on, Jules, take a look at her. We'll get *her* to come to the show!" Sam was prancing around with excitement.

"Well, okay," Jules agreed. The two of us trailed behind Sam as he cut through the Feeney's backyard.

I had expected some kind of funny remarks from Sam about Sally and the dance, but he didn't say a word either. Maybe the two of them were ashamed of dancing with a girl, now that it was over. Well, whatever the reason, I felt relieved that I was their friend again.

"You talk to the new girl, Jules," I said. "Tell her about the show, and tell her we're charging a nickel to get in."

"Wait a minute," Sam looked as if a light bulb had gone on in his head. "I got an idea. Let's have some fun. Don't tell her right away about the magic show. First tell her we have a club, and we want her to join, and she can join if she goes through an initiation."

"What initiation?"

"We'll make it up. Hard stuff that she has to do—so hard that she won't be able to do it."

"It shouldn't be anything impossible," Jules said. "That's not fair. But it wouldn't be a bad idea to have

her do something that'll help the club get money, or
have her do something funny."

"Yeah," Sam said. "Something funny. I'll be in charge
of initiations, okay?"

"I guess so," Jules said.

I felt a little annoyed that Sam was taking over, but
he was vice president and I was only treasurer. When
we came around the side of the house the new girl,
Betsy, was still sitting with Willie on the porch steps.
Sam pulled us down in the bushes so we could watch
and listen for a few minutes without being seen.
Through the leaves I caught a glimpse of frizzy hair. I
laughed and poked Sam.

"They aren't talking loud enough," Sam whispered,
as he yanked us both up. "Come on," he said. The
three of us came out of the bushes and approached the
steps.

"These are my friends," Sam said to Betsy. "We have
a club."

"Greetings," Betsy said with a wide smile. I took a
good look at her face. She did wear glasses, but she
wasn't ugly. She might be a brain; you couldn't always
tell. Sibby, for instance, looked sort of brainy but was
really a moron.

"I'm Betsy Harris," she stood up. "I come from Syracuse, New York." She did sound different. Sam was
right about that.

"Want to join our club?" Sam asked. He was pretending to be very friendly.

"Who are they?" She nodded to Jules and me. Sam was no good at introducing people.

"I'm Jules. She's Ellis. We live back there." Jules pointed to Milford Square. "Our club's giving a magic show."

"It's a magic club?" Betsy joined us now, leaving Willie alone on the steps. She had probably already discovered what a baby he was.

"It's the Milford Square Good Citizens' Model Airplane Club," I told her, "but we do all kinds of things. Mostly we help the war effort."

"Want to join?" Sam prodded.

"I might. Are there any fees?"

"Fees?" The three of us exchanged glances. "You mean money for dues?" Jules asked.

"Or membership fees when you join?" Betsy gave him a direct look. She must have had a lot of experience belonging to clubs.

"Well, there *is* a membership fee," Sam started talking fast, "but there's mainly an initiation. If you don't pass the initiation you can't get in."

"What does the initiation include?"

"That's secret," Sam said. "You want to join or not?" He was rushing her, I thought.

"Well, you have to give me some clue about the initiation," Betsy said. She sure wasn't dumb.

"It's nothing bad," I told her.

"Who else is in the club?"

"The three of us," Sam began, "and . . ."

"The *four* of us . . ." Willie grunted from the steps.

Sam was impatient. ". . . and my sister, and Ellis' brother, and a kid named Tim and a girl named Sibby. Want to join?"

"Tell me what I have to do for the initiation, and I'll let you know."

"It's all secret. Come to the Milford Square mall," he pointed, "at two o'clock sharp. We'll tell you then what you gotta do."

"Okay," she agreed. "I'll ask Mama."

"Mama!" Sam snorted. "Where's 'Mama'?"

"In the house now, but she's leaving soon for the office."

"What office?"

"Her office. She's a lawyer."

"Oh, yeah?" Sam looked as if he didn't believe her. "Then where's your father?"

"He's in the Army," she said.

"Oh, yeah?" Sam looked at her in a slightly new way. His father was only an air raid warden. "What rank?" he asked.

"He's a captain and a doctor." Sam didn't have anything to say to that.

"Come on," he motioned for us to follow him. "Hey!" he called back to Betsy. "One more thing. The first part of the initiation is if you talk to anybody in the club before two o'clock you get paddled." He said it with a laugh, as if he expected her to make the mistake of answering right back. But Betsy didn't. She shook her blond head up and down to show Sam she understood. "And one *more* thing," he giggled, in a high voice, as she turned toward the house. "Say hello to 'Mama' for us!"

"She's not so bad," Jules said as we walked back through Feeney's yard. "What do you think, Ellis?"

I hadn't thought she was so bad, either, but I didn't like the idea that Jules was sticking up for some new girl. "Except for her frizzy hair, and funny accent and her 'Mama,' she's wonderful," I laughed. Jules gave me a surprised look.

"Yeah, I guess her hair does stick out," he said. That made me feel better. Suddenly I was really in the mood for teasing Betsy.

"What things are we going to make her do for the initiation?" I looked at Sam.

"I have a good one!" He grabbed Jules' shoulder and whispered in his ear. The two of them laughed.

"Tell me!" I said, but they only laughed louder. Boys were making me sick.

"No, I was just kidding around," Sam went on. "This is really it. Come here." We formed a huddle, and Sam whispered his plan. Even I agreed that it sounded pretty funny. I couldn't *wait* for the initiation to start.

Twelve

About one thirty I sat leaning against a tree on the mall. Jules and Sam hadn't come out yet. I felt confused. On the side against Betsy, she *was* sort of different. It would be a big insult if Jules started hanging around with her instead of me. And who ever heard of calling your mother "Mama"? On the positive side, I knew that the way somebody's hair looked didn't matter much, she had stood up to Sam pretty well, and it might be very interesting to have a friend whose mother was a lawyer. After all, Nancy Drew only had a *father* who was a famous criminal lawyer. That was a lucky break, but it wasn't so special. Having a lawyer *mother* might really help a girl get into detective work. If I got to be friends with Betsy Harris maybe I would have a chance to get into that field. All of this, of course, would only be possible if Betsy was interested in being a girl detective. From our first meeting, though, I had a hunch that she might.

Jules and Sam, carrying a paper bag, came out of the McConagy's house just as a truck pulled into Milford

Square. I knew right away that it was Sibby being delivered by her father's handyman. I had telephoned earlier to let her know about the club initiation. Tim Feeney, Mick and Ruthie joined us on the mall.

"Where is she?" Sibby asked eagerly, before she had gotten out of the truck. "Where's the new girl?"

"She's supposed to come at two," I said.

"Poor her!" Sibby gloated. She loved having someone worse off than herself.

"What are we going to do to her?" Sibby wanted to know. But I didn't have time to answer. By the hedge around the Feeney's backyard I saw a frizzy head coming toward us. We all sat silently in a circle watching her. Behind Betsy trailed Willie Pflug. We had one hundred per cent attendance.

"The meeting will come to order," Jules said, when Betsy stood outside our circle. "Sam is vice president. He's in charge of initiation of new members. Now he'll take over." Jules sat down and Sam, with his paper bag in his hand, got up as if he were a dictator.

"Sit in the middle," he motioned to Betsy. "The first part we all do," he said. Sam dumped the bag out on the ground. At first I didn't recognize what was in it—it looked like a gooey porcupine. Looking closer, I saw that Sam had dug up soft tar from the street, rolled it into balls about the size of walnuts, and stuck each ball on the end of a stick. In the bag his tar "lollipops" had formed one big blob, with sticks coming out like porcupine needles.

"Special initiation lollipops," Sam said. He pulled

them apart and gave one to each member. "You can talk now," he told Betsy, but she shook her head and pointed to her watch. It must have been a couple of minutes before two, and Sam had said no talking until two.

"This is the first part of the meeting." Sam announced. "Everyone must lick a lollipop. Otherwise you're out of the club."

"Yuk!" Sibby made a face at the tar ball, but I winked at her to show that we were just going to pretend.

"These are delicious," Sam said. "A new kind of licorice invented during the war." He drew the lollipop close to his mouth and smacked his lips as if he were enjoying it. Jules, Sibby, Tim and I imitated him.

"Best thing I've tasted since watercress!" Sam shouted.

"I'm not doing it." Mick said. He got up, threw his lollipop on the ground and headed for the house.

"You sissy—you're out of the club!" I called after him.

"So what!" he said, slamming the door.

"Okay, Betsy." Sam stood over her, hands on his hips. "You gonna eat it or not?" Her tar lollipop, stuck all over with bits of leaves and fuzz, looked disgusting.

Betsy checked her watch before speaking. "Yum, yum!" she murmured, pretending to lick it as we had done.

"For *real*," Sam said. "Your tongue's gotta touch it."

Betsy touched her tongue to the tar.

"It has a delectable flavor!" She was a pretty good actress.

Sam smiled as if he was satisfied. "Willie, you too," he said. Willie gingerly put his tongue on the tar. If his mother had been there, she would have had a fit.

"Oh, my gosh, Sam," I said, "look at Ruthie!" While the rest of us had been faking, or brushing the tar against our lips, Ruthie had stuck the whole thing in her mouth. There was a ring of black around her lips, and she was chewing on the remains of the tar.

"Make her spit it out, Sam," I begged.

"Ruthie!" Sibby cried. "You're going to die!"

In the middle of all the screaming, Sam stayed calm. He raised his hands to quiet everyone down.

"It's true," he said quietly. "The people who *really* put the lollipops in their mouths are going to die. The rest of us were just pretending. The tar is poison."

Ruthie didn't care. She was still chewing the last piece of tar, even though I tried to force it out of her mouth. Betsy was snickering to herself. She seemed to think the whole thing was a good joke. But Willie Pflug was scared. His face turned pale, and his chin quivered.

"I'm going home," he said, starting to cry.

"Wait, no you don't," Sam stopped him. "We don't want your mother to see you like this." Sam sat him down on the ground. "Look," Sam said with pity in his voice. "It's affecting him already. He's got ear lobes. Did you ever notice that before, Jules?"

"No, I didn't," Jules said seriously. "Poor Willie's got ear lobes."

"And he's got tear ducts," said Betsy.

I wasn't sure what they were, but it was probably

something normal like ear lobes that just sounded bad. Sam and Sibby, who weren't very good at keeping a straight face, doubled over with giggling at Willy. I personally was still worrying about Ruthie, who had really eaten a blob of tar.

Willie sat sobbing with his head between his fat knees. "I'm gonna die," he wailed. "Let me go home!"

"No," Sam said, "we can't do that. The disease you get from the tar is catching. Everybody sit down! Because of this terrible thing that has happened—three kids eating poison, but mainly *two kids,* Ruthie and *Willie*—we're sending Betsy on the next part of her initiation." Everyone listened closely. Willie even choked back his tears for a second. "Betsy, you have to go up the hill to Windsor Avenue and knock on the door of the Gruen Funeral Home." Sibby gasped. "Tell them that two kids aren't long for this world, and you want Gruens to come down here in their black hearse and get 'em."

A scream from Willie started low and rose higher and higher. "Help!" he shouted, struggling to get away. But Sam sat on his legs and wouldn't let him up.

"Ellis," Sam ordered, "you and Sibby go with Betsy to make sure she does what she's supposed to do at Gruen's. Jules, Tim and I stay here to guard the victims. We can't have 'em spreading their disease around."

"Okay, Sam," I answered, "but for Pete's sake, get Ruthie to wash out her mouth." I was pretty nervous. I didn't think the tar could kill Ruthie, but I wasn't absolutely sure. And I wasn't looking forward to going to Gruen's Funeral Home. That place gave me the creeps. Sam always had to carry things too far. Maybe Sibby and I could start walking in that direction and then let Betsy off without doing her initiation test.

Sam, struggling on top of Willie, grunted to Jules, "Give Ellis your pencil and pad. Ellis, you write down what Betsy says at Gruen's." I saw that it would be hard to fake it.

At first the three of us walked silently up the hill toward the funeral home. I would have liked to just talk to Betsy, to find out whether she was interested in being a girl detective. But the club initiation and the orders from Sam made me act a little bossy.

"What am I supposed to say when we get there?" Betsy asked. She was taking the whole thing like a good sport.

"You're supposed to tell them that two kids on Milford Square aren't long for this world," I said. "Tell 'em to send the hearse. Sibby and I'll just stand on the corner while you go up to the door." I didn't want to go any closer than I had to.

"How will you write down what I say?"

"Don't worry, I'll hear."

The Gruen Funeral Home looked forlorn in the summer heat. The sun beat down on us as we stood on the corner waiting for Betsy. She made her way up the steps to the front door.

"What if there's a funeral going on right now?" Sibby asked. I didn't answer her. I planned to run if anyone came to the door at all.

Betsy rang the bell. "I wouldn't do that for a million dollars," I told Sibby. We waited. Then after a minute, the door was opened by a man in a dark suit. In spite of what I had planned, out of curiosity, I stayed rooted to the spot. Betsy stepped inside, and the door closed behind her. Sibby and I looked at each other.

"Ellis, what if she never comes out!" cried Sibby.

"Don't be a simp," I said, but I was thinking the same thing myself.

Though we had no watches, I saw the minutes ticking by on the big clock of the Windsor Hosiery Mills in the distance.

"What's taking her so long?" Sibby whined. I shook my head helplessly. The two of us sat down on the hot pavement.

"Let's go," Sibby said after another few minutes. "Who cares what happens to her. She's not our friend."

"We can't leave," I argued. "We were sent here to guard her. Let's pretend we're girl detectives." There was nothing I felt less like doing than sneaking up on Gruen's, but I figured that if I was really going to be a Nancy Drew I'd probably have to do much worse things. "Follow me," I said.

I crept up to the front porch without making any noise. Slowly I tiptoed up the steps with Sibby hanging behind me. At the front window I tried to peek in, but the venetian blinds were in my way.

"Around the back," I whispered. The back was spookier than the front. Shiny black cars were lined up by the garage. There were two entrances, one by the garage, and one through an enclosed porch. I was sure that the one by the garage led to where the bodies were kept. Inching my way along the side of the house, I went up the steps by the porch and leaned over to look in the window. Suddenly a face peered out at me, and the porch door creaked at my elbow and made me jump so hard that I knocked against Sibby and we both fell off the steps.

"Help!" I cried.

"What's the big deal?" said a voice. Betsy stood at the top of the steps laughing at us. "Good-bye," she waved to a man and woman inside the enclosed porch. "Thank you!" I recognized the woman as Marybeth Gruen's mother.

"What were you *doing* in there?" Sibby sputtered, as soon as we were out of earshot.

"They gave me lemonade," Betsy said. "They were very nice. That was Mrs. Gruen and a man who works for Mr. Gruen."

"What did you say at first?" I asked.

Betsy laughed. "Promise you won't tell the others?" I nodded. "Promise you'll put down what I tell you in the notebook?"

"Yes." I said.

"Okay, write down that I asked the man in the black suit to come down after Willie with the hearse, and that the man turned into a vampire and started chasing me, but I got away."

"Sam won't even believe it," I laughed. "What did you really say to that man?"

"I said, 'I'm new in Wissining, and I got lost. May I use your telephone?' "

"Did you use the phone?"

"Yes, but I knew no one would answer—Mama isn't home. Mrs. Gruen wanted to drive me around looking for my house. Wouldn't that have been something, to pull into Milford Square in the hearse?"

"Poor Willie," I said. "It's good you didn't let her drive you."

"When I saw your face at the window, I said to her, 'Oh, there's my friend. She'll show me the way home.' "

"Mrs. Gruen never knew it was a joke?"

"Nope," said Betsy. "She thought I was really lost. I can be very sneaky when I want to."

"Sneaky enough to be a detective?" I asked.

"Oh, sure," Betsy said. "I often do detective work."

"Do you read Nancy Drew?"

She gave me a look something like the looks I usually give Mick. "Nancy Drew is infantile," she said. "I *used* to read Nancy Drew. Now I read Judy Bolton mysteries. Want to see my Judy Bolton books?"

"Yeah!" This was turning out better than I thought.

"Why do you call your mother 'Mama'?" Sibby interrupted. She was probably annoyed that Betsy and I were talking about mystery stories and getting to be friends. " 'Mama' sounds like baby talk," Sibby sneered.

"Because 'Mother' sounds too formal, 'Mommy' sounds too ordinary, 'Mom' sounds too boyish, and French '*Maman*' sounds too affected. Besides Mama likes it, so it's good enough."

"Is your mother—your mama—by any chance a famous criminal lawyer?" I asked.

"No, she works for the government. But she knows a thing or two about criminal law."

"You're in our grade, aren't you?" I asked. Betsy nodded. "That's good," I said. "We can walk to school together in the fall, if you want."

When we reached the bottom of the hill, Betsy nudged me. "Get out the notebook. Try to fool Sam."

"Willie must have fainted by now," I said, as we turned into Milford Square. "Is he still screaming?"

The three of us looked toward the mall, but it was deserted.

"Hey, what happened to those dumbbells?" I looked around, half expecting Jules and Sam to jump out of the bushes. "Sam?" I yelled. Sam was sitting alone on his porch. When he saw us, he ran full speed across the mall and fell into step with us.

"She did it!" I grinned. "She went into Gruen's!" But Sam grabbed my elbow and made a sign for me to hush.

"Initiation's over," he said. There was something strange about his voice.

"Did Ruthie get sick from the tar?" I asked.

"No, Ruthie's okay." He stopped walking. "While you were gone a messenger came to Jules' house. Jules' mother got another telegram about Les," he said very softly.

Thirteen

That evening a strange quiet settled over Milford Square, and by the next day all of Wissining knew that Les had been killed in action. The War Department said they regretted to inform the McConagy's that the new list of war dead in the Pacific included Les' name. The Sunday morning edition of the *Windsor Times* printed the same picture they had run when Les went away. I cut it out and stuck it in my notebook at the place where my story about Les stopped.

In our house we spoke in hushed voices. My mother had been the one to tell me the news.

"Have you heard?" She had met me at the door when I had come in from the club initiation.

"Sam told me Mrs. McConagy got a telegram." I was breathing hard and my insides seemed to be melted, even worse than they felt while I was waiting for the results of the Citizenship Award.

"The news is bad," she said, twisting the edge of her apron. We stood in the dim hallway looking at each other. "Les is dead. He was killed in action on the island of Iwo Jima." My mother reached out to put her arm around my shoulder, but I pulled away.

"The dirty Japs!" I shouted, running to my room and slamming the door. I felt like smashing everything in the world made in Japan and Germany and any other countries that were Axis Powers. I waited by the door for a minute, half expecting my mother to follow me, but when she didn't I flung myself down on the bed. Though I had expected to cry, no tears came. "Cry!" I told myself. I just felt numb.

Then, while I was lying there, a lot of pictures went through my head, some real and some that I made up. Mrs. McConagy's face when she saw the telegram; Les hiding in a foxhole and a grenade exploding; Judy—Les' old girl friend—kissing the soldier on the Fourth of July; Mr. McConagy shaking his head sadly and not caring at all about who wanted iced tea for supper. The one person I couldn't picture was Jules. What was Jules doing and thinking? He hadn't cried in front of me since we were babies. Was he crying now? Would he stay in his house, or would he come out and play as usual? What would we say to each other the next time we met? I tried out different things to say, but they all sounded stupid.

At supper no one spoke except my mother asking if anyone wanted anything. Even Mickey understood that things weren't normal. I went to bed early, but I couldn't sleep. The spooky Snow White bookcase started haunting me again. Once, when I dropped off to sleep for a second, I woke up suddenly, thinking that I saw the flash of a hand grenade, but it was only a light from outside reflecting off my Citizenship Award plaque. During the night it seemed that Les was alive and had come to present a flag to the school, but when I woke up I realized it had only been a dream.

On Sunday the whole family went to church. Usually in church I passed the time by drawing on the church bulletin, but on this Sunday I sat absolutely still. "Please make it not true about Les," I kept praying over and over. But I knew that that was useless. You were supposed to ask God to help you accept things as they were, not to ask Him to make people come back to life.

As soon as we drove into Milford Square after church we saw the police car in front of the McConagy's house. I figured it had something to do with the news about Les. It wasn't until we pulled up in front of our house that we noticed the bunch of people talking to Pat the policeman and to Officer Sharky, the Chief of Police.

"What's all this on a Sunday morning?" my father asked. The Shoppe's grown-up daughter leaned in the car window.

"Jules McConagy has gone and run off," she said. "As if that poor woman didn't have enough trouble!" She nodded toward Mrs. McConagy, who was standing next to the Chief of Police.

"Run off?" My father couldn't believe his ears any more than I could.

"Run off," she repeated. "Took off early this morning, they think. Now why would he do that? That poor woman." She shook her head.

My father got out of the car. "Stay in here," he told Mick and me firmly. A peculiar soupy feeling spread all over me. My eyes blurred, and I felt as if I were dreaming again. Jules—run away? How could he? What for? I couldn't bear sitting in the hot car.

"Please let me get out!" I begged my mother.

"Daddy says to wait."

"Please, I'm going to be sick!" I pushed my way past Mickey, out of the car, and into the house. I ran straight to the bathroom, and when I heard my mother's footsteps on the stairs I locked the bathroom door. "I'm all right!" I called, but my voice sounded as if it belonged to someone else.

"Ellis, open the door."

"I'm all right. I'll be out in a minute." As her steps faded away, I ran to the window and raised it until I could see the McConagy's porch. Mr. and Mrs. McConagy, followed by Chief Sharky, were going into their house. Pat was talking quietly to the neighbors, who seemed to be breaking up and returning to their own homes.

Suddenly I started sobbing and sobbing. To make sure my mother wouldn't come running, I threw myself down on the bathroom floor and buried my head in a towel to muffle the sound. When my body stopped shaking I knelt by the bathtub with its funny claw feet and pressed my forehead against the cool edge.

"Ellis!" my mother called.

"I'm coming!" I answered. But I didn't move.

I must do something to help, I told myself. I must try to think why Jules would run away and where he would go. Why would Jules run away? Because he was upset and angry and sad. But that wouldn't be like him. He wouldn't purposely want to make his parents worry at such a bad time. He must know that running away wouldn't help matters, unless . . . unless Jules had gone someplace that he thought *would* help.

Maybe he had received a message about Les—not a real telegram, but one of the special, mysterious messages that only came to him. Was it possible that Jules had gotten a message about Les and that he hadn't believed what the government telegram said? Once in a while there were stories in the newspapers about the War Department's making a mistake. Just a month before, a soldier from Windsor had turned up when his family had thought he was dead. Jules had gone somewhere special, I was sure. He had gone because he had *had* to. But where? If it was far away there was nothing I could do. Well, for certain I couldn't be of any use sitting with my head pressed against the bathtub.

"Ellis!" my mother shouted again.

"I'm coming!" I unlocked the door and went downstairs.

My father was sitting in the living room with his jacket off and his hands on his knees.

"Ellis," he said, "can you tell me anything that will help the McConagy's find Jules?"

"How do they know he ran away?" I asked. "How do they know he didn't just go for a walk or something?"

"Mrs. McConagy heard him in the middle of the night, but his bed wasn't slept in. They think he may have taken some of his things, and they think he took his money." I remembered that Jules had had about five dollars saved up. "Now, Ellis," my father leaned forward, "can you think where Jules would go?"

I didn't know what to say. First of all, I really didn't know anything, but second, even if I thought of something I wasn't sure whether I should tell on Jules. I was absolutely positive that he must have had a good reason for doing what he was doing.

"I know where he *usually* goes," I said, "but I don't think he's at any of those places now."

"How much money did he have—do you have any idea?"

"About five dollars, I think."

"That's good," my father said, turning to my mother. "Five dollars won't get him far."

"Ellis, did he ever say anything to you about going away?" My mother looked as if she were about to start crying.

"No."

"When did you see him last?"

"Yesterday—early in the afternoon. We were having our club initiation, and Sam sent me and Sibby up the hill with the new girl. I didn't see him after that."

"Is there any reason you can think of why he would

run away? Would the shock of the telegram affect him like that, do you think?" my father asked. I thought about whether or not to mention Jules' messages, but I decided not to. No one else knew about them, and I had no proof that a message had made Jules leave.

"I don't know why he would run away," I said.

"Come outside and speak to Pat." My father took me by the elbow. "Tell him all the places you can think of where Jules usually goes."

Pat smiled at me as if things weren't so bad. "Where do you and that fella hang out?" he winked. "Got any secret hiding places?" He seemed to think Jules was nearby, in hiding because he was so upset about Les.

"Well, we go up to Windsor Avenue. The Mingus Magic Shop, the Rialto, the Wee Nut Shoppe."

"Any clubhouse?"

"No, but we play in the woods behind the pavilion at the playground." Naming that spot made me think again of the Fourth of July dance. "And we go to the creek, by the springhouse, where you found Mickey that day."

Pat nodded. "I've already looked down there," he said to my father. "Would he be likely to go near the mine hole?"

Pat's face had a strange expression, as if he wondered whether Jules would jump in on purpose.

"If he did," I said, "you wouldn't have to worry. He's a good swimmer."

"Tell me, is there any place outside of Wissining that Jules has ever talked about wanting to go to?"

"No," I said, "not that I can think of. Unless . . ." suddenly I remembered our talk the day before. "Unless, the Windsor Fair . . . he wanted to go to the Windsor Fair to see Mingus."

"Mingus the magician—that's Charley Wertz . . ." Pat seemed to be talking to himself. "Well, that's a lead," he said. "Thanks, Ellis. You're a good girl."

I didn't see what I had said or done that was so good. In fact, I felt almost *bad* mentioning the Windsor Fair because I was sure Jules hadn't gone there, and I felt sorry when I thought about Pat and Chief Sharky wasting their time running around the fairgrounds looking for Jules and maybe calling Chas. Wertz over the loudspeaker. The last thing Jules would be doing on the day after the telegram came would be enjoying himself at a magic show.

"Come in the house now," my father said gently. "Stay inside." He seemed to be trying to protect me. Maybe he was afraid I might run away too.

When Sunday dinner was over, the afternoon dragged on forever. My father went out to meet Chief Sharky. Some of the men in the neighborhood had offered to help in the search. I begged to be allowed to go, but my father had said no. I sprawled out on the living room rug to read the funnies, but nothing in them was funny, and every time I head a sound I would jump up to look out the window toward the McConagy's house. The blinds were pulled shut at Jules'; there wasn't a breath of air or a loud sound in all of Milford Square.

I thought of trying to see Sam, but his house looked

closed up. I couldn't imagine breaking the silence by calling "Yo," or even by ringing a doorbell. The radio was no help in getting my mind off things. On the program "One Man's Family" a grandfather with a quivering voice had a pile of children and grandchildren who had nothing but troubles, and the old man got stuck with all of them. In the background I could hear my mother talking to Grossie on the telephone, probably telling her about Les and Jules. I was going to ask to speak to Grossie, but the idea of talking to anybody seemed awful.

About four o'clock, just when I thought I would explode if there wasn't some news, I got the idea of going over to Betsy's house. If she was home I could at least ask to borrow one of her Judy Bolton mystery books. And maybe she could give me some advice about how to help Jules. Leaving the house without telling my mother, I walked through the back alley to Betsy's. When I first stepped into her yard it looked as if no one was at home. Then I saw Betsy's frizzy hair blending into the bushes beside her house. She was holding a Mason jar in one hand, and when she saw me she made a sign for me to be quiet. With a lunge forward, she came out of the bushes cursing to herself.

"Salutations," she said. "I missed the bloody thing."

"What?" I didn't know what she was talking about.

"Almost got a grass snake. I missed the bloody thing by an inch.

"Was it bloody?"

"No! That's a very bad swear word in England. Don't

use it there or you'll get your bloody mouth washed out with soap. Where've you been since yesterday? What was that telegram that came?"

"You don't know about it?"

"No."

"Well, Jules has run away from home."

"Jules? Because of the telegram?"

"In a way. Jules' brother Les was missing in action. We were all hoping he'd turn up safe, but that telegram yesterday said that Les was killed."

"How horrible." It was a strange time to notice such a thing, but I couldn't help hearing that Betsy had a special way of saying "horrible." That must have been the way they said it in Syracuse, New York. "And Jules ran away because of his grief?" she asked.

"I don't know. The grown-ups sound like they think he might be in danger—you know—trying to hurt himself because he's so shocked, but I don't believe that. He'll be very sad, sure, but I don't think he's in danger."

"Where could he have gone?"

"Search me," I said. "I haven't told anybody else this . . . but Jules sometimes thinks he gets messages, you know, feelings that things are going to happen."

"You mean E.S.P.—extrasensory perception?"

"I don't know if it's that or not. He said he got a feeling before Les was reported missing. And another time my brother was lost in the woods, and I think Jules got a feeling that day that if we climbed up over the pipe Mickey'd be okay. We did, and he was."

"You think Jules got a message about his brother?"

"That's the only thing I can imagine that would make him go off. He wouldn't just hide because he was sad. Can you think of anything I can do to help him?"

"I'd go around to places where he might have gone and look for clues. For instance, did he get money out of the bank? Did he take clothes along? Did he take food with him?"

"He took his five dollars, the police said. They haven't told any other information, though."

"Then you'll have to do your own detective work. Judy Bolton would make a list of possible places, and then she'd check them out. I'll help you make a list." She tossed her jar on the grass. "Forget the bloody grass snake!" she said.

I felt a little better when I walked back from Betsy's house with my checklist. Still, as I slammed the screen door, I held my breath wondering what might have turned up while I was gone. Though it was early, the sun had gone down and the house was dark.

"Daddy!" I shouted, but he didn't answer.

"He's not home yet, Ellis," my mother called from upstairs. "I'm going to give you supper now. We won't wait for him." The thought of the three of us sitting alone at the kitchen table, pretending to eat, made me depressed.

After supper Mickey and I were curled up on the floor next to the big radio listening to the "The Jack Benny Program" when I heard my father come in the door.

"No news," he said quickly, as the three of us came

running. "They're pretty sure he didn't buy a ticket on any bus or train out of town. But we've combed Wissining—he's not anywhere here." My father sank into a chair and passed a hand over his eyes. My mother and I looked at each other and then back at my father.

"If he's not found by noon tomorrow," he said, "they're going to drag the mine hole."

Fourteen

I could tell by my father's face at breakfast in the morning that everything was exactly the same. He excused himself quickly. "You stick close to home today, young lady," he said to me, as he went off to work. I didn't answer. I had decided, no matter what, to look for clues. It made me feel bad to pretend to obey, but there was no choice. I checked the newspaper—it was full of news about the war, but there was nothing at all about Jules.

As soon as my mother was busy running the vacuum cleaner and Mickey was playing upstairs, I took my checklist and half a loaf of bread and left the house. Betsy had offered to go with me, but I had told her I'd rather go alone. Going with someone would have made it like a game. This was no game. Number one on my list were stores where Jules might have bought something to eat. If he had left home without breakfast and had taken money with him, he might have stopped for food.

First I tried Priscilla's Candy Store by the library, but she said Jules hadn't been in. Next I walked up to

Van Horn's Bakery and the Wee Nut Shoppe. Neither owner knew Jules by name, so I had to describe him each time. It was all pretty useless, since in both places they ended up saying very cheerfully, "If he comes in we'll tell him you're looking for him!"

While I was up on Windsor Avenue traffic was stopped for a railroad train. It suddenly occurred to me —what if Jules had jumped on the couplings and had ridden the train out of town! They said he hadn't bought a ticket, but riding the train free would have been a lot smarter. If Jules had gone somewhere, maybe it was to Washington, D.C. It might make sense to go to Washington, if you wanted to check on a government telegram. I even asked a man at the Rialto Theater where the train was headed for. He told me he believed it was going to Baltimore. Well, that's it, I thought to myself. Baltimore's near Washington. That must be what Jules did.

For a while I was so sure about my Washington hunch that I almost gave up looking for clues. I don't know what kept me going. Circling around purposely to avoid the mine hole, I headed for the creek. I knew Pat had already searched around the springhouse, but I just felt like walking someplace peaceful. I could hardly believe that the people I passed on the way were going about their business as if everything was normal. When I walked down the path at the bridge grasshoppers were singing happily in the fields. I felt miserable. I sat down on the bank to take off my shoes and let the water ripple over my feet. I ate a piece of bread. It must have been getting pretty late in the morning, but I didn't care. Then I stood up, tied my shoes together by the laces, slung them over my shoulder and started to walk in the direction of the sewage pipe.

As I got close to the cement pipe I remembered the day when I had been so scared because Mick was lost. That same wave of weakness and fear came back to me now, as I stood near the spot where Jules had dropped his watercress. There was Jules' jar, in fact, overturned but unbroken.

I climbed the bank, clutching at roots and rocks as we had done when Jules was helping me look for Mick. Crickets hummed, the earth smelled rich and for a second I forgot how bad things were. At the mouth of the pipe I hoisted myself onto the cement shelf. With my back to the opening, I looked through the trees over creek, field and winding road below. And when I dared myself to turn around for a quick look into the dark interior, I saw Jules. He was lying in the gentle curve at the very beginning of the pipe—asleep.

"Holy moley!" I said under my breath. I stood like a statue for a second, until it really sank in that I had found him.

Jules' head was resting on his arm, and he had a corduroy jacket flung over him like a blanket. Next to him was a cloth sack tied to a stick. It looked as if he had studied the way hoboes carry their belongings. The only other thing I noticed was Les' high school year-book, which lay at Jules' feet. I debated whether to wake him or to sit by until he woke himself. The thing that helped me decide was the picture in my mind of the police dragging the bottom of the mine hole. If I could get Jules to show himself before noon then maybe they wouldn't have to stir up that cold, black water.

"Jules," I whispered. "Yo, Jul-lee," I said very softly. He opened his eyes.

"Ellis . . . he's dead." Jules spoke in an even voice, as if he weren't even surprised to see me, and I realized that he was half dreaming.

"Jules, wake up." I touched his arm. He looked me full in the face, his eyes growing larger. Then he propped himself up on one elbow.

"Ellis," he smiled and sort of chuckled quietly. "Ellis, I don't know where I am. I'm half asleep."

"You're in the cement pipe. Jules, why did you run away?" He sat all the way up, blinked, and pushed back his hair.

"Oh. . . ." he groaned. "Now I remember."

"Jules, everybody's very worried. Why did you run away?"

"Wait a minute—let's get out of here," he said. "It smells like garbage." He picked up the yearbook and dragged the cloth bag and jacket behind him. I followed him out onto the shelf where we sat with our feet dangling over the edge. The sun shining through the leaves made speckles on Jules' face.

"How did you find me?" He was fully awake now.

"It was just plain luck. I *never* thought you'd be here. I made a list of places to look, and the pipe wasn't even on it. I just wandered here by accident. I thought I was seeing a ghost when I first saw you! Jules, *why did you run away?*"

He stayed quiet for a second. "Well, I may as well try to explain it to you, because nobody else'll know what I'm talking about. They'll get it all wrong."

"Go on."

"When you went away with Betsy at the initiation," Jules began, "Sam and I were still sitting on top of Willie Pflug. Then this motor scooter drove up to my house; 'Hey,' Sam yelled to me, 'who's that guy on your porch?' I saw that it was somebody in a uniform. I went tearing into my house. The messenger was just going away. My mother was holding a telegram and staring at it. She didn't even open it. I was . . . sort of embarrassed. I pretended I had to go upstairs, but when I got to the top, I hung my head over to hear what she would do next. I waited a minute, and then all I could hear was this awful low sobbing that didn't stop. My father wasn't home yet. I didn't know what to do. I went into my room and shut the door. I guessed what the telegram said." Jules cleared his throat.

"Then what?"

"When I was in my room, I got this *feeling*. It wasn't exactly a message. It was sort of like an *order,* something I *had* to do, even though I didn't know who was ordering me."

"What was the order?"

"It was strange. The order was, 'Find the tree that Les and Judy were sitting under in the yearbook picture.' "

"What for?"

"It was as if some message about Les would come to me there. As if I wouldn't be sure about Les until I got to the tree."

"Where is the tree?"

"I didn't know *where* it was—then. And I couldn't run out at that moment to look for it. My father came home, they showed me the telegram, they telephoned people, everything was terrible. And it got dark. I decided when I went to bed to go looking for the tree as soon as there was enough light to see outdoors."

"You should have left your mother a note."

"I didn't want anyone to come after me while I was looking."

"Did you find the tree?"

"Yes, finally. It's not far from the springhouse. But I didn't find it until this morning. That's why I stayed out all night. I looked all over yesterday."

"Didn't Pat or Chief Sharky see you?"

"Were they looking?"

"There's been a big search, Jules. Pat even told me he checked the springhouse."

"I didn't get there until this morning. I was all over the woods of Wissining yesterday, checking every tree. Pat must have passed right by me."

"How did you know which was the right one?"

"The shape. Look at the picture." He opened the yearbook to the photograph of Les and Judy. "Come on, follow me. I'll show you where it is. Take my jacket!"

I was anxious to get Jules to go home, but I figured

I'd better do what he wanted me to. He scurried down the bank as fast as he could go with the book under his arm and the stick over his shoulder. When we came to the creek bed, Jules led the way over mossy rocks to the field in front of the springhouse. Though I had never noticed it before, I saw now, almost immediately, the tree he meant. It was the one in the picture. Jules pulled up short at the base of it and sat down in its shade.

"This is it," he said.

I threw down his jacket, my shoes, and the bread, and knelt, looking at the tree. "What happened when you finally found it? Did you get a message?"

"No." Jules let out a long sigh. "I don't know what I was expecting. My hopes were all built up, so I thought maybe I'd hear a voice, or something. You know, in the Bible people are always hearing voices and seeing signs from God and stuff like that. But when I saw it, it was just a tree."

"It's a nice one, though," I said. The fork was low enough to make it a good climbing tree. I stuck my bare foot between the two main branches and hoisted myself up to the lowest limb.

Jules looked up at me through the leaves. "Then, when I didn't hear any voice," he went on, "I looked around for a written note, or something carved on it, or *anything* special."

Just as he was telling me about looking for signs, my eye hit on something amazing on the limb above me. "Jules!" I shouted. "Look at this!" He stared right at the spot, but he didn't move. He shook his head sadly.

"Jules!" I said, "it's L.M.—Les' initials, carved right here on the tree!"

"I know."

"Isn't that special? Isn't that a sign?"

"*I* carved them there, this morning," he said.

"Oh." At first I felt let down, but the more I thought about it, the more it seemed right. I didn't really like the idea of a mysterious sign. It was nice to know that the initials were there because Jules had carved them. "Then you don't believe in your messages anymore?" I asked him hesitantly.

Jules stood up and clasped his hands around a low branch. "I guess not." He thought about it. "Maybe I never did. Well, I guess I used to . . . when I was younger." We were both quiet for a minute.

"How come you carved the initials?" I asked.

"To make my own message. To remember Les."

"Now it's his tree," I said.

"In a way," he nodded. "But you can sit in it."

" 'Don't sit under the apple tree with anyone else but me,' " I smiled. I didn't mean anything special by it—I was just saying the words to the song.

" 'Till I come marching home.' " Jules added the last line to the song.

"Do you think Judy knows Les won't be coming home?" I wasn't sure if Jules felt like talking about Les, but it seemed as if he did.

"She must know by now. It was supposed to be in the paper. She won't care, though." He made a face.

"Why not?"

"I saw her with somebody else on the Fourth of July," he said.

"A soldier?"

"Yeah."

"Where did you see them?" I asked him.

"In the afternoon, fooling around at the swimming pool, and kissing in the woods just before the dance."

"Before the dance? Did it make you feel bad?"

"Yeah, I guess so." Jules looked at me for a second and then lowered his eyes.

"Hey, Jules," I asked him, "now that you found the tree, what're you going to do?"

He picked up his jacket. "Go marching home," he said.

Fifteen

Coming back from the creek, Jules and I agreed to pretend we had met on the street near Milford Square. Neither of us felt like explaining the whole business about the cement pipe and the tree. As we came into the square through Feeney's backyard, we saw Jules' father standing on their porch. Jules dropped his jacket and hobo pack and ran toward him. Mr. McConagy didn't usually show how he felt, but when he saw Jules he threw his arms around him and hugged him hard. The word that Jules was back got around the neighborhood fast.

"He felt sad and wanted to be alone," I explained to anybody who asked me. My mother wondered where I had been all morning, but in her relief at Jules' coming home, she didn't push me about it. The police called off the dragging of the mine hole.

Once Jules was safe and the first pain of Les' death passed, things settled down a little bit in Milford Square. The hot days of July flew by, while all the time the war was "winding down," as they said in the newspapers. The McConagy's changed the silk hanging in their window from one with a blue star to one with a gold star, and at the end of July they held a memorial service for Les. Lots of people in town came to the service—friends of Jules and his parents, teachers from the high school, and a few of Les' buddies in the army. Judy was there. The minister who spoke said that Les had given up his life for us but that he was still alive in our hearts and minds. He *was* alive in my mind, building model planes, and playing first base and sitting under the tree that now had his initials on it.

Even though it was a sad time because of Les, good things happened too. There was a feeling of closeness between people. The Milford Square Good Citizens' Model Airplane Club finally held a magic show, with all proceeds going in Les' name to a veterans' hospital. We even got a mention in the "Around Town" section of the *Windsor Times*. "Local magicians conjured up a substantial $17.95 yesterday as a contribution to the Brandywine Veterans' Hospital," the paper said. "The contribution will be made in the name of Leslie H. McConagy, killed in action on Iwo Jima, 1945." We never would have made so much money, except that Shoppe's grown-up daughter gave us ten whole dollars.

The members of the club stuck together pretty much through the summer. Jules and I stayed close friends. Even though we never mentioned it, there was a sort of secret bond between us after the day I found him in the pipe. Even Sam Goff stopped being so terrible. Maybe it was because he felt sorry about Les, or maybe it was because his stepmother was home now and could spend more time with him. Her defense plant had closed on account of the war winding down. As far as the rest of the club went, Tim Feeney helped his parents a lot in their victory garden, but when he wasn't busy, he hung around with us more than with the St. Agatha kids. Willie Pflug, Mick and Ruthie were always underfoot as usual. Sibby called me one day at the beginning of August to tell me that she wasn't going to see me much anymore. Her father was going to send her to a private school in Windsor in the fall. I pretended to be sad, but I was really relieved that I wouldn't have to keep putting up with her.

Another reason why I knew I wouldn't miss Sibby was because of Betsy. Betsy's moving to Wissining turned out to be the best thing that had happened all summer. Naturally she had passed the club initiation. Sam still teased her off and on about her Syracuse way of talking and about her "Mama," but she never let it bother her. He also tormented her when he found out she couldn't swim or ride a bicycle. But even Sam had to admit that Betsy could do a lot of other things well. She could do card tricks, draw pictures of people's faces that really looked like them, identify bugs and mount them on pins and talk very fast in Pig Latin. I saw right away that I had been stupid to worry about whether she was pretty or not. She *was* pretty in a way, when you got to know her. Jules liked her, I could tell, but he didn't love her.

In the early days of August the whole bunch of us would go to the swimming pool to try to teach Betsy how to float. "You're all horrible! Glub, glub . . ." she'd yell at us as we laughed and she sank. Afterward we'd buy Popsicles from McKinley, who parked his orange cart in front of the pool in the afternoons. In the evenings we'd play Capture the Flag and Spud on the mall until our parents called us in to bed.

On one of those evenings there was another dance at the playground. I made sure to point out to Betsy who Sally Cabeen was. Sally was there with the same Tarzan boy she had danced with on the Fourth of July, and Marybeth Gruen whispered to me during intermission that Tarzan and Sally were going steady. This time there wasn't any big rush to dance with Sally, either; in fact, Jules and Sam stayed outside and played Giant Step and hide-and-seek with Betsy and me during the whole thing.

On August 6 two serious things interrupted the calm of those summer days. The first one affected the whole world. The headlines in the newspaper said: "First Atomic Bomb Dropped on Japan." This was supposed to be good news for Americans because it meant that the Japanese wouldn't be able to hold out much longer against us. I felt mixed up. I certainly wanted us to win the war—I even wanted to get back at the enemy because of Les, but the idea of a bomb as powerful as 20,000 tons of TNT scared the wits out of me.

The second serious thing affected our family. Grossie went back into the hospital. "It won't be for long," my mother said. I wasn't sure what that meant.

"Can I get to see her again?"

"I'll let you know," my mother said. When I went to bed that evening I had a nightmare. I dreamed Mrs. Lane got angry at me and locked me up in my glass-covered bookcase.

During the next few days my mother went to visit Grossie as she had at the beginning of the summer. I was supposed to make lunch for Mick and drag him around with me wherever I went.

"Why doesn't Grossie come to our house on Fridays anymore?" Mick asked me.

"She's sick, dope," I said. I wasn't so much annoyed with him as I was with not knowing more about Grossie myself. "Anyway, ask Mom," I told him. It was easier for little kids to ask personal questions. That evening he asked her.

"Grossie's very sick," I heard my mother tell him, as she was tucking him in bed. Things always sounded more important at bedtime, as if God was listening.

In the other room I heard Mick ask, "When'll she come to our house?"

"I don't think Grossie will get well enough to come to our house anymore," my mother said in a strange voice. I buried my face in the pillow and kept it there until the pillow was soaked with tears. I had guessed for a while about Grossie, but until that moment I hadn't admitted it to myself.

"They've surrendered!" Sam jumped over the porch divider and banged on our front door. "Yo, Ell-lee . . . the Japanese've surrendered!"

I didn't know whether to believe him or not. That was exactly the same thing he'd said two days before, when it had turned out to be a joke. Jules joined him on the porch.

"It's true, Ellis," he shouted through the screen door. "Turn on your radio!" I opened the door for Sam and Jules as my father tuned in the living room radio. My mother and Mick came running, and the six of us stood in a semicircle with our hands behind our backs as if we were at a ceremony.

"We repeat," the radio blared, "President Truman has just officially announced the unconditional surrender of the Japanese." The six of us drowned out the announcer's voice. Jules and Sam jumped up and down hugging each other and dancing around the living room. Then Jules, Sam and I cheered while Mick banged on the piano. My father and my mother, even though she was tired from going to the hospital all the time, smiled and clapped in time to Mick's beat. We could hear the same commotion from other nearby houses.

"Spit, spit, right in the Führer's face!" Sam shouted.

"Off we go, into the wild, blue yonder!" sang Jules, as the six of us stomped out the front door and into the street where everyone was gathering.

"Ring all the doorbells!" Sam told Mick and Ruthie. "Tell everybody to come out!" The two of them scooted around to every house while I ran to get Betsy. By the time I got back, almost every neighbor in Milford Square was outside, on the porches or in the street. Jules' parents were a little quieter than some of the others, but I could see that they were really happy. Then, all at once, without anybody suggesting it, everyone moved onto the mall. People who usually never spoke to each other were chatting and laughing together.

"Look!" I cried. "I can't believe my eyes!" I tugged Jules' shirt sleeve. "*Mrs. Lukesh is on the mall!*"

"This is the happiest day of my life," Jules said.

Then all the fathers gave the kids money, and we went in a group to Priscilla's Candy Store for ice-cream cones. Each of us carried three or four cones with a piece of waxed paper over the top to protect them, and when we got back to Milford Square we handed them around. They were all squishy and melted, but nobody minded. The next two days were declared holidays, and we stayed outside as late as we wanted.

The war was over.

Nothing you could see changed overnight after the surrender, but the whole world seemed safe at last. On V-J Day, the official day of celebrating victory over Japan, Jules and I took a walk down by the creek to look at Les' tree. When I got home, there was a note for me from my mother, saying that she had been called to the hospital suddenly. I saw that the world would never be safe all the time for everybody.

During breakfast the next morning the telephone rang. My mother answered it, and when she came back to the table, her eyes told us the news first.

"Grossie's gone," she said. "She never regained consciousness. Uncle Frank will come for me in an hour or so." She sat for a second with her head lowered. Then she pushed back her cereal bowl, got up, and did what I thought at first was a strange thing. She went upstairs, and soon we could hear her moving heavy things around. When I got up from the table I climbed the stairs and saw that she was cleaning out closets. "Just something to keep me busy," she said to me quickly.

Going to my room, I closed the door, lay on my bed and stared at the mark on my ceiling. I didn't cry—I had already done that. After a minute I got up and took the blue poetry book off the shelf—the book of Mary Ellis' that Grossie had given me. I rubbed the leather cover with my thumb. Grossie must have known when she gave it to me that we might not see each other again. I flipped through it, reading the first lines of a lot of poems. I had a feeling, from looking at the book before, that there was one in particular I wanted to find. Then I saw it. It was a little hard to understand, but I thought I had it figured out.

> *The bustle in a house*
> *The morning after death*
> *Is solemnest of industries*
> *Enacted upon earth, —*
>
> *The sweeping up the heart,*
> *And putting love away*
> *We shall not want to use again*
> *Until eternity.*

That's what my mother was doing in the closets, I supposed—keeping busy to take her mind off sadness, bustling around, sweeping up the heart and putting love away—love for Grossie. Just as Jules had bustled around carving initials in the tree, where he put away his love for Les.

I stared at the poem, thinking what a hard time it was—the end of so many things. Some of those things were the hardest I'd ever faced, like the end of Les' life and now of Grossie's. But some endings were good, like the end of the war. And some were just *there,* like the end of the summer. It seemed that such a lot of time had passed since the trip to Sibby's, the Citizenship Award, and the Fourth of July. Before I knew it, though, school would be starting, and there would be all sorts of beginnings again.

Suddenly I felt the same thing my mother must have felt. I felt like sweeping, or running fast or swimming hard—anything to be busy. Just about the only thing you *could* do when you put away for a while your love for one person was to start loving other people more—and to keep yourself very busy.

I wasn't exactly sure what to get busy at, but I put the poetry book under my arm, and passing by the room where my mother was still moving around, I ran as hard as I could down the steps and out the back door toward Betsy's house.

ROBIN F. BRANCATO grew up in Wyomissing, Pennsylvania, a suburban town which provided inspiration for the setting of *Don't Sit Under The Apple Tree*. She majored in creative writing at the University of Pennsylvania and has been doing graduate work in English at Hunter College and the City College of New York.

For the past ten years, Robin Fidler Brancato has taught high school English and journalism in Hackensack, New Jersey. She lives in Teaneck, New Jersey, with her husband, John, and her two sons, Christopher and Gregory.

J
F
B816d   Brancato
            Don't Sit
            Under the Apple
            Tree

DATE	ISSUED TO
	MARTIN ROSS
FE 18 '80	JEAN HOWER
JY 14 '80	Mabel Orth

MY SISTER
LOOKS LIKE
A PEAR

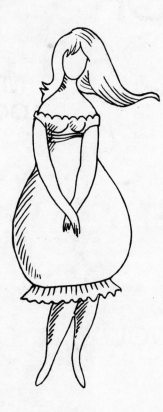

MY SISTER LOOKS LIKE A PEAR

awakening the poetry in young people

DOUGLAS ANDERSON

HART PUBLISHING COMPANY, INC. NEW YORK CITY

TO LEONARD RANDOLPH

COPYRIGHT © 1974
HART PUBLISHING COMPANY, INC., NEW YORK, N.Y. 10012
ISBN NO. 08055-1131-8 (paperback 08055-0190-8)
LIBRARY OF CONGRESS CATALOG CARD NO. 74-79926

MANUFACTURED IN THE UNITED STATES OF AMERICA

contents

To look at you, my son,
to know you came from me,
but you are you.
You have your father's eyes
but you see things differently.
Such an impish smile,
what are you thinking, my son?
Are you going to pull the cat's tail?
If I look away I know you will.
The cat will scratch you,
don't you know?
Now I hold you while you cry,
my son, don't cry. Now you know.
You have to learn yourself.
And I have to learn with you.

MY SISTER
LOOKS LIKE
A PEAR

At the conclusion of each chapter, I have presented one or more poems written by students. These poems are enclosed in boxes for easy identification. While they do not necessarily relate to the specific chapter they follow, the poems do illustrate the larger point of this book—that there is a poetry in all young people, waiting to be awakened.

DOUGLAS ANDERSON

1. "i never did like *poetry,*

but this is really good"

This book is a carnival of emotions. There are happy musical carousels here, and there are death-defying feats of personal risk, and horror shows, and cotton candy, and demolition derbies, and little gardens for the lovers to go off and hide in, and shooting galleries of the soul, and tonic salesmen, and some of those crazy mirrors that make you look like you're made out of silly putty.

But mostly, the carnival is one of shared love. Because there is a deep, simple music in every human being. No exceptions. Sometimes the music is buried or hidden away, or it has a lot of trouble getting out of the cages we keep it in. But it is always there. It is always longing to be free and to sing.

So, much of what is in this book is by, for, and about word-singers, roughly 15,000 of them whom I've worked with in *Poets in the Schools* programs across America and at all grade levels.

This book offers about 2 per cent of the writings of these 15,000 students. By conventional standards, some of it is "good," and some of it is "poor," but all of it is interesting, alive. The book also includes specific tools for teachers and students to let the music come out, and some pointed travel notes from my own distressed and mischievous conscience.

But this book is not "another anthology." Nor is it an ax-grinding, guilt-fueled tirade. This book is an attempt to pump a lot of vitamins into our country's ailing poetry. Lately, our poetic health as a people has been suffocating in private imagery and academic tedium. That's sad, because poetry is a powerful and intimate force that can start us to communicate more with one another, to begin closing the grim chasms in our common faith and our sense of worth. Poetry is a public art. It is for everyone, because the music is in everyone.

In my travels for *Poets in the Schools,* I've had chances to share student writing with many people who are not teachers, not poets, and have no technical training in verse. Their general reaction has been, "You know, I never cared for poetry, because I could never understand it. But this stuff's really good." By this I do not mean to imply that I have diluted or oversimplified this book in the least; I hope many of the verses here will delight and challenge highly trained poets. But the music is for everyone. The music, and therefore the book.

One more thing. I originally said Yes to working in *Poets in the Schools* programs *partly* because I got paid for it. I remembered the numbers of dishes I've washed, and apples I've picked, and basements I've dug out, and beers I've drawn, and wet concrete I've slung, and clocks I've punched, and ships I've moored, and cartons I've packed, and floors I've mopped, and johns I've cleaned, and meals I've missed. And I said Yes.

Not that I *minded* any of that experience: I wouldn't trade off a minute of it. But all that time, when anyone asked what I "did," I answered I was working at being a writer. I'd always had it in mind that one day the world might let me support myself doing what I wanted to do.

The *Poets in the Schools* program let me do that. I wish to thank the state arts council administrators of Minnesota, Oklahoma, North Dakota, South Dakota, Alabama, Nevada, Washington, Alaska, Colorado, and Hawaii for providing me three years of honorable and joyous work.

Every time they say:
Shut up! (stupid kid!)
Don't swear! (Ya little bitch!)
Walk straight! (Lazy child!)
Turn that off! (Tasteless!)
Oh come *on*! (Unsophisticated!)
Don't kiss him! (Slut!)
Who do you think you *are*? (Nobody)
Retard! (Reject!)
Just look how lucky you are! (Ungrateful!)
You don't know what you're talking about
You lazy stupid little bitch
Who is always wrong and never
Right and is a whore and
Whose side of the family could you
Have gotten your big mouth from
I just don't understand
Your kind you don't know
Anything no you can't *they're*
Not the right age group
What can you be thinking . . .

I am going to smile and agree!
And it will scare the hell out of them.

                                    CYNDY BRUMLEY

2. my chest's

hairier'n your chest

Who does not have things inside, important things he's always wanted to bring out and share? And who does not fear being laughed at, or scorned, if he dares to show them? And since our fear is so strong, most of us end up settling for silence: we end up strangers, not only to our closest friends, but—far more important—to ourselves. It's less a writer's problem than it is simply a human one.

Making the rounds for *Poets in the Schools,* I've often traveled with Dan McCrimmon, a first-class songwriter/guitarist whose music has turned a lot of students on to poetry. The two of us are seldom able to stay in any one school over five days. So the question we always have to contend with, and are often asked by resident teachers, is: How do a couple of music-and-word freaks walk into any public school in any part of town and, in five days or less

1. Ease the students through the clumsiness of working with strangers

2. Turn them on to poetry

3. Inspire them to try writing some of their own, and

4. Get them not only to turn in their efforts, but to share their poems with their peers?

It's easier to get through to elementary students, because they haven't learned to fear each other yet. But even with grade-schoolers, you have to begin somewhere. And Daniel's got the guitar with him. So one thing we do to break the ice is teach the young people a song, then invite them to make up more verses.

Tom Paxton's written a lot of neat kids' songs. Or maybe they're kids' songs for adults, or adults' songs for kids. Anyway, they're neat. In one of them, Paxton wrote a whole string of verses which are boasts. We teach the students the melody, then invite them to make up more verses on their own—about something bigger than, or funnier than, or prettier than, or smellier than. Then we can all sing their new verses together.

We begin communally. Three or four people propose ideas, and we vote for the one they like best. (Children's taste is flawless.) So the first line's gonna be,

My chest's hairier'n your chest

Okay, so why is it hairier? Once again, a lot of proposals. Pleasant pandemonium—Daniel strumming and saying "Huh?," everyone giggling, tossing out ideas, and me writing them down as fast as I can.

And pretty soon you don't have to vote anymore. Everyone knows on instinct when the craziest, most creative idea surfaces.

So now we know why "My chest's hairier." But the reasons *don't fit the lines.* We keep tapping out the rhythm, until *they* find how to make it work. If they finally can't, then either we make a suggestion, or else they scrap the idea altogether and go looking for another verse.

About two-thirds of the following verses were composed communally, the others by individuals (some anonymously).

My chest's hairier'n your chest
My chest's hairier'n yours
My chest's hairier 'cause I eat lima beans
My chest's hairier'n yours

⁕

My teacher's uglier'n your teacher
My teacher's uglier'n yours
She's got muddy hair, her name's Mrs. Strawface
Her teeth are all rotten with holes

⁕

My wahine's sexier'n your wahine
My wahine's sexier'n yours

She wears a teeny weeny yellow polka-dot bikini
My wahine's sexier'n yours

❋

My watch is slower than your watch
My watch is slower than yours
It's made of tinker toys and it ticks backwards
A minute is an hour too slow

❋

My house is stinkier'n your house
My house is stinkier'n yours
We burn skunks and there's pigs in the bathtub
My house is stinkier'n yours

❋

My bike's cheaper than your bike
My bike's cheaper than yours
Cardboard frame and the chain's made of licorice
String-bean tires that go flat

❋

My teacher's groovier'n your teacher
My teacher's groovier'n yours
'Cause she's not mean, and she takes our insults
She ain't a granny no more

My peanut butter's stickier'n your peanut butter
My peanut butter's stickier'n yours
It sticks to bread better, goes good with dog food
My peanut butter's stickier'n yours

※

My glub's flubbier'n your glub
My glub's flubbier'n yours
They flub blubber 'cause their eyes are made of rubber
My glub's flubbier'n yours

※

My smile's bigger than your smile
My smile's bigger than yours
It's six inches high and three feet wide
My smile's bigger than yours

SANDRA CARNES

She grabbed the slender white chalk
and her eyes went down to the book.
She looked up and at the same time
the chalk ripped down the board with a screech.
Little bumps crawled up and down my spine.
She sneered.

LAURA ROSEVEAR

I was in the bushes
playing hooky from school.
I hear footsteps! They're coming to get me!
Well, surprise, surprise—
it was just an ant!
Lucky, lucky me.

LAURIE MEECHAM

3. the program

and how i first got into it

The *Poets in the Schools* program is jointly funded by the National Endowment for the Arts and state arts councils. It began in 1966 as an experimental pilot project. Because of the immense enthusiasm expressed from all sides, the program has now grown out into all fifty states.

The purpose of the program is to expose students to artists, to encourage a generation of young Americans who —though few will become artists—will have an increased ability to appreciate and enjoy fine art. An equally important feature of the program is to offer interested teachers materials and suggestions which will help them carry on with the work after the visiting artist is gone.

Generally, artists are recruited locally by state arts councils. The choice of which artist is to work in which school is left to the cooperative discretion of the state arts council and the local school. The majority of the artists work exclusively in their home states.

The range of writers working in the program includes everything from Ph.D.'s to college-dropout street poets.

The only two official requirements for getting in are (1) that you've been published, and (2) that you relate well to students in schools.

My own involvement with the program began in Denver in 1971. I was one of five to fifteen people (depending on the season and travel schedules) living in a commune. Most of us were in our mid-to-late twenties, and were trying to make it as some sort of artist: songwriter, guitarist, poet, painter, puppeteer, leathersmith. We all lived in one house because we needed moral support, because the rent was cheap, and because we could usually get straight answers from each other—positive criticism for our art, and loving criticism for our hangups.

My communal brother Randy Martines was in college at that time. One day, he read a couple of my poems in a class. The teacher liked them and asked to meet me.

She turned out to be the director of the Colorado *Poets in the Schools* program, and wanted me to work in it. Employment!

I said Yes.

Then, through another timely introduction, I met Leonard Randolph. Leonard Randolph is a warm, kind human being, and exceptionally gifted both as a poet and as director of *Poets in the Schools*. He said he wanted me to travel a little in the Far West, to do more work for the program: specifically, he wanted me to straighten out a problem.

A particular state arts council had hired three poets to come in from San Francisco. And they were doing really well at first—turning the students on to using their imaginations—until one of these poets printed FUCK on the board, in very large letters, in a high school classroom. The program was subsequently suspended.

What Leonard Randolph had in mind was that *I* was supposed to go in there and....

I said NO: I haven't had much experience, who am I to, and what if, and are you sure you want, and I might not be able to, and look here this program's really important and what you *really* need is someone who can....

Inside two weeks, I was on an airplane west.

And I was *scared*. Until I stepped into the first classroom. From then on I loved it. Along with writing, I love working with students more than anything else I've ever done.

It was not long before I got more offers to travel. I immediately balked. It meant I'd be away from Denver—in particular, the people I loved and needed—most of the '71-'72 school year. I resolved the problem by convincing Leonard Randolph to hire my old friend Dan McCrimmon, and to allow us to travel together.

Daniel and I met in 1964, in the old *Café Les Tarots* coffeehouse in Denver. I was still wallowing in a mire of very long words then, and he was just beginning the guitar. Since 1964, he'd performed in a hundred-odd folk clubs, loud bars, and college gymnasiums across America, and even in a couple of recording studios.

And we'd done some collaborating. I believed that poetry is *by definition* a public art. Up until the age of print, that's how the Muse had always spoken—out loud and communally. Reading a poem in silence is like trying to hear a symphony by looking at the score. To prove that poetry still communicates best in the open air, Dan and I had performed together in public: my verse, with his spontaneous music.

Besides, I told Leonard, he's a published songwriter, and he ought to be supremely capable with the students. And we could keep each other going through all that traveling: neither of us would feel quite at ease out there alone in the motel suites of America. Besides, it would be good for the program: a sort of traveling medicine show.

Leonard said Yes.

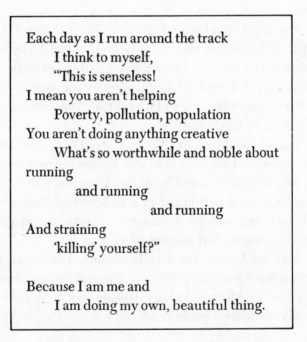

Each day as I run around the track
    I think to myself,
      "This is senseless!
I mean you aren't helping
    Poverty, pollution, population
You aren't doing anything creative
      What's so worthwhile and noble about
running
        and running
            and running
And straining
    'killing' yourself?"

Because I am me and
    I am doing my own, beautiful thing.

4. getting to know you

The reputation of poetry has been improving a little in recent years. But a lot of students still groan at mere mention of the word. For there are still many school systems where poetry, and the arts in general, are "taught" in the same way as geography, math, and social studies.

You must memorize "alliteration," "pentameter" and the first verse of "Evangeline" for the same reason you must memorize the capital of Montana, $C = \pi d$, and the preamble to the Constitution: if you don't, you'll flunk the test. And don't let me catch you writing about spinach monsters or the death of love or skating on the rings of Saturn when you're supposed to be studying complex verbs. Because school is *serious business*. You're here to pay attention, follow directions, and stay in line.

That approach makes it impossible for students to find poetry enjoyable, or to relate it to their own lives. It's just one more bad mouthful: you cram it halfway down and let it stick in your throat just until you can retch it back up on a test paper. Then you forget the whole mess as quickly as possible. The only thing you remember, for the rest of your life, is the bad taste.

Besides, poetry doesn't really matter. The arts are frivo-

lous: nice games for the idle rich, but fundamentally irrele-
vant to the hard struggle to get a job, make a living, and
survive. So why bother?

But many American students—particularly by the time
they reach secondary schools—have been painfully introduced to the difference between economic survival and
spiritual growth. They know—they want to know—that
there's more to life than a living. They know that the insides of things are not always what they look to be on the
outside, and that life is as often unfair and irrational as it
is fair and rational. And if you can share poetry with young
people which explores these truths—poetry they can *understand*—and if, along the way, you can show them that artists
are not ideas put in bodies but *people*, like themselves, then
poetry can become vitally important in their lives.

One of the first keys an artist can use to open up
any group of students is his own life: not as a showcase for
personality, but as a medium of communication. Students
have a lot of questions; as you coax these questions out, and
answer frankly and warmly, you can feel the stiff distance
between you and the students relax and close. Gradually,
the "idea" of poetry becomes as real to them as smiling and
breathing:

"How did you start writing? How old are you? Are you,
married? How did you get here? Where are you staying?
What do you think of Rod McKuen? Do you have a dog?
What was your first poem? Why do you wear hiking boots?
What do you think of our town? What grade level is your
favorite? Does poetry have to rhyme? What's your opinion
of dope? What do you think of coarse language in poetry?

What are your hobbies? Have you ever been to the Grand Canyon? Do you make a living from writing? How do you get published?"

The opportunity to have a writer's life at your disposal, and to ask him all the questions you want, is an important feature of the *Poets in the Schools* program. At first, it's like having a book you can ask questions. And it's not long before the students' fascination shifts from the poet to the poetry.

> Death, their sour faces looking
> grieving not for him but
> for themselves.
>
> STEVE ROWELL

> my hand is crying
> tears of ink
> the poetry is lost
>
> LISA JACOMB

THE UNBOUNDED ZERO

Oh zero, how can they say you're nothing!
Oh 0, the nerve of them to say you're nothing!
I know you're here, 0, I know you're everywhere
to me you are greater than 1
to me you are greater than 101
to me you are greater than 1 billion and 1
Because to me, 0, you're not a number, you have
    no limits
you are unbounded and limitless
you are boundless like the ocean
you are unlimited like the universe
they know that the ocean and universe are something
But yet they still say you're nothing
If only their hearts were as unbounded as you
to me, 0, you're the greatest

JOE PANICO

If happiness were truth
my life would surely be a lie.
    JOHN MC CRADY

5. eating soup

with a fork

A second powerful key to awakening the poetry in young
people is to read them verses written by others their own
age. They seldom want a teacher to lecture at them. In my
case, as an itinerant poet, I was not there to be a teacher
anyway. And people seldom want to hear a lot of words
they don't understand—at least not at first, they don't. They
want to hear, and to write about, things they know—*their*
dreads, *their* dreams, *their* joy, *their* anger, *their* love—not
someone else's idea of how they're *expected* to feel. So I
often begin with their peers' writing:

> *Even though I believed*
> *your hands upon me*
> *were a gesture of your love*
> *I still feel sick*
>   *when you pounce upon me*
> *with that sinful lustly liplick look.*

You have told me
      that it's good,
it will bring us closer

Well Hell anyway
      turn off the soft music
and puke up the wine!

Then what do you have?

      Two people
Two paper doll people
who can't find
      real love . . .

                              COLLEEN HENRY

✳

GIRL TALK . . .

Hi have ya heard about Teresa who hadda
get married yeah well you know how cheerleaders
are oh wow is Bobby a fox don'cha think so well
hasn't she gotten fat this year I really hate
her anyway and that creepy chick she hangs
around with is such a gossip don't you hate
gossips I make it a rule never to gossip and
have ya heard about . . .

GUY TALK...

Goddam Goddam heh heh heh howdja do
at the game I really scored and I wasn't even
playing football heh heh heh and Saturday we
went to the speedway saw some farout
machines man did ya see the K.C. lights
on the Nova hey man getta look at the head-
lights on that one what model no that was
no car it was Sandy heh heh heh ...

TAMRA JENKINS

※

Getting born into society is a pain
Society is a python squeezing
until you are a dry, lifeless, juiceless,
broken peach pit of a corpse of a person
And have no more to give, then puts
you on welfare and drops you by the trail
and moves on

SCOTT LEE

As Dan and I read these things, we make it clear to the students that we don't have any preconceived ideas about how a poem is supposed to be written. It can be rhymed or unrhymed, three lines or thirty, zany or grim, pretty or ugly, euphoric or horrid.

That's not to say we have no standards. When you write about something important, you don't use just *any*

words, and you don't want to be caught with a load of ex-
cess baggage. You want to get right in there, and get right
back out. And when you throw away many of the conventional crutches, you take on the added responsibility of
finding the true form for whatever you're writing about.
Whether it takes you five minutes or five years, a poem is
not an easy thing. It wants care.

Though Dan and I try not to be personally judgmen-
tal, we do impose a technical prejudice: we prefer writing
with *things* in it. For instance, we ask students which of
these two pieces they prefer:

> *Hating someone for his color*
> *is like eating soup with a fork.*

※

> *Why is the world full of so much prejudice?*
> *It's stupid to hate someone for his color.*

Nearly always, a majority prefers the first one. We ask
why, accepting all answers as valid. "The first one's more
the way people really talk." "It's better because it compares
prejudice to something else." "I just like it better." "It shows
instead of tells."

And what about *the language*? We keep on directing
questions, until someone mentions *things*. The first poem
has soup and a fork in it—things you can taste or touch. The
second poem does include nouns, but they're all abstract.
You know how when you get a Hallmark card you think,

"If I took the name off, I could send it to just about anyone, and just about anyone could have sent it to me"? That's what the second poem's like. But it took a person, a *particular* person, to write the first one. Writing carries more power when it speaks through things.

Sometimes we'll even pass out a mimeographed list:

life	*love*
hate	*loneliness*
truth	*beauty*
happiness	*evil*
war	*peace*
great	*good*
bad	*Soul*
feelings	*experience*
Man	*ugliness*

We recommend that the students write about these *subjects* all they want, but stay away from these *words* as much as possible—unless they use them well, we add.

These are useful examples. But how do we actually start people writing? How do we find something everyone in the room can write about?

How about a couple of universals? Love and hate, say.

Before starting to write, though, we repeat our bias for *things*. We read something like this (by an anonymous student in another state):

> *Isn't it wonderful, sharing*
> *all the beautiful feelings and experiences*

and all the pain and heartbreak
of being in love, growing and living
together?

We make known our frustration. The piece could have been written by a husband to his wife, by a trainer to his prize dog, by an old man to his rocker, by a gardener to her favorite begonia—by just about anybody to just about anything they happen to feel good about.

So much beauty has been lost because the writer has left us in the dark. *What* beautiful feelings? *What* love? *What* heartbreak?

On a picnic, beneath a tree that casts melting shadows.
I lie on my back as your hair falls, a secret tent.
You eat the iced cake from my hand,
And lick its crumbs from my fingers,
Missing the one above your lip.
And I can't help but smile.

※

You turn around and nothing's there
yet you can still feel the
presence of his body. The touch of
his lips, the smell of his clothes.
But am I feeling this for him
or me?

ANNETTE FRANKLIN

If I slugged you in the mouth,
don't mind.
It's a lot of meaning,
no lie.
I'd touch your unbrushed teeth,
poor fist.
Let the germs come to me,
mingle germs
That's feeling, man, true feeling.

※

Love is like a pebble in your shoe.
Even after it has been removed
A tender spot in your sole remains.

That's better.

Don't down or knock a person,
He dies for himself, not you.

You're walkin in the john
you know you're gone,
There is a moke* with a knife,
you try to save your life
The moke says "Get wise, punk"
and you reply in return "That's why
I come to school, Jack"

*In the islands, *moke* is slang for tough guy.

6. starting stuck pumps

There are always people who have trouble getting started. That's partly our own doing, because we prefer to work with a wide range of students, not just the ones already known to be eager and talented.

Why are they having trouble? Not interested in writing about love or hate? Okay: no one's *required* to write about just that (to require creativity is a hilarious contradiction of terms—and it's utterly futile).

So what's the problem?

"It's too early in the morning." Okay: write about what it's like when it's too early in the morning.

"Poetry's for fairies." Okay: write about Fairies I Have Known.

Or maybe the original topic—love and hate—can still work. Because it doesn't have to be just love or hate between *people*. How about love for cars, or love for violence, or for music?

One at a time, Dan and I draw the students out, nearly always by listening: "What do *you* know about?" And we never coerce. Occasionally, students have sat in, just watching for three or four days, before they finally wanted to write.

Partly, they want to feel us out. Some of them simply don't trust us. They don't believe we really try to accept each person on his own terms. They don't believe we're really not going to hand out grades.

We want them to come out of their shells: we keep on inviting; and we keep on offering options. We operate on the highly "idealistic," yet feasible, assumption that if we can't make what we're doing interesting, then we have no business forcing anyone to listen.

For three days, a Hawaiian high school student insisted to me that he was embarrassed even to try to write. He'd been taught all his life to be a loser, and he'd learned the lesson well. He was sure that his words would all be spelled badly, that the grammar would be wrong, and that I couldn't read his handwriting. Besides, he wouldn't have anything worth saying.

We finally got past that. He wanted to try. But he was still plugged up. "I just can't get anything out."

At first I simply replied, "Well, don't sweat it—some days you can write, some days you can't. It's the same way for me."

Five minutes before the end of the period, it finally dawned on me: but of course! "Make your frustration work *for* you," I told him. "Write *that*."

Five minutes after the period, I was on the way to my next class. Panting, he caught up with me. "Sorry, I didn't get started till the last few minutes. Hope it's all right."

It's too bad I can't do anything
when I suppose to.
It's too bad my tongues gone when
I need to express myself
I can't find my hand, it left me
alone, here with a sheet of paper.
Lucky thing my tears are here,
here to stay, with me
So I give you my drops of tears.

I was late to the class. It's hard to get yourself together just after someone freely gives you something so beautiful that you want to weep for joy.

He was quiet—when he was—which he was—
    most of the time.
He was kind—when he was—which he was—
    most of the time.
We all loved him—when we did—which we did—
    most of the time.
He's dead.

MARK SWART

Evening comes
a small sad song
sung inside a closing flower
the earth speaks a lullaby
in answer to a cricket
writing his timeless tune upon air
the moon gives a silver smile
and the stars wink goodnight
touch my hand, world
among the sleeping birds
take my hand, dear one
 and lead me by the weary mountain

CAROL BERRY

7. self-esteem

The single most important thing I strive to awaken has little to do with writing. It has to do with personal worth. Personally, I thrive on competitive challenge. But I do not accept that an education system which raises up the excellence of the few therefore *has to* devalue the many. By and large, American public education, like America itself, ignores losers. And the category *losers* includes, by and large, all but the winners. Paul Brase, my friend and colleague in the program, quips, "Sorry, kid: you've only got a B-minus soul."

Dan and I try to cultivate self-esteem. For instance, when any class writes, we give back to that same class, on the following day, a typed and dittoed collection of their work, including at least one entry from each person who wrote. Everyone represented. Nobody first or last for any particular reason.

Then we try to get the students to read through the whole collection aloud. No one has to read his own, we say; just pick one you happen to like, and read it out.

Depending on how reserved the class is, that can take a lot of coaxing. But the effort, and the occasional long silences, are worth it and more. (You can get around the silences by simply taking each piece separately: "Now who wrote this one? Would the author like to read it? . . . Anyone *else* like to?" If not, I read the poem myself and go on to the next one.)

It's worth it to try to draw the students out, because each person is somebody: with his own creative vision, and his own pure language—if he can be made *aware* of it. It doesn't matter whether you're supposed to be one of the pretty people or one of the ugly people; whether you're an intellectual superstar or a remedial reader; a jock, a fink, a soshe, a hood, or a teenybopper. EVERYONE has a gift, no matter how deeply buried, and no matter how awkward its first steps into the light.

At the beginning stages of working with a class, we value every effort on the ditto sheets equally. For instance, these two entries appear side by side:

a hitchhiker walking down a road

✳

Ebbing tides
    Sunlight painting
        golden lines
to make a break between sky and sea
Sprays of gentle waves,
        an old memory caught once
            again through an ancient scent.
A tired old woman

> *searching along the shore for*
> *something she never understood*
> *Youth is gone.*

SANDY GROUX

We value such poems equally because we don't want to chase the more introverted young people back inside themselves. For many students, to have written *anything* is a rare act of courage, and a rare gesture of trust in us. To use these students' initial efforts for purposes of comparison—"This one's brilliant but that one's lazy and clumsy"—is heartless and arrogant.

You never know how much of the beauty is hidden. If, for instance, you simply *value* the first of the two pieces above; if you say it looks to be the seed of a long poem, or maybe of a short story (which it *is*); if you express an interest in hearing more ("*What* hitchhiker? Why's he hitchhiking? Where's he going?"); if you don't slam the door on their sensitive, often vulnerable feelings, you never know what might come out the next time around.

You'll never know what a "semiliterate, troublemaking, disadvantaged loser" (or any other human being) is capable of, unless he knows you respect him.

In the junior high school at Lovelock, Nevada, the Chicano son of a migrant wrote one line in three days, and so illegibly I had to ask him to help me decipher it:

I always slept in a dirty bed

That's at least as good as, "I have measured out my life in coffee spoons." I don't *care* that the boy can barely read at third-grade level. I don't care that the world has given up on him. And I don't care that I'm only given three days with him. I'm going to let him know how fine that line is. And when his line is read off the ditto sheets along with everyone else's work, I'm going to praise hell out of it. And, after the others are through giggling at his worn-out shoes—as junior high students have a way of do-ing—and they see that I'm not joining in, then maybe next time they'll look at the creative person and not the shoes.

Teachers often remark, "You know, little so-and-so hasn't done a thing all year. Can't get him to respond to anything. But now he's writing like mad."

There's a reason for that, and it goes beyond my novel advantage as a special guest and my experience at getting people to write. Much of the success I've had in classrooms derives from dealing with students—even elementary stu-dents—as adults.

Perhaps the one most unfortunate thing I've observed in classrooms is the universality of, in the language of Eric Berne's *Games People Play*, Parent-Child transactions. The teacher plays Parent, and the student is constantly and subtly maneuvered into playing his Child. And this all tends to reinforce what Thomas Harris calls the "not OK" feelings in the student. And that *partly* explains why stu-dents are so often afraid to write, and why they so often claim "I really wouldn't have anything worth saying any-way."

Using Berne's scheme again, the one thing I work to

establish at the outset is an Adult-Adult contract with the students. Yes, I have more experience at writing than they do. But I'm not any more potentially creative than my students: no one is. I'm not faking it when I say to them, "We're all writers working equally together. And as a writer, you have as much to say as anyone else on earth."

Everyone can blossom.

The worm not only turns,
he often does it without giving
the proper signal. That's life . . .

THE ACT OF LOVING

It doesn't matter who you love
or how you love but that you love.
For in the end,
the act of loving any man
is the act of loving God.
The good in men is all the God there is.
And loving contributes to that good
And to that only God.

KAREN CULVER

I smile from the knees up
because from there down I must be a little sad

Trees are keys
to the breeze.

TERESA MILLER

I'm always so much colder wearing all the clothes I own
than when I'm being naked with you.

JANELL WELZ

A wanderer amid confusion
Locked inside
an invisible door.
Panic coming
    upon me.
Scream, scream
    No one can hear
Tears fall,
and explode when they hit.
I am blown, my mind
    into pieces
by my own
    sorrow.

SHERRI CAMPBELL

8. i wouldn't say this
if i had to sign it

If what Dan and I are doing doesn't interest the students, we see little point in requiring attendance. So we offer free passes to the library.

But if a student *does* want to come, he can often get a pass out of a regular class to join ours. Hence, we draw a few people who just wanted to get out of geometry. That's okay: you never know what a student who thinks he got away with something is going to pick up in spite of himself.

Further, we encourage, *but do not require*, students to sign their work. If students *had* to sign, there would be many things they wouldn't write about in school, for fear that their "friends" would know.

One of the problems of putting an artist into a classroom is that he is committed to the whole distressing process of self-discovery. And it is hard for Ralph and Jeanie to get down to life's nitty-gritty on paper without worrying about the smirks of Carol and Jim and Pete across the aisle. This is not to say that the artist should be content to have his students write entertaining tripe and thus shirk the drama of personal search and confrontation without which an artist-in-the-schools program—at least in secondary schools—cannot be significant. But you can't force that confrontation to happen all at once.

Another factor which inhibits students from signing their work is that junior high and high school boys often have an image of "the poet" as a frail, anemic type with girlish lace at his collar and cuffs. Add to that the adolescent struggle to establish a sexual identity, and the still powerful American myth that physical prowess is the measure of a man. Add to that the frequently televised image of manhood as the rugged, 44-caliber, Two-Fisted-Macho-with-a-Barbed-Wire-Soul. All this has been changing considerably during the last five years: boys aren't nearly so afraid as they once were to express honest feelings. Still, it's not easy for a boy to put his name to his writing.

On the first day we write, anywhere from 5 to 80 per cent of the students sign. But by the second or third day, it starts becoming obvious that creative writing is not only a form of self-expression, but an assertion of self-esteem, for men as well as women. There's dignity in it. I keep pointing that out: "This writing deserves a signature." Over the course of a week, it's not unusual for the percentage of signers to rise from say 30 to 90 per cent. This increase can be attributed to the "strong" pieces of writing we read from other schools, to our own enthused, unsissyish presence, and mostly to the students' increasing willingness to write.

I wish to go see my grandmother
so she can make me clothes
That makes her happy

BEVERLY FISH

I wish I was a book then
everyone would pay attention to me
and better be careful too!

SUZANNE PEASE

Days I have most fun I'm running in fields
as wild as the wind. Wearing black striped
robe. I love grass rubbing my legs. I like to
stand by the river watching the shadows in
the moonlight. At daylight I watch for my
enemy, the man.

SUSIE SMITH

9. your face

looked like moldy bread

Tell about the moment your skin didn't fit. Sometimes that happens when you meet someone for the first time. Like there's this chick you've been circling around all year, and finally you get up enough nerve to start a conversation with her; so there you are at last, talking with her, and you suddenly realize your fly's open.

Tell about one of those moments. Make light of yourself. Start out your poem with "My skin didn't fit right," or "The first time I met you, I felt like . . ."

There she is
over there, across the room,
by herself.
I wish I was like Don Juan.
I could just get up and
sit by her and talk with her and—and
and who am I trying to fool.
I could never do that.

I'd be so scared stiff I'd
bumble it all up.
She's getting up,
walking this way,
she's coming closer, closer, closer.
She sits down beside me. My heart is
a woodpecker on a tree. She says "Hello"
I mumble something.
She stays silent.
I think back, a Don Juan
gathering courage
I turn to her. Nothing.
She asks me what is it.
I say "Would you like to dance?"
On the dance floor with her in my arms,
I think Why was I scared?

⁜

The first time I met you I felt like butter
because your face looked like moldy bread.

SAM BELYER

⁜

Being in a crowded room
Meeting people and trying
To enjoy yourself but you
Still have that empty feeling
In your stomach.

Everytime I look at you
It seems you search my soul
You suck the corners of my brain
You rip me apart at the seams
You suck
You pull
You draw me in
You tempt me with false smiles
But I'm no fool; you lose.
I'm weak, but I still belong to me.
Smile, someone hates you.

RICK SEELHOFF

10. the nearest open door

Since my purpose is to get students writing poetry, why not use as models the poetry they're already close to? Rock and folk-music lyrics.

There's dim garbage in quantity on top-40 radio. But there are also a few lyrics which stand by themselves as poems: in parts of the rock operas *Tommy* and *Jesus Christ Superstar*, and in many of the songs of Joni Mitchell, Gordon Lightfoot, Bob Dylan, John Lennon, Paul McCartney, Paul Simon, and a number of the traditional black blues men.

One way to study poetic technique—and to make a traditionally boring exercise alive and meaningful—is through those lyrics: ask students to bring them in. Type them off onto ditto sheets, and invite everyone to dig in and see what makes those lyrics work, in the same way a good mechanic digs into an engine.

An even better way to examine poetic devices is to ask students to discover traditional techniques—however half-formed—in their *own* creative writing. When they can see it there, or in popular writing that speaks to them, then they're far more receptive to discovering, and appreciating, those same devices in Homer or Bryant.

i gonna smother your ass in mashed potatoes
and i gonna make gravy out of your hands
    and when I through i gonna serve you in the lunchroom
to all the good boys and girls.

11. you don't have to love music

to love me

Another way to use music is to invite students to write to it. In this case, of course, I mean music without lyrics.

I discourage students from writing *about* the music. "Don't say 'This sounds like,' or 'It makes me feel like.' Instead, BE the music. Change identities. Crawl *inside* the music, and write from the inside out.

"And since you're using your imagination, there is no right or wrong answer, and nothing you can't write about. If the music makes you want to fly, then become something that flies; if it makes you feel ugly, write an ugly thing. Become something mellow, or jagged, or joyous, or gory. Feel what you will: but try to translate your feelings into *things*, instead of just writing about feelings in general."

I begin with examples of other student writing. For instance, I'll play a few bars of a super-low-pitched male, Russian voice, chanting the Orthodox liturgy; then I'll ask the class at large what it might be. "A tape recorder at the wrong speed." "A car trying to start on a cold morning." "A suffering tree." "A building creaking." "Fog."

Then I'll read examples of what others have written,
all to the same piece:

> *I'm a deep dark cave so lonely I feel sad enough*
> *to bury myself until I don't exist and take*
> *everything with me.*
>
> RICHARD SHERMAN

*

> *I am just awakening*
> *From a long, deep sleep*
> *Someone is talking*
> *But it doesn't register*
> *I fade back down death's long corridor*

*

> *In a monastery*
> *Every one of us*
> *Very old man in the lotus*
> *Evening falling, very dark*
> *Voices from all around*
> *Astronomy dominee*
> *Stars filter through the dark-tinted glass*
> *We have to go on further than ourselves*
> *Nor can we even if we wanted to*
> *   Someone said*
> *"Everywhere I look I see only my own desires"*
> *   and I believe it*
>
> MARK LINEHAN

Since different spirits need different stimulants, I play several pieces of music. "Write one thing to each piece," I say. "Or write one thing to all of them; or just write one, or just two—however you're moved."

One of the prerecorded tapes I've used includes three or four minutes each from the Moody Blues' *Days of Future Passed* album, a section of the rock group Pink Floyd's "Come in Number 51, Your Time Is Up," a brief Gregorian Chant, some squirk-and-bleeple electronic music by Stockhausen, and Gabor Szabo's guitar rendition of the old rock hit "Walk Away Renée."

The trick is to find music which is not too specific in its associations: Halloween ghost sounds, for instance, usually produce only predictable triteness.

Other pieces I've used include: orchestrations of Erik Satie's "Gymnopedies"; John Fahey's "The Singing Bridge of Memphis, Tennessee"; parts of Sir Ralph Vaughan-Williams' "Sinfonia Antarctica" and "Fantasia on a Theme of Thomas Tallis"; Moog Synthesizer music; part of the "Underture" from The Who's rock-opera *Tommy*; "Songs of the Humpback Whale"; the climax from the first movement of Mahler's Symphony #10; Indian street music by "The Bauls of Bengal"; and the aria from Villa-Lobos' "Bachianas Brasileiras #5."

Because I have so little time with a group of students, I'm able to use only very short selections. I'd much rather have a whole week to really get into the music, using much longer pieces. One that comes to mind immediately is Alan Hovhaness' "Mysterious Mountain."

Occasionally, a student will write a complete poem in

response to the recordings. But what you usually get are kernels, seeds, promising fragments:

> *Isn't it great, it runs so straight, so swift, so*
> *fast, quickly changing directions each time*
> *a hoof touches the ground. What a life elud-*
> *ing hunters dodging bullets, always moving*
> *on, wouldn't that be exciting? I wish I was*
> *a deer.*
>
> CHARLES CANDELARIA

There's a potential poem in there, if you can just get the student to coax it forth. But it is the student alone who must finally do the creative work, for there is no profit in convincing a student of his potential unless he can recognize and cultivate it for himself.

As with the other writing exercises, the "music writing" is transcribed onto ditto sheets, so that everyone can see everyone else's responses. The result is not only the communal joy of seeing how differently people responded to the same pieces; it's also an opportunity for serious, extensive, workshop sessions.

After reading aloud all their responses to the music of the day before, I'll ask the students, "Pick one you like— any one."

So someone chooses.

"Okay. *Why* do you like it?"

"It goes with the music." Or, "It just feels good." Or, "It tells it like it is."

"Okay. But *how* does it accomplish that? What words, on the page, make it work?" I keep returning their attention to the writing itself, until someone says, "Well, it's that verb," or "He made a likeness," or "It's the way he used that color," or "It's the rhythm," or "It's the way he left words out," or....

In this way, students discover for themselves devices *anyone* in the class can imitate. For if students can see how their own peers use poetic techniques well, the natural reaction is "Well, if he can do it, why can't I?" That impetus, plus a lot of individual attention through positive criticism, makes most of the inferior writing disappear without any embarrassment to its authors.

Here as elsewhere, I do not judge pretty writing better or worse than morbid writing. For instance, a junior high student wrote,

> *Some chick screaming her guts out in an alley*
> *and the guy's having a lot of fun.*

It was unsigned, and no one would claim it. I guessed it was written by somebody playing the game called "I'm a smartass and I'll prove it by grossing you out."

But instead of dumping on it, I took the effort at face value and made an extended point out of it. I said I thought it worthwhile to write out, so plainly, that strange part of us which *enjoys* things violent and hurtful.

I have no idea whether what I said made the anonymous author examine his own thinking. But I figured I had a better chance that way than by coming on like Mr. Morality.

You don't *need* to preach that selfish violence is bad. Everyone already knows that. Everyone *has* known it, for 5,000 years and more. You don't change evil with sermons. But recognizing evil where it really lives, maybe that helps out a little.

I've used music to spur the writing of something over 5,000 students at all levels. I'd like to barrage you with about fifty pages of their responses. As it is, here's a few.

"The Day Begins," from the Moody Blues' *Days of Future Passed* album:

> *I am a deer running through the fields and then coming upon a pond and seeing myself for the first time ever.*
>
> **GABY STEPHENS**

※

> *I am long hair on a girl's head being blown in the wind. Then she puts on a scarf and takes away all my freedom.*

※

Pink Floyd's "Come in Number 51, Your Time Is Up" (sireneery female chorus, followed by sudden eruption of drums, guitar, and screaming male voice):

> *I am a star telling secrets to the universe.*
> *I am a person falling into time.*
>
> **LORI HUNTSMAN**

A sacrifice where a lady is going to have her legs cut off. The minute she gets her legs cut off she has to walk across a fire lake.

LORRIE MOORE

✳

I'm a very sad angel on a cloud looking about the world and then I see the light from another planet and there I see people different from ours—they're happy and they care about their planet.

ROBBIE WEAGANT

✳

I am an echo trying to find a place where I truly belong, being violently thrown from wall to wall to mountain to mountain and up into the sky to search forever.

✳

Gregorian Chant:

I am a condemned man singing in his prison cell.

✳

People with seven in the family trying to get to the one bathroom.

JAMES ARNEY

I am at the funeral of my best friend. I really loved him. He was my bird.

MARTIN FITCH

✳

I am trying to explain love to hate without being mean.

COLLEEN LYONS

✳

I am spirit now.
I am watching my friends at my funeral.
Let me tell you of my friends.

✳

I am a teacher lecturing her students about the significance of the irregular cornice of the Greek architecture. Even I am bored.

✳

Electronic music, from Stockhausen's "Kontakte":

Man's first step on the moon,
trapped in space.

EDWARD WESLEY GARRETT

I am a glubfish going glub-bub, glub-bub
WILLIAM HARVEY

☀

I'm in a time tunnel and never get out. It's so deep long it has psychedelic sound that makes me drowsy. I'm hot and hungry. All of a sudden an explosion was boomed and I was set free into the wilderness.

LORI BOHN

☀

I am a scientist using my miniaturizing machine. I am putting my cat in it to see how it works. The cat got so small it vanished and all that was left was its meow.

SUSAN PEDROL

☀

*I work at a computer station
listening to the sun all day.*
PAT HALLOCK

☀

I'm a monster's stomach with an ache for love but all I get is indigestion and heartburn.

RICHARD SHERMAN

I am a bowling pin bombarded by your heavy balls

＊

*I am the mainspring of the world
and I am dying.*

＊

Indian street music, by "The Bauls of Bengal":

*I crush the corn
And sing my song
Cross-legged for hours before my stone
I sit and crush the corn
The children play before me and
I sing my songs
I crush the corn
So we may eat during the long winter
I crush the corn
The children play before me
And I sing my songs.*

＊

*I am singing praise to the sunrise, that gives
us life. Sometimes so cruel but so fulfilling.
Life all that I have. Glory to the sun.*

DONNA DEZSI

Someone is being hurt,
because I can hear the beat
the beat of a heart in the distance.

✳

I am a elephant. When I walk through cinnamon
I go crunch, crunch, craaaack ahhhh.

RICKEY CLYNE

✳

I am a Spanish lady's voice box. I am like
a cigarbox with its lid flipping.

LORI PROCTOR

✳

The Camarata orchestration of Erik Satie's "Gymnopedies III":

I am a butterfly harmoniously moving from note
to note, ever so softly touching on each.

✳

I am a piece of silky smooth milk chocolate
melting in a warm mouth

LINDA ARMSTRONG

56400

I am a pair of old shoes nobody wants to
wear. But then a poor old man comes by
and takes me out of the garbage. Now I will
start life all over again.

ANTHONY MARTIN

✳

Gabor Szabo, playing "Walk Away Renee":

Every simple summer second
Filled with smiles
And "Stay awhile" s
And Sunken sun
Just careless fun.

ANAMARIE MICHNEVICH

✳

I am trying to make you happy
I'm not too fast
I'm not too slow
I am soothing and relaxing
I have a good beat
You don't have to love
music to love me.

LORY LEFF

Not all these efforts are complete "poems." But they all show clear evidence of creative discovery. And, though some of them would work better in poems without the "I" voice, I want students to discover the poetic spirit in *themselves*: initially, many think that poets could only be *other* people. So the "I" is a powerful tool.

The writers represented in this chapter are about evenly spread out from fourth grade through high school. I could list their grades, but I think that marveling over how creatively they write *considering their ages* begs the point. Each is an aroused human being at a moment of discovery.

Or I could have listed the parts of the country each lives in, or labeled the writing "ghetto," or "suburban," or "Chicano." But the difference between two people who sit side by side in the same room is likely to be far greater than the difference between, say, an Alabaman and an Alaskan.

This is the planet Earth. These are human beings.

"Why don't you get a haircut."

"It's my head. I'll wear it the way I want."

"If you don't get a haircut, you're gonna have to leave. Why don't you get a haircut."

"You're not asking me, you're telling me. I'm not gonna do it."

"I work for eighteen years and what do I get, a long-haired hippie freak. You only think of yourself all you can do is listen to that damn music and play that damn harmonica."

Crash, smash, kick!

"Hey that's mine, you can't do that."

"Are you telling me what I can and can't do. If you don't get a haircut I'll kill you."

"Listen man, I'll just leave, okay?"

"How can you be so passive."

"You ask me how I can be passive. Because I love you."

12. embarrassing simplicities

Sport is best in slow motion.
For when you watch the bullet
Tear into the deer's flesh—Oh
How pretty.

JOY BELL

When I first saw this poem, I was more than green with envy. I was embarrassed. Because, if in five minutes and in twenty simple words, only three of which exceed one syllable, some little fourteen-year-old can say something so exquisitely, then what am *I* doing mucking around in my own eighty lines of polysyllabic dreck?

Working with young writers, especially with the very young ones, has powerfully altered my own style.

Yes, even up through high school, they have the "unfair advantage" of their innocence. Adolescents seldom appreciate the torturing moral complexities we are all, sooner or later, given to cope with.

But as Wordsworth wrote, "the child is father of the man." I believe our young writers are not behind, but far out in front of us, and pointing the way to a genuine rebirth of poetry in America. They write very simply and directly; but somehow, they're doing it without flattening the deeper meanings. They are trying to show us how to make poetry, once again, a *public* art.

I can't stand the touch of her hands and
despise her innocent look
Shut the ugly voice that comes from her
things she wants make me sick
but I want her I need her she
needs me I love her but I hate her

I counted your smiles today,
More numerous than yesterday.
Will you allow me to pride myself
With the permanent wrinkles
    around your mouth?

13. dirty words

The point of the *Poets in the Schools* program is to liberate people's imaginations. You *don't have to* liberate the language. The children have already done it.

When a student writes with "four-letter" words, I generally try to conform to the particular community's notion of "taste." Either I talk with the student privately, and keep his work away from all other eyes; or I read it aloud to the class, but keep it off the ditto sheets. Or I read the work aloud *and* put it on the ditto sheets. With respect to the ditto sheets, either I leave total blanks where such language occurs, or I replace all but the first letter of any "dirty" word with hyphens, or I print the whole word. I try to be "mindful of community standards": Kindest personal regards to the Supreme Court.

The best way I know to reduce coarse language is to allow it: Because most (but by no means all) occurrences of such expression simply boil down to exhibitionism: using forbidden naughties to get everyone else to say Ain't I Cute. When you quit forbidding naughties, and start treating them as words which are common, ordinary, and perhaps a bit dull, then the thrill evaporates.

There are, however, some kinds of content about which

you can't write honestly unless you *do* use coarse language. You'd be cheating if you didn't. And when a subject like that arises in a classroom, and I want to read something which includes objectionable words, then I make a little speech in advance—saying I fully respect the rights of anyone who does not wish to be subjected to street language, and I invite anyone who might be insulted to leave.

No one ever has.

Yet there is a much deeper issue underneath all this. It has little to do with whether a community is going to hypocritically pretend coarse language doesn't exist. What it has a lot to do with is whether we're going to pretend there's no such thing as coarse, visceral *thought*.

The one piece I've read in classrooms which has drawn the most fire is my own humorous comment on the quality of drive-in food. I wrote it in the form of a television commercial, to advertise the "Sh-Boom Donald Duck" hamburger. Here are the "questionable" lines:

Sink your teeth into one of our Astro-Gastros:
a thick double bum of maggoty celotex
around three juicy layers
of rare, vitamized sewer patties
garnished with bubonic rat snot
steaming hot barbecue hog vomit
and generously sprinkled with that drooling aroma
combined specially for Sh-Boom
from drano and powdered roach carcass.
And don't forget our scrumptious
Sh-Boom I-scream, served fresh

from our runny white diarrhea machine.
Yes folks, that's why we say with pride,
'When America eats out, America eats Sh - - Boom!'

My "purpose" (if there needs to be one) in reading that
is not to open Pandora's box: it is to acknowledge the
normalcy of our "ugly" as well as our "pretty" fantasies.
Such thoughts are, to a point, as natural to man as breathing. What elementary school student, for instance, doesn't
learn, somewhere along the line, the song, "Great green
gobs of greasy grimy gopher guts/Covered with monkey
vomit"?

Such fantasies want exposure. For there is a part in all
of us which is fully capable of inventing things far more
morbid than rat snot, diarrhea machines, gopher guts, and
monkey vomit.

In nearly any "advanced" civilization, dark feelings are
methodically repressed, "civilized," and, whenever possible,
extirpated. But the point is you *can't* extirpate these feelings: and when you try to, you either cultivate a terrific
overload of guilt, or you encourage people to keep those
dark feelings inside themselves for so long that the feelings
finally begin to breed and mutate, turning ugly and sexually
vicious and homicidal: yes, people finally get around to
declaring war.

So I encourage the expression of these black visions:
not so that people will indulge them, but to get the trouble-
some thoughts out in the air and the light. That way we can
at least see them for what they are, and maybe find con-
structive ways to employ them.

BLIND CHILD

Blind child sitting there in a world of your own.
You do not speak, feel, or see.
Or do you?
Do you not speak because they do not listen?
Do you not feel because long ago they forced you not to?
And do you not see because hate, sin, and greed
have blinded you?
Blind child I know you and I'm reaching out to you
Blind child you are me.

14. never never met you, never never intended to

Sometimes my colleague Daniel beats out a rhythm on the guitar (you can do it with pencils, or just by clapping hands). *Any* old rhythm. Then he asks everyone to listen. What do you hear in that rhythm? What sound? *Any* sound.

Try to write it out.

Don't like that rhythm? Okay, here's another. Try this one, or this one, or this one. Or maybe you've got one of your own. *Any* rhythm. Doesn't matter *what* you write, no matter how plain or nonsensical: just so you get into a rhythm.

> *never never met you*
> *never never intended to,*
> *walking down the street*
> *one day around five o'clock*
> *I say, saw a man standing there*
> *he said to me how are you*
> *I said very well*

then he shot me. and I
fell to the ground. and said
never never met you
never never intended to.

JEFF BUERKE

✳

Mr. Sun come shine on your face
Oh Mr. Sun come on, come on
Mr. Sun come brighten our day
Oh Mr. Sun

CLAUDIA AHRENS

You said you're gonna get a motorcycle
and we're just gonna trip all over this
summer. Yeah, if it all works out, we're
gonna head to Texas some day. And just
stay in the country, for a day or two.
Hey, M.D., if it don't work out, you
know we can go back to walking.

MARGRETA LAND

Sometimes I commit suicide in my mind
and I try to imagine who would care
and I am amazed at how fortunate I am to be loved.

15. sex

Underground "ribald classics" have circulated in our public schools for generations. The juiciest of them have been passed from hand to hand, copied and recopied, generation after generation. Occasionally, even a teacher will say, "Why I saw that when *I* was in school." Here's one of the oldies:

MY FIRST EXPERIENCE

The sky was black
The moon was high
We were alone
Just her and I

Her hair was soft
Her eyes were blue
I knew just what
She wanted to do

I didn't know how
But I tried my best
I put my hand
Upon her breast

Her hair was soft
    Her figure was fine
I ran my fingers
    Down her spine

I trembled with fear
    My fast-beating heart
As she moved
    Her legs apart

At last I'm through
    It's all over now
My first experience
    Milking a cow

Here's another, sporting the same title.

I leaned back and let my lap straddle his knees. I put him off many times. I knew I must give in to him, but the growing fear pulled me back.

I knew there was little time left. He kept assuring me the after-effect would be wonderful. I felt his soft hands touch me. But I moved away with fear. A soft voice finally convinced me to let him touch my tender spot. Then he started to work, and gently told me he would try not to hurt me.

He moved slowly and gently. I relaxed at
his request; I opened wider and wider so he
could slide it in and out easier.

Then a chill ran down my back. I couldn't
control myself. I screamed DON'T—TAKE IT
OUT.

He said the faster it comes out the less it
will hurt. By that time I didn't have much
courage left. But I gathered up all I had,
and I could feel the fear and coolness go
through me as he twisted it out.

He turned to me and smiled. Then, in a stern
yet gentle voice, he said: "There, now that
tooth won't bother you any more."

Whenever someone tells me the poor dears simply
aren't mature enough to handle matters of such gravity, I
show them these things, and read them pieces of student
writing about sex. For junior high and high school students
are not only capable of handling the *subject* of sex; many
have had the *experience*. And if you give them half a
chance, they can write about it with a sense of intellectual
candor, and of positive acceptance, sufficient to put many
of their elders to shame.

God—I love
your touch
and when you
press my breast

my nipple grows
and I want to
move like the surf
in the fluid
motion of your hands—
I am clay, my artist
mold me
and I can move
with love
and a heartbeat
is the rhythm.

*

As my hands rub down your soft hot back
and my feet tangle with yours,
that's the first time I've ever done that,
it ain't evil but it ain't love.

*

"LATER!"

Let's go in the bedroom
No, let's stay here and watch TV
C'mon, this show is no good
Later.
Make love to me
I don't even know you
But I love you

How could you in this short time?
I can't explain it, I do
Later.
How do I tell my parents
Don't worry, I'll get the money for an abortion
No, I can't destroy something you and I
have created! Please hold me and tell me
you love me.
Not now, Later!

TONI KING

Nearly all student writing about sex comes in un-signed. The authors fear retribution: they, and most of their friends, have been taught to think of sex as some-thing nasty and shameful.

Poets in the Schools is not a sex education program: but when the subject arises naturally through student poems, I would like to conduct open discussions. I would think it extremely unlikely that any such discussion would develop perverts. And I know such talk would defuse some of the fear young people have of sex. For they've not only been taught guilt, many of them don't *understand* sex. Their ignorance occasionally gets them into serious trouble. I do not believe knowledge corrupts.

Nonetheless, because of the program's vulnerability to public pressure, I'm generally not overly explicit in dis-cussing sexual issues which arise in students' writing. An alternative is to read things of my own, and works by other students, which, though they are as semantically pure as the driven snow, nevertheless reflect candid and healthy

attitudes toward sexual contact. One of my favorites is by
Carlene Cummings:

> *The first time we tried*
> *I was too nervous and small*
> *And you were much too big*
> > *to fit inside*
> *So we laughed at ourselves*
> > > *and were innocent*
> > > *one day longer*

It's mirthful. It finds a way out of that adolescent hairshirt
or sexual self-consciousness. And it's such a *relief* to young
people to hear such a poem—to consider at least the possibility that sex is not the ultimate life-and-death, manhood-
or sissyhood risk they've been taught to fear.

LOVE RELIVES

See how the snow melts;
its glisten fades and
yields to golden rays;
its beauty cannot last.

Taste the sweetness of sugary ice cream;
Bite, lick, swallow . . .
its once creamy smoothness disappears;
its beauty cannot last.

Smell green musk in summer trees;
they shiver in wind, relish the rain;
but mother calls them to die . . .
their beauty cannot last.

Fiery jewels glide in the tarred night;
they march and display a divine show,
then dawn conquest;
their beauty cannot last.

Love graces two lives;
such a web has no spider woven;
naught can surpass the warmth, passion,
excitement it instills
yet such are easily cooled . . .
its beauty cannot last.

(continued)

See how winter falls each year.
Taste of ice cream rolls on the tongue
many times.
Fiery jewels dance after each war with day;
So shall love grace two lives again.

Why mourn?

16. i would give you

a cloud of colors

There are these people, see. The wee folk. Even when they're full grown, they're no taller than the pupil of your eye. And they're nomads. They travel in boats.

But not boats on water—*wind*-boats. They make 'em out of leaves.

You know how the sky gets colored just before dawn? That's because the wee folk are sowers and harvesters, too. They fly up there in the wind-boats, and plant seeds. Then they sing, in a music older than the stars.

All the sky blossoms.

They take seed from the blossoms, then plant them again just before sunset.

One morning I heard a tapping on my window. Thought it was just a stick or something. But I looked anyway.

And what do you know! A whole wind-boat full of the wee folk.

They asked me to hold out my hand, and they gave me a bushel of the seeds. The seeds are so tiny that a whole bushelful filled up only a little bit of one of the creases in my palm.

I started to ask the wee folk a lot of questions. But they said they had to be going (*born,* in their language): so away they flew.

I never got my questions answered.

Suppose *you* were one of these folk. Where do you go at night? What do you wear in the winter? What places have you been that no one else has? Do you have friends? Animal friends? People? What tricks do you play?

> *I wear a coat of flowers to keep me warm. I sleep in the weeds and use flowers as blankets.*
>
> ROCKEY KURZENBERGER

※

> *We have children, we teach them ourselves, no school. All the sick people take care of themselves. We all live for at least 80 years. Mice are our cars.*
>
> SANDRA BACHMEIER

※

> *I fly an inch a day.*
> *I eat pimples from people.*
> *I rode on a falling star to get here.*
> *I wrap peoples hair around my feet for shoes.*
> *And I ride grass for skis.*
>
> SCOTT LATUSECK

The grass will be my jungle. The flowers will be my trees. I sleep in kleenexes. Butterflies would be airplanes.

BEVERLY FISH

✳

I would wear an oak leaf hat and spider web shirt and apple skin pants.

KRIS KUYKENDALL

✳

My friend would be the person who made me up. I would go as far as the farthest star. I would sleep in a leaf bed. And if you are good to me I would give you a cloud of colors.

DEBBIE KAY BRANNUM

✳

I'd swim in a tear, live in a nose, and take rides on the toothbrush and visit the teeth.

MARY DREXLER

✳

I would sleep on a mattress of bees.

TINA DAL SANTO

Our clothes are paralyzed snow drops wove in with grass blades colored our favorite color by the color fairy.

DOROTHY J. DE CORDE

✳

I'd put a flower seed in my button hole and then it would grow to be a Bachelor's button.

NANCY BRUCE

✳

I would go in a woodpiker hole and hope that the woodpiker was not there. I would use a leaf and use a vine to hold the leaf on. My hold would not be very nice but it is better than nothing.

BRUCE JOHNSON

✳

My dog would be an ant. My house would be an upsidedown coke cap. I'd go skiing on an ice cube. I'd scuba dive in mud puddles. My rocket ship would be the one I made from popsicle sticks.

STEPHEN LEE

I would shave every day but probably cut myself in half. And I sell clouds for a living. I would eat ants for a chicken and for clothes would be the sunset.

BARBARA MAC DONALD

✷

The people have problems such as starvation, shelter, and they might be squished.

✷

I would go to the library and borrow books about Abraham Ant-Lincoln and draw Ant-Washington too.

RONALD LOWERY

✷

I would sleep under a tiny mushroom. But if it got cold I would sleep inside someone's beard.

CYNTHIA SIMMONS

✷

I would have some string for a pet snake. I would ride around the woods on a snake's back. I would eat moon flower seeds.

BILLO WILSON

*I would have big white doves for friends.
They would let me fly on their back. I would
eat tiny clover petals. I would have a shirt
of silk from silkworms.*

KRISTIE SHARP

✳

*If someone didn't like me I would take out a
needle and thread then I would sew them in
their house I would meet superman and
beat him up.*

DAVID ZOLLER

Try it. *Any* story like that. For instance, my friend
Bob Jaeger read a poem called "Little John Bottlejohn,"
by Laura E. Richards, to fifth and sixth graders. Here are
the first and last verses:

*Little John Bottlejohn lived on the hill,
    And a blithe little man was he.
And he won the heart of a pretty mermaid
    Who lived in the deep blue sea.
And every evening she used to sit
    And sing by the rocks of the sea,
"O, little John Bottlejohn, pretty John Bottlejohn,
    Won't you come out to me?" . . .
Little John Bottlejohn said, "Oh yes!
    I'll willingly go with you,*

And I never shall quail at the sight of your tail,
   For perhaps I may grow one too."
So he took her hand, and he left the land,
   And plunged in the foaming main.
And little John Bottlejohn, pretty John Bottlejohn,
   Never was seen again.

Well, what became of him? Where did he go? How did he live?

   Any story like that. Except tell only half of it. Let someone else finish it. That's the best way.

do you remember the day
we switched jeans
and laughed till our knees rubbed holes?
your hands moved old paper
to a kite
that tattered the breeze for us
cherry pop wine dribbled
and you loved me
in yellow chalk on the sidewalk.
I lay close to the dirt
in the grapeyard
till you shook
the china leaves and
saw my tennis shoe.
christ and then we were twelve.
the baby in us yelled and molded.
popsicles were petty and not
worth the mess
one two three
        and everyone was out.

CLARE ROSSINI

17. the tormented ones

There sits
in front of me
a crumpled tissue.

It seems
so very
dejected
and rejected.

Somebody
took advantage of it
and then
left it
to rot.

You know . . .

It looks a lot
like
me.

L. D.

And he is not the only one. They are the strange ones—the
"weirdos" whom their peers often jeer at, or simply,

efficiently, ignore. They are "in" school in body. But in their minds, they're forever pressed against a window, looking in—sometimes with great longing—from the outside.

And they suffer. Their skin hangs on them like a heavy curse. Their hangups wrap around them like a shroud. And to the questions which distress and haunt them, what few answers they find are so painful that they sometimes regret having been born.

They seldom excel in the scramble for grades. They are often obnoxious in class, turning off both their less articulate peers and those teachers who can't or won't understand them. Or they are excessively drawn in: "Don't notice me. Can't you see, I'm nobody, nothing, a zero. Just let me pass through unnoticed. Give me my C, and forget me."

There is often beauty—great beauty—inside them. The very curse they are under throws the beauty up closer to the surface. Creation often arises from conflict—in the tormented strangers who live among us, as in the world at large. And since the only weapon these young ones have is the imagination, they often employ it with a vengeance.

These tormented ones are among the most valuable resources we have. As someone who has been where they are, I believe they are worth saving not only because philanthropy makes us feel good, but because we *must* save them. Because, no matter how offensively or erratically they go about it, the tormented ones are struggling to keep the wise, innocent child intact within them. One secondary student I worked with wrote, "I've decided that when I grow up I'm going to be a kid." That is more than a reassuring credo: it is an imperative for our collective survival.

Keeping that ingenuous child-heart alive through all our adult growth is all the difference between being afraid to risk and having nothing to hide; between calculating our every move, and being playfully honest; between carrying our fears around on our backs and standing up straight with a smile.

They are the strangers, the misfits, the tormented, the lonely, and sometimes the desperate ones: the potato-faced plain Jane who doesn't get invited to parties; the smartass black whose disruptions and sulkiness can irritate the hell out of you if you let him, or can turn to creative gold if you encourage him; the retarded one with the speech problem, who knows that people can be mean and nice all at once; the C-minus student with the high IQ, who is interminably browbeaten because he's "not working up to his potential" and who is invariably tardy to or absent from all but the one class he cares about; the athletic superstar who'd like to be let out of his cage of praise.

The divine seed of creation is in each of them. They are the key to our own creative survival. And remembering the tormented ones, seeking them out, overcoming our own hangups enough to give them a chance to blossom: what more worthy, significant work can one be privileged to do?

I want to be a movie star
    I want to be a wife
I want to help the sick and poor
    I want to live on life

I'd love to travel oceans
    I'd love to see the moon
I'd love to learn an Indian call
    I'd love to see these soon

I grew up and married
    I never fulfilled my dreams
I locked them up for all my time
    To never be heard or seen

And now I'm old, and oh, so grey
    My dreams have not been fulfilled
I think of them and cry sometimes
    For I know it was them I killed

You who are young and strong and brave
    Don't lock your dreams in your heart
For they won't be used, the doors will close
    Open them, before you depart

BONNIE BAYES

18. fighting

for permission to piss

Write about the school. But don't just spout off your opinions: be original. Make a *likeness*, or use a mess of neat,
sound-alike words. For instance, "I hate school because it's
a drag" doesn't say much of anything new. But, "This school
is like a person trying to crawl into a hollow icecube" (Bob
Celski), now that's got class.

> *My school has snakes, snails*
> *and snoopy snotty snickery snoopers*
> *and dotty potty cotty fotty rotty reachers*
> *smeachers creatures and big fat teachers*
>
> DEBORAH SMITH

※

> *My school is like administrators instigators*
> *agitators emancipators eradicators and alligators*
> *fighting for permission to piss*
>
> PENN DILWORTH

Or if you live in a city, try to write about your block.
What is the craziest thing on your block? The saddest?
Meanest? Happiest? Show the most important thing you
know about your block, just like it is.

On my block there are
bars and two liquor stores

On my block there are
drunks and bums,
But that doesn't bother
me at all, because I've lived
there for six years.

On my block there are kids,
mean kids and nice kids
fat kids, and even baby kids.

On my block, there are dogs,
Old dogs, new dogs, crabbly dogs.
Just like you and me.

DARCEE SHURSON

FLIGHT

The wind it whistles past me
And the ground below looked like
        thumbtacks and marbles
Little rats scurry along,
While the sky lays at my face,
And I throw the scary eyeballs
At the Devil,
Who looks at me
From a cliff, and sucks his pitchforks,
And bites his tail,
And envies at my flight.

MARK DOUGLAS

I met him, it was a strange feeling that had
come over me he was himself that was the
first day of life the first time of the sun not
of the darkness, the first time of first times
the day of love, of song and joy, the day he
came into my life the day he was there and
then and the time was the only time, the
right time, filled with happiness that filled
my dreams. A time of love, only love.

LUCY TUTTLE

19. you feel so closed in

"Loser" Junior High is in a neighborhood where you can generally find two buildings—a Slavic orthodox cathedral and a bar—every fifth block. Most of the parents are blue-collar folk; many speak Lithuanian, Polish or Russian at home. Hence, most children have little English when they start school, and their native languages, of course, are not spoken by the teachers.

A high percentage of the young will never leave the city—or even the neighborhood where they grew up. The general attitude of the students is that you stay in school only until you're old enough to get a job in a gas station or a factory.

The school building has many broken windows. Two years ago, a burglar alarm system was installed. Evidently, the one creative talent the students respect—indeed their one sophisticated art form—is theft.

Classrooms are depressingly silent. After ten minutes in the first session, it was obvious to Dan McCrimmon and me that the children's spirits had not been subdued, but squashed. In ghetto schools, at least you find a little rage; at "Loser," you find resignation.

About eighty students came to our voluntary "library"

session the first day. (But the class wasn't actually held in the library: the librarian insisted that not a single chair be moved from its position at any single table. So we all went outside on the lawn. Next morning, the principal forbade that as well.) The second day, in the boys' gym, the same session drew about 170. When the bell rang, I was in the middle of a poem; about two-thirds of them stayed to hear me through.

A handful of students turned out some extremely high-powered writing. But, for most of the people, the sheer thought of creative writing—much less the act of sharing it; less still, that anyone would consider their work valuable —was threatening, if not embarrassing. In comparison to other junior highs, "Loser" presented a student body whose general estimate of their personal worth was lower than any I've ever encountered.

For instance, in the first session, I saw two students throw their writing in the waste basket. After the class, I dredged the writing out of the can—and found not just two, but *eight* papers.

Dan and I asked a few questions of the young teacher who had invited the *Poets in the Schools* program to Loser. We learned that the students had been taught that the yardstick of "good writing" is proper mechanics. If they turned a paper in without a heading; if they misspelled a single word; if their grammar was not flawless; if they smeared the ink with the side of their hand while writing— then they were disqualified out of hand.

This same young teacher coaxed one of his classes into writing personal letters to us. Here's what they had to say:

I don't feel like writing . . . theirs bad lighting . . . it hits me once in a while when I feel like doing something else. No I just don't feel like writing.

※

When we were outside yesterday, I thought you guys were really great! Everything was so neat sitting in the grass with the sun shining . . . I'm not writing this just to be nice either. . . . When you are in a classroom, you feel so closed in.

※

I used to write poems in third grade but my mom said I was crazy.

※

I don't hate writing but I just got a lot of things I have to think of so I am never in the mood to do anything!

※

I don't feel like writing I'm tired, I wanta get outside and walk home to get out of these hot clothes.

. . . in the school I went last year every time
I wrote something and really told how I felt
about it . . . I always would get a bad grade
because I didn't spell a word right or I didn't
put it in a right paragraph. But I always
hated it because you had to write on some-
thing they told you to write on.

As with all the other classes, Dan and I dittoed the
writing from the class in which eight papers had been dis-
carded. And we *included* the discards on the ditto collection. We read the work back to the students aloud. They
seemed pleased.

So I carried it all a step further. To their obvious
amusement, I took up chalk, and wrote some tongue-in-
cheek "rules" on the board:

1. Be cra-a-a-zie
2. Don't kare if speld rong
3. Frags OK
4. No heading

I then said, "Yes, well sure there's a kind of writing
where you have to get everything proper. Is that why some
of you threw away your papers—because you were afraid
you'd made mistakes?" Many nodded yes. So I said it didn't
matter. The writing they'd done yesterday was just fine as
it was, and I didn't want them to worry over mechanics. I
read some free-form writing from other schools to illustrate
the point.

Then I passed out unlined paper; asked them *not* to put on headings; and suggested that they all try to start somewhere near the middle of the page, and write outward, in spirals or crazy curves.

"What should we write about?"

Well, how about anything that spreads—maybe like a spiral (e.g., a tornado, or a top)—or just plain spreads. So what spreads?

"Ketchup. Ice cream. Germs. Mud. Blood."

Okay. Try it.

They had *fun*. All but one or two people wrote, and they wrote an average of three times more then they had the day before. Most students wanted to read aloud their work themselves: others wanted us to read for them. Most of them signed their names, and no one threw away his effort. Their spelling improved by at least 200 per cent.

Dan and I first used this "spread" exercise at "Loser." But as we tried it at a few more schools, the exercise began to produce a modified form of what is called "concrete" poetry. Eventually, students would not just write about things that spread, but about *anything*—they'd just form the words into a picture of what they were writing about:

The rolling hills are like two people frolliking in the park.

SUSAN MILLER

Anyway, at "Loser" Junior High the tide turned on Tuesday, and for the rest of the week the students barraged us with writing. I let up on almost all tendencies to either edit or criticize. I had typed and dittoed almost everything every student wrote in every session. We went through ten reams of paper in a week. The office staff complained; the students were delighted.

By Friday, our voluntary sessions were running attendances of over 300. Amazingly, that many students, packed into a cavernous gymnasium, were quiet enough to listen to their friends read their own efforts at creative expression.

Daniel had taught them all a Shaker hymn:

> 'Tis the gift to be simple, 'tis the gift to be free
> 'Tis the gift to climb down where we ought to be
> And when we find ourselves in our place just right
> We're in the valley of love and delight

And how they did sing! They sang till the air broke, sang so that the third floor heard.

'Tis a gift to be gifted to give: if the gift we bring were the clinging kind, which depends on us alone, I could not bring myself to set foot in another school.

But all we really have to give the students is themselves. And as Daniel remarked after we left "Loser" Junior High, "The whole sense of what we're doing simply destroys the concept of *performance*. It's all so much more real."

MY DAY BY DAY OF LOVE

Though we see each other day by day
But it seems to me that every day is a calmly day
The shame that hides my face from seeing you
is the things that makes me far away from you

I could not think anyone else as pretty as
        you are cause you're so bright as
        the morning star
I could not take away my eyes from seeing you
cause it's the only thing that makes me
        close to you

I hope that this poem is a part of my body
        to you cause it's the only way I
        can tell
I really love you
I know that your love can make me happy
and I do my very best to make you happy.

FELIX DAHILIG

If I was like a sunrise
I would have many colors of love.
They would change every day
but never lose their beauty.
Not for one second
would I cease to amaze.
I would open each new day
shining out upon the people
of every land of every color
I would bring light into their eyes
and warmth into their hearts.
And I would let them know
that as long as there is a sunrise
there is hope for another day.

SHERRI CAMPBELL

20. debbie

At age fourteen, Debbie is still in fifth grade. She has either
a mental disorder or a nervous disorder, which makes both
her speech and her script very slurred. By *Teen* magazine
standards, she's not very pretty. And a number of her classmates make fun of her on the playground: they've been
lectured to be more considerate, to no effect.

But by the third day of working with Debbie's class,
a general atmosphere of self-esteem and mutual respect
had begun to sink in; and it involved Debbie directly.

She had written, along with everyone else, a "picture"
poem on a ditto sheet *(see opposite page):*

Debbie's teacher wrote me a word-for-word transla-
tion, so that on the following day, when it came Debbie's
turn to read aloud, I'd be prepared to help. But when we
reached her piece in the packet, I never got my mouth
open. The *students* helped her. They were all bent over her
work (each had a complete set), squinting at the words,
helping her get through it. Debbie's poem read:

> *I love to be a bell, rang on Sunday and Wed-*
> *day after Wedday and Sunday and this way*
> *and any way and Sunday and Wedays, ring*
> *on Sundays and Wedday.*

DEbbie

I LovetobeaBell
raNg OIVS UNDayandwedda
ychapterwedayaNdSuNday
atthesWayaNdaywayaNd
SuNday and wEDayrINgON
SUNDaya aNd WEDDay

Whatever her handicaps, Debbie has a gift for poetic
rhythm. I read the piece again, aloud: we'd already talked
about how rhythmic repetitions can strengthen writing,
and her classmates had no need to fake respect for her work.

Later in the hour, I looked up to find Debbie watching
me. Eye contact. A smile. And after class, just for a minute,
I put my arm around her.

The next day, she brought this to me:

> *Rain Drops Fall on My Head*
> *and fall on my head because I keep explain-*
> *ing. Keep on explaining. Rain drops on my*
> *head because I keep explaining. Crying be-*
> *cause it is good for you, Crying.*

How many are there?

Debbie was easy to spot as one who needed extra care because her deficiencies were so obvious. But there's at least one "special case" in every classroom, and I know I've failed with all but a very few of them. Most of them I didn't even notice.

And it's not just the Debbies, or the students in the "special education" classes. The children who need more attention are the "average" ones, the "ho-hum" ones, the troublemakers who aren't quite annoying enough to kick out.

Every one of them has a gift. No exceptions. A *rare* gift. And each one of them can blossom just as beautifully as straight-A Susie who's your pride and joy.

No exceptions. But finding that gift—finding the patience in yourself to *want* to find it, and then finding the trigger which will release it—that's where the work is.

I always wanted to call
    myself on the phone,
so I did
    but the line was busy

MAD LISA

Wow! Are you from Mars?
No, three stars up the road.

SCOTT MEREDITH

The sharp whirling blades of the "iron bird"
appeared to be moving in all directions—
clockwise, counter-clockwise, up, down, in,
out. They were moving so fast it looked
slow—like the wagon wheels on cowboy
movies. I walked right through these pro-
pellers and it didn't even hurt.

21. a kissing king

Take one of your initials, or one of your best friends' initials. Build on it. Say something that makes sense, or say pure nonsense; something pretty or ugly, true or false, dead or alive. Just build on the sound:

Hi ho had hiked hills and hid in a hunk of hippos.
MIKE HASKINS

✳

A kissing king kisses a killer kangaroo.
MICHAEL KOFSKEY

✳

Rafael Rock Robles Raps Rope Round Rakes.
ESTHER ROBLES LOPEZ

✳

Gloomy goats eat glass.
PAUL GIEROW

Our house is not spotless
but it serves the purpose
We could not have children
but had enough company
between ourselves,
our dogs and cats and even Al
our rat.
There were holes in the walls
and the ceiling too.
There wasn't a washing machine
so I washed in the sink
no modern conveniences
except a stove that didn't work
and a hot water heater that only
worked when it wanted.
But it was our house.

He worked at a car wash
at $1.65 an hour
I went to Catholic Welfare
once a week
and got $7.50
We were vegetarians
and vegetables are cheap
It was the dog food that was
expensive
He worked from 7:00 in the morning
to 7:00 at night
I cleaned house and waited

(continued)

Cooking our brown rice stew
I'd be so impatient
Then the dogs would bark
I'd beat him to the door
"GOD, honey I missed you,"
A peaceful dinner No candle light
No talking
Didn't need any
Our souls were attuned
We go to the front room
sit in our Early American
Salvation Army recliners
and listen to music.
No matter how bad off we were
we always had music
unless our electricity was turned off.
Very early to bed
It's a short night.
Naked
Lying hip to hip
Content
Dreaming thoughts of each other
And what we would do
When the alarm rang
At 5:30
Stretch
Open our eyes
Look at each other
Roll into each other
All at the same time

(continued)

To come together
To love
To start another morning
With each other

                DEBBY BRAULT

a smashed bird
lying on rocks
mangled body
crushed beak
feathers torn
wretched in pain:
looks like a tear stained image
of him
last night
silently suffering
alone
on the floor
immobile.
white pain
shining around his eyes.
bare vulnerable body—
solid structure
of anguish

                LOUISE LAUER

22. pigbird:

goes oink tweet

At third-grade level and below, children have trouble with the simple, manual labor of writing things down. It's so difficult to form all those strange shapes.

But their minds are pure lightning. So, while a student is cooking up 300 words of astonishing original myth, all he'll produce on paper is, "I dreamed about my dog."

Well, then why not bring in some help?

I brought high schoolers, enough so that there was one big person for each little person. To their obvious amusement, I told the little people that the big people were there just to be their secretary-slaves. That erased any traces of fear of the giant-size strangers.

Then we all sang a song together, and got down to work. I tossed out ideas everyone could get started writing about. The suggestions were hardly out of my mouth before *everyone in the room* was happily working. No one had much trouble getting started, because everyone had a helper. And there was no "discipline" problem, even with first and second graders.

These collaboration sessions are, far and away, the most joyous and productive I've ever taken part in. It's the dream of the Perpetual Motion Lovesong Creative Writing Machine come true. And the older students serve splendidly. They know by instinct that they aren't there to put words in mouths, but simply to ask, encourage, and record.

I always try to get the high schoolers back the next day, for the communal reading of the previous day's work. Often, one of the little people asks his big helper to read for him. And it is a significant learning experience for all the little people to see, in print, words they often use out loud but have not yet learned to read.

In another school, I even employed fifth- and sixth-grade secretaries in second-grade classrooms. I figured that about fifteen minutes would be the most I could dare; the session went on for nearly an hour without waning. Again, this may have had something to do with my offering the fifth- and sixth-graders an Adult contract. Before we went into the classroom, I told the ten- and eleven-year-olds, "Look, I can toss out an idea or two. But the real success of this depends on you. I want you to be to these second-graders the same thing I've been to you. It's your show."

Of the many exercises I've used in these sessions, one of the most joyful and productive is the invitation to make themselves into some kind of fantastic animal, constructed from the parts of many animals, and to invent names for their animal selves. Here are some third-grade responses, recorded by twelfth-grade servants:

ALLIGALION

This ugly alligalion has an alligator's head.
His big feet have warts all over. He has no toes.
He is fat and long and has a red tail, blue head,
*   yellow legs, and orange body.*
His teeth are like fangs all coated with blood.
He lives in a lonely cave with bats and fires.
He eats people by gobbling them up.
His hair is all full of bugs and mice, which
*   crawl in his ears, and climb in his eyes.*

RHONDA CHRISTENSEN

✳

Pigbird—the bottom like a pig, front is like
a bird. Goes oink tweet. Fly into the air
around a star, to land on a star, eat like a
pig, fat on bottom, skinny on top, bird beak.
I'd be pink and blue like an ostrich, a curled
tail. I'd live in a nest, eat and lay eggs all
day. Keep eggs warm, teach baby pigbirds
to fly. Eat hay, corn, steak, french fries,
mashed potatoes—drink milk, water, take
medicine. Really fly good—everyone thinks
I'm weird looking but pretty.

BRIAN CONGER

A GOBBLE GOOBLE

I'm a pig with feathers . . . I wear black, purple, hot pink, and baby blue tennis shoes. I have pink yarn hair. I love to eat material and grass and red beads and hands on wash machines and rings. I'm getting married and the lady's name is Howdy Doody Gooble. I don't have any eyes or nose and I sneeze through my toes.

LESLEE WOOD

O Lord, stretch my soul until
the agony fulfills me, and pain
contains my very existence
making all love and happiness
yearn to die.
Squeeze my brain until all
I know oozes out.
And rip my heart until
the pain is equal to that
of being in love.
And then & only then, my lord,
will I shed my pride and
beg you to love me.
And I will tear myself
apart in a mad attempt
to love you.

SUSAN SHIPPEE

23. a pound of
purple petunias

Sometimes when a class is particularly sullen—or even when it's *not* sullen, but I just want the students to start out by having fun—I'll pass out dittoed copies of a list like this:

red	snarl	wind
quick	coo	swan
still	sing	velvet
broken	weep	pickle
bright	tease	puppy
silent	race	lion
blue	smile	dishes
gold	stink	giraffe
clean	lie	wart
rotten	fly	leaf
high	sail	ring
green	bump	rubber
sticky	surprise	ocean
delicate	lick	ribbon
icy	chuck	steel

sleek	shoot	birth
silver	pound	hippopotamus
purple	dream	bullet
white	shout	peanut butter
brittle	sparkle	ghost
wee	chime	monkey
loony	chase	blood
rusty	scratch	wheel
cross	crackle	angel
humongous	mutter	junk
jagged	dance	wizard
cool	flapdoodle	clown
flaming	open	moose
stringy	grow	petunia
juicy	waddle	cake
deep	mooch	pussy

To make the list, I picked mostly short words with neat sounds, and left out most abstract words.

"Take as many words as you want from the sheet," I tell the class, "but get at least one from each column. Scramble them into an image. You can change nouns into verbs, add endings, or fill in with prepositions or articles. But no *other* words, *unless* you make them up. Just do this one thing: *put words together in a way no other human being ever has in the whole history of the language.*"

This is a specially good exercise to use with people who solemnly promise you they've never had a creative thought in their entire lives. Give them all the makings of poetic instant coffee, then see how pleased they are with their own results:

open wind sparkle
icy shout of the ghost
a pound of purple petunias
red loves velvet
the silver pickle spills its juicy ocean
jagged cake looks like a velvet cliff to a crumb
white wind eats the moss away
the juicy blood dances with the purple ribbon
delicately chiming birth

Other variants of this exercise include word-poker: print a word on each card of a deck, then deal each person a hand and confine him to those cards. Or cut pictures out of magazines and put them into two or three different boxes —a box for "pretty" pictures, a box for "ugly," a box for "informative"—or any other categories you feel like setting up. Then have each person draw one picture from each box, and ask him to make one image, or one poem, including all three of the pictures he drew.

It's unpredictable as hell. Just like life.

Joyce Petty, who teaches third-graders in Las Vegas, encourages her students to make up fantastic poems or stories from their spelling words. In this way, she converts an ordinarily boring exercise into lively, creative play.

I tore the tag off my mattress
They're coming to get me
I'm a wanted man
Listen
The sirens
          "Come out with your hands up"
Look what society has done to me
          "We have you surrounded"
I hate you society
          "Give up peacefully"
Up yours
          "Come out"
I'm tearing the tag off my mattress!!
          "Don't do it
          Stop or we'll shoot"
No!
          "All right, Fire!!"
They got me
I'm dying
All I did was tear the tag off my mattress

ALLEN LEVY

yes mama, we walked alone
        one night
no mama, it wasn't all
        his idea
yes mama, we stopped &
        made love
no mama, it wasn't all
        his idea
yes mama, we got rid of
        the baby
no mama, it wasn't all
        his idea
yes mama, he's
        gone now
no mama, that was
        my idea.

CHYRISA BACE

24. lovelock, nevada

The whorehouses are still open, though I'd guess not as many as in the boom days. Those institutions gave a name to Lovelock, and to the town just up the road, Wadsworth (where you get your wad's worth).

First thing I did in Lovelock was drive around. A lot of small frame houses and unpaved streets. A single mini-casino. The one movie house, open on Wednesday and every other Sunday, shows year-old winners. No losers.

It had been a fine drive through desert valley—up I-80 from Reno. And I'd slipped into that high lonesome groove the road sometimes gives you—not a down blues, but a rolling, unwinding, freedom blues.

Late spring thunder shifted huge and freely in the sky. Why is the sky bigger some places than others? In Nevada, a whole storm takes up just a corner or two. I'd driven in and out of rain all the way, and stopped the car occasionally just to smell.

The moisture brings perfume out of the sage. You can climb one of the low rock ridges—those buff-green hills both smooth and creased like dinosaur hide—breathing that thick, seductive sweetness deeper and deeper into your body. It's like being near the navel of Mother Earth.

The first room I walked into, in Lovelock's elementary school (*all* the schools are on one block, and that's all the schooling for a radius of fifty miles), was an outright gift from the gods. I rubbed my eyes. By my body clock, it was still nine *a.m.* in the middle of the night; I'd not had but one cup of coffee yet, and I could have been hallucinating.

There was no oaken desk. No skinflint weasel brandishing a hickory stick, and croaking, "A is for Apple, B is for Bird."

Friends, I mean to tell you there was MUSIC in that room. The rock group Blood, Sweat & Tears on a phonograph, and a lot of other records which *the students* can just play whenever they want. And desks strung out in crazy clusters. And colors, colors, crayon flowers and trees and birds, and the words "spring" and "love," most of them down at student eye level, all over the walls, even covering large areas of chalkboard.

And there, hunkered down eye-to-eye with a fourth-grader, was this sandy-haired, honest-faced, smiling young dude in far-out (and I do mean far-out) clothes.

That's Mr. Waller. But the students call him Bill, or sometimes Captain Willy. He's not a hallucination, either.

One of Bill's former students had transferred in from California. All his "permanent records" labeled him a "reading problem." Bill wouldn't believe that until he tried for himself. Inside two months, the boy was reading above his grade level.

And the "problem child" started writing poems. Bill showed me some of them, cold, before he told me the author was only nine years old. The poems showed the un-self-conscious, creative exuberance of a very gifted spirit blossoming early.

Then the boy moved up to fifth grade. Bill asked him how he was doing.

"Well, I wrote a couple more poems; but the teacher and the others made fun of me. So I don't think I'll write any more poems."

Lucky I went to Bill's classes first. Initial exposure to the junior high or the high school might have shut me down before I had a chance to get started.

The high school teacher I worked with is a sensitive, introspective man who's been teaching in the Lovelock school for eight years. At the beginning of his seventh year, he finally got up the nerve not to shave off his yearly vacation mustache. The resultant hassle cost him God knows how many confrontations with the Super and the Board; but he's still got the mustache. He'd have had less trouble with it in the United States Army.

The first day in this teacher's classes, I ran right up against the same wall. Lovelock High is where most urban high schools were ten to fifteen years ago. Booze is still the biggest thrill, followed by football glamour and closed cliques of cowboys. When I compare the political narcosis of Lovelock High to the inflamed political activism of, say, the Chicanos at West High in Denver . . . well, really, I find both in some ways unproductive. But better knowledge than nothing, and at West High at least the students care enough about what's been done to them to get angry. But at Lovelock High, only two or three in the school (total population 190) even write about such issues as "pollution," and mostly in sentimental moralisms. Nothing about racism, nothing about ethnic postures, nothing about governmental spending choices.

Throughout Lovelock High, boys and girls sit on opposite sides of the rooms. By choice. And on the first day, the side row of boys sat with their fists propped into the cheeks of their turned away faces, and ignored me.

My choice was either to retreat into my *own* provincialism, or try to come out further. I was working alone, but I had Dan McCrimmon's LP along. Some of it's genuine, solid, country music, so I brought it to class. They liked the songs I played. Then I read a Denver student's poem, written from the point of view of a Vietnam soldier who feels that the young folks back home have it too soft. Then we all went out on the lawn, and composed a class poem about football.

That day, I made a public-relations touchdown. But on each following day, it was like starting all over again at the bottom of the pit. I'd come along at least five years too late.

I finally got one class of eleventh-graders to open up and talk. I kept asking questions until I had their story straight. Here's what they said:

"From first grade and before, we were told to shut up. Almost nothing we did was right. When we were younger and we talked a lot in class, it wasn't right for ten- and eleven-year-old kids to be talkative. They sent us to the office. They said we were bad. And in this school, sure, they say they want to know how you feel, but they never listen when you tell them, and it doesn't do any good anyway.

Teachers, administrators—they don't care. So why speak up, when you know it won't mean anything and all you do is get in trouble for it? And if they don't listen to us, why should we listen to them? Fuck 'em. Fuck school."

I won't defend that attitude. It's as selfish and futile as that of the administrators. But the losers are the children. The percentage of students at Lovelock High whose desire to learn has been permanently obliterated is as high as in any urban ghetto. If these young people had even one teacher a year, or every other year, like Bill Waller, at least some of them would still have a chance.

But here again, the school is not at the root of the problem. Across America, schools are pretty much as their communities desire them.

I love the sheer physical beauty of Lovelock, Nevada. I-80 is still Main Street. Lovelock is handmade houses; home-baked pie and good coffee in the cafes; a lot of people with strong smiles and honest dirt on their boots; a seductive eternity of sky; clear air; green, blooming beauty everywhere you turn.

There's something to the rural distrust of big cities: the thought of 10,000 people or more packed into a square mile evokes sheer defensive horror among country people. I got a taste of that feeling on the Friday afternoon of my first week in Lovelock, when I drove out of town for the weekend.

I just had time to get over Donner Pass, into San Francisco, down to Civic Center, and into the symphony hall, before the first notes of the Sibelius Symphony #2. My mind didn't catch up with me till about halfway through the first movement. Sproi-yoi-yoi-yoi-yoing.

I started seeing things. The backdrop behind the orchestra shifted from the Pacific Ocean at night, to the Nevada plains, to the set granite face of the Lovelock High principal, to a steaming apple pie, to a Marlboro commercial, to the beautiful smile of Bill Waller.

At intermission, I went downstairs to the cocktail lounge: people in evening dress, with cigarettes and drinks in their hands, speaking easily a language which, to people in Lovelock, might as well be Japanese. For example, Sandburg, Frost, and Longfellow are among the only traditional poets who even mildly interest regular classes at Lovelock High; I recalled the general attitude of most "symphony people" toward these particular writers.

Lovelock tumbleweed and *champagne entr'acte*—like two, free-floating islands, passing, miles distant, on the Pacific Ocean at night, and communicating only by wireless, if at all. My mind was ripping in half.

I tried to call up that fine, weird streak of Zen wit— the god—the sheer insane glee of so diverse a creation. After all, son, it's all an illusion, see? All done with mirrors.

I had trouble remembering that. For how many lost Americans are out there bobbing about, both little and large, everyone crazed with amnesia, pretending there's been no disaster; everyone safe in his little rubber lifeboat.

Lost Lovelock, looking with queasy suspicion at its own cowboys herding cattle on Hondas; at the strangers who stay in town just long enough to bleed all over a couple of fifty-cent slot machines; at freaks passing through on big

Harleys; at the astonishing remarks somebody else's daughter made in a classroom. The whorehouses still stand, welcoming truckers, railroaders, traveling salesmen: well, after all, they're only in town for a night, and they take their filth with them when they go. All they leave behind is their money.

It's hard not to think of it that way. And in Lovelock, they *are* thinking of it that way: strange people may pass through, but the town remains unchanged. "Not here."

The editor of the town paper, he must have had a lot of drive once; spent a lot of time in places like Philadelphia, and left a string of his guts plastered against the world's brick walls. "No, I'm not gonna change nothing. I'm what you call a casualty of *the war*." He knows the war's on the way to Lovelock, Nevada, and he's going to watch Lovelock lose with a mixture of genuine compassion and malicious glee.

Though the population is dwindling, Lovelock may not die. Maybe it'll end up as another gas stop between Cheyenne and San Francisco, with one of those hand-painted "Population 82" signs. Or perhaps the town will dry up altogether—and leave, in a string of rotting ruins, the ghosts of a prostituted dream.

Like one of its own one-armed bandits, Lovelock, Nevada, is rigging its own game: to lose. Football is not adequate preparation for "the game of life."

THE WOLF

I heard the wolf
He gave his call
from seven to three o'clock that night,
over and over again
The wolf is out there
in the darkness of the empty woods,
Nowhere to go,
The empty woods is like an empty home.

BERNADETTE JONES

Well wall, today I'm going to tell you all
the things I hate. I mean you hate things too
I'm sure. Like my posters all over you.
Pictures smiling at each other across wall to wall.
Well, sometimes people just don't turn me on.
Like me and you. (We're not people but we have feelings.)
I know you don't like when I get mad and pound
my fists on you. Because I know you can't fight back.
But I guess if you don't like my ways sometimes
I don't like yours sometimes. We're even.
Well, nice rapping. Keep the cold out.
Good night.

DORIS SANTIAGO

The staple came out of my pages of life . . .
at last.

MAD LISA

Hi Sue, wanta ball?
No, not today, I have a headache.
But we have to practice for the tournament.

SCOTT MEREDITH

remember when i ran across your stomach,
running i broke my ankle in your navel.

RICHARD RUSCH

25. bugs

I wrote a poem called "Women" (and another called "Men")
in this style:

>Women in leather and silk
>with honey and milk
>
>Women with roses
>and porcelain noses
>
>hanky women
>hanky-panky women
>
>Fire and lyre women
>
>Boy women
>Troy women
>
>Station wagon Joan of Arcs
>Chorus line Evangelines
>
>Wicker women with cats and bamboo canes
>gummy smiles
>mocking the frisky whores next door
>
>show-it-all-in-public untouchables

Goes on like that for pages—like a catalogue. While reading part of it to a class, I got the idea of "catalogue" poems. Pick a subject, any subject, and exhaust it. For instance, lines, or circles, or parents, or walls, or cars, or. . . .

One student tried "bugs." Brought me a list of about twenty. She looked to be the type who could stand a little goading, so I said, "Aw, c'mon: you've hardly *started*." Thirty minutes later, she delivered.

BUGS

I like bugs
big bugs
little bugs
fat bugs
skinny bugs
long bugs
short bugs
bugs with spots
  stripes
  colors
  lights
bugs with wings
  feelers
  teeth
  rings
I like bugs
sad bugs
happy bugs
joyful bugs

sorrowful bugs
oozy bugs
black bugs
creepy bugs
red bugs
blue bugs
green bugs
red, white and blue bugs
bugs that love
   hate
   sing
   cry
bugs that crawl
   rip
   bite
   lick
I like bugs
spooky bugs
scary bugs
weird bugs
dopey bugs
Lady bugs
Men bugs
Beatle bugs
grouse bugs
flying bugs
swimming bugs
ground bugs
air bugs
water bugs

I like bugs
bugs that jump
bugs that leap
bugs that screech
bugs that peep
bugs that talk
I like Bugs

I cried on your shoulder
You held my heart;
As the darkness was gone
And the path ahead
Held warmth and sunshine,
You took my lips
And curved them upward
Into a thankful smile.

If I had to choose
between loving you hard or loving you soft,
your response would be my only answer
rage or melting ice,
diffusing like a light bulb,
showing itself off before dying.

DANA HALL

It's strange to feel love
for somebody only because of
their twisting and curving features,
only to find you hate them because
you love somebody with an interesting
and appealing mind.

O how strange and frustrating
it is, to love the appealing
mind, or the appealing body

Why does he hold me and love me when the sun has
    gone to bed
yet when we awake with the sun I am
thrown aside like the sheets and bedspread.

26. classroom ecology

The buildings which make up the typical "modern" elementary school are often one-story, cinder-block rectangles slung together like chicken coops. By the door into each room there is one window, about eighteen inches wide and four feet high. And that's all. They must be preparing for an invasion.

Packed into these rectangular cartons, you quickly lose your sense of the colors and natural curves and normal music of the real world. What you get instead is that green, snarling, fluorescent poison which breaks into your eyeballs like splinters of glass.

Nietzsche contended that 90 per cent of metaphysics is physiology. Much of who we are and how we feel depends on our simple, sensory relation to such fundamental elements as light. Over a million years and more, man's eyes developed in direct relation to natural, point-source light: sunlight and firelight. When you suddenly project into that relationship an artificial glare which, among other things, destroys natural shadows, then you foul that relationship. You're tampering with the visual habit of thousands of generations. And when you introduce that "light" into a *learning* environment, not all the ingenious teaching techniques and learning machines on earth will restore a natural relation: because you have cut the tree at its root.

A good many of the "problems" in our schools derive from simple, environmental mistakes.

In a particular high school I visited, the weather was warm, so the windows were open. There's a lot of lawn, and someone was mowing it. Mowing LOUDLY.

This went on all week. In fact, it goes on all week, two weeks a month, through nearly half the school year, at every school in that city.

With eighty students before me, and the day as muggy as it was, I finally had had enough of it. I stopped in mid-sentence, and announced to the class, "Will someone please go out there, RIGHT NOW, and get that thing STOPPED?" I don't think anyone in the room had realized just how loud the mower really was until, about forty-five seconds later, it did indeed stop.

After class, I got to talking about the mower with a young male teacher. It wasn't obvious from his demeanor, but I believe he was just slightly resentful: between the lines, he seemed to be saying, "You can get away with this because you're a special guest."

What he *did* say was, "Well, we're *used* to it. It's one of the things teachers have to put up with."

I responded openly but firmly: "*Why* do you have to put up with it? *Who* made the policy? You've even got a *union* here. And school's in session less than half the daylight hours. So what comes first—education, or landscaping?"

I hope I didn't shut him off. Because it's important. *Real* important. Lighting, space, scheduling, and noise level have every bit as much to do with whether people can learn as anything else does.

In another school, instead of being trucked around from room to room, Dan and I were given a room of our own. Classes came to us. The room had a door we could close, and four huge windows, and comfortable furniture, and no desks.

We established a zone. We had a couple of shelves of poetry books brought in. And when we weren't conducting classes, and when Daniel wasn't playing, I had a tape going, which includes a lot of pleasing, low-key music, classical, folk and jazz.

Students often sat with us for hours—listening, reading, quietly talking, writing. The room became more than a room—a little island of creative, musical peace.

> And the ranger rode up and down the mountain ridge
> five days a week, twice a night. Silver took him
> anywhere—desert, river, mountains
> And the people asked as he left
> Who was that masked man in love with his horse?

27. me, the king
of the human race

Imagine the exact moment of your birth or death. What was (is, will be) going on? Tell about specific things—scenes burned into the deepest parts of your being. Let us come with you. Take us there. Help us to live in that moment.

Or make up the ultimate fish story. Maybe, for instance, you were born of a tree, or a swan, or the ocean, or rain, or a star. What was it like?

> *Somebody jumped off a bench which he hit a pole and the pole hit a tree. The tree was rammed into the ground so far that it hit the devil's head. Then he screamed so loud it made an angel fall on an ostrich then she laid an egg. Then it was hatched and that's how you were born.*
>
> BERT BROWN

One night I got very sick and was about to die. Then it happened. I did it, I died. I could feel my blood. I could feel my nose needed a Kleenex but I was in the coffin and didn't have a Kleenex. When I finally could feel my dog licking me I knew I was dead. It was cool in the coffin but no heater. But all of a sudden I couldn't feel I couldn't hear, I, I, I—Good Bye—it's the end for me. But look for my Spirit. You'll know it's mine because it will have a Kleenex.

SIGNE FEATHERSTON

✳

When I was born on a glish-glosh day the sun was green and the moon was gray. The hour was brown and the day was pink, the grass was blue and the trees were purple. When I was born on the wings of the sea the water was rough and happy and gay, the time was then and is the same now for you and me somehow the time and time and time, we had now is gone and the time is bad, oh so bad, it tells you what you are and what you were to be soon and soon it will be gay it will be gay and gray on the wings of day, the wings of day . . . time and day, time and day.

LUCY TUTTLE

I was in an uncomfortable slime
With the alien voice of time
Falling on me like an anvil
And the leg of Mother Torture
Stomping on me
Squashing my bones
Like crushing ice.
I am in an egg of sweating bog,
Of Walruses with their tusks in me
Getting smaller, smaller, smaller
A hand reached me and pulled at me
It strangled me and choked me.
I saw a light
I am free.

MARK DOUGLAS

✳

One day there was a man from Mars. He
flew to Earth and crashed. Some people got
him but he died. I am his ghost. That is how
I was born.

SCOTT SCHMIDT

✳

When I was dead,
My mother baked bread,
Because it was the only
Thing she could do in her head.

MICHAEL DARWIN

*In my death I'll have fun. I'll . . . swim in
a tank full of sharks, whites preferred. I'll
try to flagpole sit on my toes, and have a fit.
I'll sit on a bus, eat ice cream, I'll stick my
tie in a printing press. I'll have such fun I'll
die of a heartache.*

JOHN BRAME

✳

*When I was born my mother
was smoking a cigar,
My father was playing his guitar.
The doctor had a smile on his face,
as he looked at me, the king of
the human race.*

MIKE POLODNA

✳

*I think of dying as a rush of purple color
flowing through my body and mind, washing away all opinions and beliefs, till finally
in a giant wave, it flushes out my soul and
sets it free.*

MARY JANE FARROW

Can anyone see me?
I have nothing on but the rain

Please stop beating me
I'm tired of your kind of love.
DARANCE CARTER

Love of mine,
can it alas be you
who float in time's great
glories that only my eyes
could once caress?

Come, let us make
fire for our
marshmallows of long
time separation,
and melt them together
in bliss.

You are mine, and I
yours, and this long
awaiting shall no longer
be an ache, just a
taste of humanity's teachings.
LISA SUMIDA

28. my sister

looks like a pear

Rattle a sheet of paper with your fingers (Kenneth Koch reports this idea in *Wishes, Lies and Dreams*). Rattle a sheet of paper, and ask, "What is this?"

Some people would say, "What does it *sound like*?" But I prefer "What is it?"

So someone says, "It's a sheet of paper rattling."

Great. But what *else* is it? If it'll help, try closing your eyes.

Then someone says, "It's rain."

"Rain doing what?"

"Rattling."

"Rattling on what?"

"Rain rattling on a tin roof."

Then someone says it's rustling leaves, it's distant thunder, it's a fish flopping in water, it's a thousand birds walking on a paper floor, it's a flag flapping in the breeze, it's a typewriter, it's fire crackling, it's popcorn, it's . . .

Okay. Everybody knows it's just an ordinary ol' sheet of paper. But it's all those other things too, right? Right.

So suppose you try to find something else, a real thing you know about that's just as ordinary as paper, and then make that ordinary thing just as *extra*ordinary as a thousand birds walking on a paper floor.

I am a turtle. I am as slow as a grape
curling up into a raisin.

SUSIE TROUTNER

✳

A pig is like a rubber balloon.

LAURA LYNCH

✳

A skinny man is like a sledge hammer.

KENNY GOUSSAK

✳

The pupil of your eye
looks like a hole that never ends.

JAMES CARPENTER

✳

The top of a cattail plant
feels and looks like a caterpillow.

FRANLYNN BUGG

Hippies are like humans.

DAVID WOOD

＊

My sister looks like a pear.

＊

Bloody eyes taste like meat balls.

KEITH GOTT

＊

*My sister sucking on a bottle sounds like
a cow walking through mud.*

ALISA ROSE

＊

*A pig's tail looks like a girl
who curled her hair.*

MYRNA H.

＊

*The pressure on your ears when you swim deep
is like the world falling on you.*

STEVE MASON

An old tire is like a dog curled up asleep.

TOM MOCK

✳

A fat baby looks like an egg.

JUNITA GORIA

✳

Cotton candy is like eating the clouds.

✳

An elephant reminds me of a clogged up hose.

TONY DAZZIO

✳

A flapdoodle is like a waddling noodle.

DANNY BURNETT

✳

A flamingo looks like a pink lampshade.

HEIDI MANN

✳

Spaghetti looks like worms crawling in dirt.

DUANE MARLER

*Breathing is like the soft flapping
of a butterfly's wings.*

∗

An old person is like an extra shoe.

It's fun. And it develops the most basic of all poetic
methods. Metaphor.

THEN AND NOW

I despised her then,
And now we're friends.
We never talk about then, now.

I wouldn't have trusted her with anything then,
And now I tell her my most secret secrets.
Neither of us think about then, now.

I told people terrible things about her then,
And now I tell everybody how nice she is.
I don't like to think about then, now.

We had different friends then,
And now we have the same friends.
Still, we don't talk about then, now.

My other friend didn't like her then,
And now she likes her a lot,
                (Better than me, I think)
But *still* we don't mention then, now.

We liked different guys then,
And now we both like the same guy.
I sort of wish it was then, now.

People liked me then,
And now everyone likes her more than me.
I wish it was then, again.

COLLEEN BUCHANAN

29. teachers

The people on the school board are profes-
sional students. They go through school
getting their degrees because they enjoy
school. So when they get on the board they
don't see anything wrong with the schools
because they like them.

But the average student who really doesn't
like school and knows what is wrong doesn't
take the trouble to get the degrees so he is
not in the position to be on the board.

PHILIP ONOFRIO

A pinkish-brown, sixteen-by-twenty photograph of Lena
Juniper hangs in the office of the Sparks, Nevada, elementary school which bears her name. Under the sacred fluorescents, from the cool, bile-green plaster, she looks at the
future through rimless, hexagonal lenses, from eyes long
dead.

I looked at Lena Juniper, in her silk-print dress and
meticulous permanent wave, and smiled at the recollection
that a few bridges in America are named after poets—like

the Walt Whitman in Philadelphia. That's neat—to name bridges after good poets, and schools after good teachers. Good morning, Lady. That's a mighty nice dress you're wearing.

Teaching's a lot of work. And I always liked that passage in *Let Us Now Praise Famous Men,* about the "terrible responsibilities." But I think I liked that passage because it mirrored my convictions about a philosophy of teaching, not because it showed me the daily war of attrition in actual classrooms.

The chance to work in the *Poets in the Schools* program has shown me that war—in spades. And it has shown me a lot of teachers. In any given school, the first place the official greeter takes you is almost invariably the faculty lounge. These rooms are a telling index of the general esprit, or lack of it, in the school, and a clue to what the classes will be like.

Some lounges are tombs; others rattle with busy gossip. In one, the bridge game lasts from September to June; in another, everyone's watching televised sports. Conversational topics vary radically—from deer hunting and football to teachers' rights to curriculum to problem students to last weekend's party. At one school, an administrator walks into the lounge, and all talk freezes in mid-sentence; in another school, the administrator is basically recognized as another person, and naturally joins in. In some lounges, teachers feel compelled to be on their most practiced behavior; in others, they joke, swear a little, and trade friendly jibes. Some lounges are casually, but not offensively, littered; some so clean they're sterile; others are pigpens. Some have anti-student cartoons on the walls; others have student art on the walls. One is like a doctor's waiting room; another like a ghetto kitchen; another like an automat.

All these details are tipoffs to an artist as to whether he will be able to open up that exuberant, light spirit which lives, somewhere, in every child. In a cold school, you often have to spend half your time chipping a hole in the wall, for some teachers resent the idea that any "outsider" could possibly have anything to show his students that he couldn't show them himself. And there are teachers who use the presence of a visiting artist as a pretext to go back to the lounge and play bridge, or to sit at the desk grading papers or making up tomorrow's test. There are the teachers who believe that discipline is the first requisite of education, and, since they assume the artist is too inexperienced or too nice a guy to tell students to be quiet, these teachers take it upon themselves to play policeman. There are teachers who insist upon introducing you, and they come on—in front of their students—with a glad hand and mouthfuls of fulsome flattery, in order to disguise their confused feelings of personal inadequacy.

And there are other teachers—the many others—who are among the most genuine, frank, compassionate folks I've ever been privileged to meet. And along the way, several have left strong impressions on me:

The assistant principal in one junior high has a paddle —a real oak fraternity paddle—and he uses it on girls, too. It's painted all variety of pretty, pseudo-psychedelic colors. Two words are worked into the designs on the striking face —"Peace" and "Love."

Farrington High School in Honolulu is big—about 2,000 students—and has a reputation for being the roughest school in the area. A lot of "underachievers," drop-out returnees, drug users.

I was invited to discuss the *Poets in the Schools* program with the entire English and Social Studies faculties. The meeting opened with a teacher's report about a survey the faculty had taken of their students: Did they like English better this year than last, and why? The teacher reported only early results (which were eight-to-one positive), and said she'd have more to say when she'd had time to analyze the lengthy, careful suggestions which *teachers* had written to accompany their students' questionnaires.

Occasionally, I've found a teacher or two who genuinely wants to know what turns students on. At Farrington, the whole faculty wanted to know.

It was a warm day, so I took the elementary students I was working with out on the lawn. Many of the teachers I work with sit right down and write along with the rest of us. But this teacher stood right behind me through the whole hour, feet spread apart and arms locked across his chest like a sergeant-at-arms. He occasionally interrupted the class, to order someone to shut up or be still. He never smiled. He never said "Please." For him, people who giggled and squirmed were "discipline problems," in need of punishing.

Between classes, I sat in the men's faculty room, editing student writing. I listened to this teacher, and five others, hold a round-robin conversation—the same conversation over and over, with only the names changed—the subject of which was the hardy-har-har ridicule of the clumsiest, stupidest, and ugliest of their students.

Only a private conversation. Sure.

During a social get-together at the end of a week, a young male teacher commented to me, "Do you find, among the teachers you meet, that many of them want to see you fail more than they want you to succeed?"

He then told me he'd been teaching for only a couple of years, yet he had already found himself becoming jaded, and giving in to the "bullshit things" most teachers do rather than teach. He thought my situation—getting to start over every week, and being relatively free of administrative impunity—probably drew at least as much jealousy on the part of the teachers as it drew admiration.

I do not think Dan and I, and others in *Poets in the Schools,* vaunt our freedom. It is, nevertheless, a circumstantial inevitability. And I had only to ask myself whether, in his shoes, *I'd* be jealous.

The key difference between an open classroom and a closed classroom, between one that is intimidated and one that is self-respecting, is the teacher. Of course, there are other variables: subject matter, required texts, grading system, peer-group power, length of periods, architectural design, quality of lighting, etc. But even where all these variables were stacked against the children, I have seen lively, smiling classrooms. On the other hand, in the very best-appointed and most promising of environments, a poor teacher can turn his classroom into a tomb.

In an as yet unpublished essay about education, my friend Bob Jaeger has written:

. . . the really important thing about a teacher is not what methods he employs, or what his personality seems, but what he is. How he is. Even psychological studies have failed to show any correlation between a teacher's methods and his effectiveness as a teacher; there is no proof that an easy-going teacher teaches any better than an authoritarian one. What psychology cannot analyze, of course, is what a teacher is beyond the shallow, outer manifestations of his personality. All the important things which happen in a classroom cannot be measured or graphed, because they happen inside. And all that a teacher can do is know how to help. The most, the best he can do is extend the invitation openly and honestly. But he must remain open, vulnerable, ready to change, and even to be hurt without throwing up all those defenses all over again. He must grow always, and begin to know himself without becoming petrified in that knowledge. . . . You can only give it by being it. . . .

Some teachers try to fake "being it": they apparently believe that classroom rapport necessitates a self-professed equality of *experience*: "We're all in this together, and I don't know any more about anything than you do."

Students immediately think, "Well then why the hell are you ten, twenty years older? Haven't you *learned* anything in that time? How come they're paying you to teach us? Or is the real reason you come on this way just that you're trying to hide something?"

But an equality of *respect*, that's another matter. It simply means accepting each student on his own terms, and trying to help each student become simply and fully who he is, or at least who he wants to be—*given* his youth, given his naivetes, his strengths, his talents, his cruelties, his needs. And then grades can be used not as a branding iron, but as a means to evaluate each person on his own terms, rather than pitting people against one another.

Bob Jaeger notes that the important things which occur in a classroom "cannot be measured or graphed." However, that does not mean that teaching teachers to teach, or the profession of teaching itself, is some kind of mystical, esoteric discipline for the select few. I am unwilling to believe that *any* teacher would not know *specifically* what Jaeger's intangibles are—what it means for a teacher to be undefensive about his weaknesses but assertive with his strengths; to be willing to reveal his private likes and dislikes, but unwilling to make his own taste the primary standard for judging either his students or their work; and to keep on trying, day on day, semester on semester, to generate enough mutual respect and love in the classroom that students can criticize each other's work without hurting each other's feelings.

I know these things are possible, because I have seen them in practice in classrooms scattered throughout America. I have seen them in teachers twenty-five years old and fifty; in strict teachers and in easy-going teachers; in biology, music, English and typing teachers; in teachers with and without families of their own; in teachers of both sexes.

All in all, I have seen the essential intangibles in damn few teachers. But that is not the way it has to be.

(Two pieces written while listening to the climax from
the first movement of Mahler's *Symphony #10*)

> I am a newspaper
> I tell horrifying things
> 2 bodies found in a lake
> cut to bits
> I tell good things
> 2 girls and boys born
> to Mrs. Voodingle Bunt.
>
> **CRIS DARLING**

⁂

I could be a turtle and be 1 hundred years old and
finally be so mad of being so slow and burst out of
my shell and be really pretty and dance and then die.

LISA SMITH

The circles keep coming closer
The circles are trying to get out
they squeeze through my ears and
out of my eyes
they meet, they link together
I've got a chain around my mind

long lashes
batting every second
like a clock
tick tock

Sound is nothing more than silence
A drain being unclogged.

SHARON DAVIDSON

30. share the darkness

with a friend

This one's always good as an optional choice, and the possibilities are endless.

If a lot of students can't get started, read out a batch of "starter lines." Tell the students that the idea is to use one of the following lines as a springboard. They can make it their own first line, then follow it wherever it takes them.

I was supposed to be sad, but . . .

I was supposed to be happy, but . . .

I wish my mother (father) didn't have to . . .

I was just coming up for air . . .

Sport is best in slow motion . . .

I learned a new color this morning . . .

Stalking the wind . . .

Digging, digging, digging . . .

When you're through washing your nickels . . .

I'd hate you somewhat less . . .

Blood puddle . . .

Share the darkness with a friend . . .

You're standing in my music . . .

Felt like a walking bruise . . .

But you don't hear them aching . . .

I smile from my knees up . . .

I wanted to run out naked . . .

In the congo of the city . . .

Sometimes my dreams are like a flood . . .

Like changes in the moon . . .

Most of these lines came from student writing. You can pick up as many as you like along the way.

> Are you seeking the sky?
> Are you sharing your life?
> Stalking the wind?
> If you are, you are with me.
>
> JERRI JACKSON

Night holding its breath
trying to keep a secret
from the world—It
cannot keep it anymore
and then in a sudden moment
as brilliant as the sun it is
tomorrow!

TINA GOODIN

WHERE DOES THE WIND GO

Where does the wind go when it isn't
Blowing?
Does it play around the trees
    Or play hide and seek?
When it plays is it strong
    Or weak?

No one knows,
Not you, nor I,
Where the wind goes
    When it wants to rest.
Only He knows the place
    The wind likes best.

KRISTIN DE NEAL

31. pre-fab blues

If you start from downtown, you get there by driving twenty-five miles out on the freeway. Look for the exit marked "Wishing Well Paradise": that's where you get off.

Fifteen years ago, Wishing Well Paradise's nearest claim to a wishing well was a pitcher-pump and a water-hole for the stock.

Nice meadow. Let's pave it.

Most of the parents have scaled that easy summit of The American Dream which goes by the name "success." But if one attribute of success is self-assurance, then the natives are faking it.

I base that opinion solely upon the alarming extent to which their elementary-school-age children write about "LSD," "heroin," "dope" and "marijuana." The ghetto high-school writers downtown don't write about dope half so much. And I don't think the little suburban students *use* much; few of them can even spell the names of the drugs. But many of them feel they *have to* write about it, because, well, what will your peers think of you if you don't?

Whatever that is, it's not self-confidence.

Over the years, I've worked on construction gangs in neighborhoods similar to Wishing Well Paradise. I've seen foundations go in without a single ounce of reinforced steel bar, and without a single visit by a building inspector. I've seen a complete set of walls carted in on a flatbed truck, and nailed up inside two hours. I've seen houses go from mudhole to landscaping inside five weeks. They don't call it ticky-tacky for nothing.

That might not matter so much, except I've seen families go together the same way, and develop irreparable cracks in the foundation the same way the houses do, and inside a year. Trouble is, though the houses are ticky-tacky, the people are still real, or at least trying to be. Especially the children.

Most ghetto students are economically deprived. Suburban children are frequently reminded they've "been given" "everything."

But "poverty" concerns more than the needs of the body. And many of the children in Wishing Well Paradise are profoundly impoverished. They're so artificially mature! We now call the '50s the silent generation. Maybe in a few years we'll be calling ours The Tired Generation. Used to be that children's bodies grew up before their minds. Used to be that children were given at least a few years of adolescent innocence before they were plunged into adult anxieties. But that's changing fast—appallingly fast.

The first of the following pieces is by an elementary school writer, the other two by junior high students.

> *You might have no sight*
> *But don't worry. Maybe it's*
> *Better not to see the light.*
>
> JULIA NICHOLS

The wolf howls out his misery—
For a world dying of poison.
A man-made poison
A killing poison
A poison born of shame.
The girls walking to school
Scrawl pollution on the window of an idling car.
This world is dying.
A death without honor. A death with shame.
And we are to blame.

MICHELLE DAVIS

✳

Nobody cares
Rotting carcasses
of doom.

Good night! and it was
but then you wanted it to last until
morning. I'd rather a thick milkshake that only
lasts a slurp than an endless, watery one that
leaves me belching moistly.

The mountain top,
The blowing wind,
And the sun
Glowing like golden bands.
Grass and ferns,
Trees, swaying in the breeze
and clouds
Shaped like dogs, like birds,
like you and me.
Everything I love
Becomes you in my mind.

Daisies in a meadow,
Stars dancing in the sky,
and us dancing in our own way.
All of nature,
Birds and bees.
Everything I love
Becomes you in my mind.

32. my bubble gum

is everything

What about all those completely ridiculous, zany visions, which sometimes pass through our minds?

> *Some guy running around without any pants,*
> *Thinking about Electric Elephants.*

                        ✳

> *My bubble gum is everything*
> *Without it I'm nothing*
> *My bubble gum is my life!*
> *Without it I'm a stone*
> *Heartless, lifeless, loveless.*
>   DAVE FOWLER

                        ✳

What is a kiss but a beard full of chicken noodle soup.

You know—moments when you go giggling, freaky nuts, and the spooky little people break out of the padded cells in your skull, and go trampling all over your "serious, well-ordered mind."

Everyone has such moments. Bring out one of your own and write it down. Quick, before it gets away—capture it now, and inflict it on all eternity.

Though we generally consider these crazy visions to be unimportant or frivolous, still, we rightly value few things in life more than a good laugh—even when it's a joke on ourselves. And before anything else, I want students to have *fun*. An education without a sense of humor is worth no more than a man without one, or a country without one. It's a pity that "recess" periods disappear after elementary school.

The self-conscious burden of seriousness is already heavy enough on everyone without making poetry another nail in the cross. I want students to find in poetry something which can both approach the hardest challenges life presents, and offer us an endless opportunity for joyous, creative play.

Our schools have suffered long enough under the harsh ethic that anything fun can't be worth doing. It's time to start a little educational pie-throwing, and plant sneaky little bombs of mirth in classrooms, with the same zany glee that we might slip rubber ice-bags under the cushions of our most decorous guests.

As I hear the silent crunch of Lifesavers,
I think, Thank God for the hole.

Miss Joleen Terry
went with Harry
in the park
when it was very dark.

JEANETTE LANE

my brother thought he might roll out the window,
    the window
if he moved his bunk bed in front of the window,
    the window
so he moved it in the middle of the room,
    the room, the room

KEVIN DALLON

Winking back at a street light
Jumping the puddle on a curb
Skipping through an empty lot
Had a dance with a city.

33. but the tears

didn't help

Remember that moment? Right in the middle of it you said, "As long as I live, I'll never forget this."

Even if it was years and years ago, you can still recall every detail—even the absurd little trivia that had nothing to do with what was really going on. Maybe it was something absurdly funny; maybe it was an incredible high; or a death.

When my grandfather went away for the last time, I was about six. I remember he gave me a fifty-cent piece. One of the old Franklin fifty-cent pieces. He'd *never* given me money before. And then it was a Tuesday, and I had to get dressed in my Sunday clothes. I'd *never* been in Sunday clothes on a Tuesday. We went to this funeral home. My mother was crying. And there was Pappy, lying on his back in a silky bed with the lid flung open. His cheeks never looked like that before: they were a funny red color, like Santa Claus' cheeks. And there was a glob of something that looked like snot but wasn't, and it was hanging on his mustache like thick mascara on a woman's eyelash.

I'll never forget that moment as long as I live. Do you have a moment like that, happy or sad?

THE CHAIR

I can still remember the day my father left us, my mother cried and cried, but the tears didn't help. He just got in the car and drove away.

The bills just kept coming in. My mother and I worked hard to pay them. For awhile everything was all right, except for the chair —empty at the end of the table.

One day he came back to us, my mother was so happy, but all he did was take the chair and left again.

SCHREEN RAEL CAPISTRANT

※

The tension mounted, she was there
and it was now or never.
I was a giraffe I had no voice
An ant, I felt so small, cowardly
suddenly I was a cat growing to
a lynx, a tiger, a lion.
Would you like to dance?
Yes
The answer russeled through

the grass, yess, yessss.
I was suddenly afraid in the meadow
singing my song of joy.

Those sunny-down days
Are taking me behind themselves,
To your green-brown air breathing
(Sweet-earth-blue-sky). Watching
Moon-bright words
Leaving you,
Becoming you in me
Like sun in trees
Or fall-spring days
(With a sprinkle of salt-cold winter).
We trade eyes
For eyes,
And photograph each other's weather,
Giving rain for rain-sad hearts,
Sun for sun-glad eyes,
Give me your heart to travel down
Until we reach your new path.
(If ever that may be)
I'll leave you (watching memories)
To your lost
Found way.

34. zeat, parluka, mereek, and munchgun

Climb into a color. And do away with all the trite associations. If you're going to be blue, say, then don't talk about sky unless you can find a way no one else has ever tried. And don't just philosophize: *be* a color. Try to follow it where you've never been, somewhere you'd never have thought of going.

> *Blue is a color of beauty, the sky*
> *Yet think of the sadness of the world*
> *The war we are in*
> *One day there will be no world for this color.*
>
> **ILENE DICKINSON**

※

> *When I spit on the ground I think Blue.*
> *When my baby brother picks it up and eats it*
> *I feel all the fun colors.*
>
> **RONALD LOWERY**

Red intense demanding overpowering
       domineering
my mother is red
Gray concrete solid staunch
       reflective
and so is my father

I live in a red house accented by
       gray
I would rather be the accent
       than the issue

ROBIN RONKEN

Maybe the color you want to climb into is a *new* color. Red, orange, yellow, green, blue, purple, brown, black, gray, pink—these aren't enough anyway. What, for instance, is the color of the sea at night? Of a cat's meow? Of the wind when it's crying?

What about autumn leaves? We could say they're red, gold, and brown, but that's just using a combination of the old colors.

So try it. Play Adam. Find something that needs a new color—or smell or taste or feel or sound—and invent a name.

Zeat—the color of a pig with chicken pocks.
Cragamajag—a squashed worm with butterfly
       guts on top

CHRIS YACH & RICKY LAWSON

*Mereek is the color of the moon having hiccups
and a dog having a rabbit.
Munchgun is a candle breaking up in laughter
and the sun burning up.
Goonick is the color of Mrs. Gasho kissing
Snoopy and a cloud wetting its pants.*

MICHELLE TERRY

※

*Parluka is a dog barking Chinese,
a newspaper singing a song.*

ELIZABETH STOFFEL

The boat sits lonely in the harbor
No one to help him.
Captive of the soul
The dark chamber of your innerself
The locks are closed for ever.

BRIAN FAY

His hair is soft golden
Shining in the moonlight
In the distance, guns roar,
And I tighten my grip.

MICHELLE JAEGER

Blue of the sea
Starch white
of the sand
Blood red
of my board
Sand on my back
Cool night breeze
on my salt crusted
face.
I wake up,
feeling numb,
my mind
floating.
I grab my vehicle
and paddle out.
I sit while
my mother laps
angrily at my knees
for intruding
into her perfect stillness.
She coughs and
sends a swell my way.
Laughing, I
catch this thing
that is supposed to
get rid of me,
taunt her, cutting
her beautiful face up

(continued)

with my skeg*
until finally, she
gives up.
And dies down
at shore, carrying
me back to home.

*skeg is the razor-sharp rudder on the bottom of a surfboard.

35. forms

A Mozart symphony and modern electronic music sound very different from each other. And if we are conditioned to forms like Mozart's, we may call the electronic music "formless junk." But a form which imitates twentieth-century chaos is *no less a form* than one which imitates the comparative orderliness of eighteenth-century Europe. Every piece of art has a form.

And so with an amoeba and a salt crystal.

A tree and a black hole between stars.

A crow on a fence post and a poem in mid-air.

Standard poetic forms are useful because, as we work with them, they force our attention onto syllables and phrase lengths and rhythms and the value of prepositions and conjunctions. As a composer must learn harmonies and rhythms and octaves or twelve-tones, so must a poet learn the common tools of *his* music. Nearly any writer has to pass through a stage where he goes around wearing words like hairshirts; pitches them like darts at carnival balloons for the fleeting prize of knowing "I did it, I did it"; tries to mesmerize the words to turn themselves inside out; and falsely endows words with a "life" and substance all their own. Having to work in conventional forms forces these discoveries, and generates the freedom these discoveries will finally yield when a writer pursues them with enough passion.

But the forced study of conventional poetic forms is not a process to be undertaken by the great majority of students. And the attempt to force one form or another upon them, often by teachers who can not tell you why they are doing it, has made poetry hateful to all but those few students who are clever enough to please the teacher. Many students have acquired the unfortunate impression that they can't write "poetry," simply because they can't write in forms which may have been best suited to the people and language of centuries past.

Yet students do write in forms: not often in classical forms, like the sonnet or the heroic couplet, but forms nevertheless. I sometimes offer students a sort of smorgasbord of forms, derived from the writings of other students. I pass out a ditto sheet with samples of student writing labeled by form, and invite people to choose one form and pour their own feelings into it. My list of "categories" is neither very complete nor very developed, but here are a few of the categories I've used, with summaries of how I've explained them.

PARALLEL STRUCTURE

Parallel structure, like any good form, is useful because it comes from *life*: events, hangups, habits keep recurring in life like the moon repeating its changes, or a song refrain. And when something *violates* the regularity, we are offered a rich poetic possibility.

I heard my mother fixing dinner
I would have food
I heard my father working
I would have clothes
I heard them both cry over me
I knew I had love

MIKE HALL

This particular example also shows how easily the form lends itself to the "twist." You set the poem up to go in one direction, then alter the direction violently in the final line or two. This can produce a very serious message, or sometimes a surprisingly funny one.

REVEALING DIALOGUE

Often even our "normal" conversation is a revealing indication of underlying motives. And one of art's responsibilities is to show us the secret behind the surface. (For examples of how this can work, see the chapter titled "IN OTHER WORDS YOU'RE ASHAMED OF ME, RIGHT?" or the poem titled "Later" in the "SEX" chapter. Indeed, examples to fit *all* these "categories" occur throughout this book.)

SHORT FORMS

We often see the world as if our minds were film and our eyelids camera shutters. A moment is suddenly caught and frozen, often by accident; but it stays with us, floating up again and again to the surface. The vision may be something serious or zany, but, whatever its mood, it often wants a short, sharply cut form.

*A tiny snail
like a bold warrior
off to war*

JAN JOY

✳

*A chipped tooth
A crooked smile*

*Sparkling at me
Sunshine*

SHOTGUN FRAGMENTS

Sometimes the events in our lives occur in ways that can be described in complete sentences. But equally often, we remember the events as a montage, or as a series of idle details, many of which may not have seemed important at the time—a broken cup, the change in a face, music in the next room, a dirty window, a dog barking outside. And sometimes a poem will take this form—a series of quickie vignettes which build their own effect.

*Dancing
Getting intoxicated
Dancing
Go to the ladies room
Dancing
Order a drink
lots of excitement*

my name called
go outside
talk to two strangers
cry
car door close
no handles in car
siren
embarrassed—head down in car
door opens
quietness
strange building
strip
shower
4 walls—closing in on me
window
car drives up
inmate brought in
prisoner—juvenile delinquent

BRENDA HORNSBY

VIOLENT TENSIONS

We are taught to keep different emotions in different compartments. But life is seldom like that. For instance, you can love and hate something all at once. Or you can be simultaneously repulsed and attracted by something sickening. You can discover that something everyone else thinks is supposed to make you sad really makes you happy at the same time. (Again, there are demonstrations of these paradoxes in student writing throughout the book.) Or something beautiful can suddenly turn horrid:

Summery nights, morning glory.
We had some great times.
We had the best.
Our love was like a swan,
Soon put to rest,
By a bullet in your chest.

NOREEN ARCHULETTA

The idea is simply to cast our vague, internal conflicts into solid form—to force opposing emotions or events to occupy the same poem just as they occupy the same moment or the same life.

RHYME

Many students still think that to write in rhyme means you have to write in perfect *end* rhymes. Except for the few who have a natural gift for it, those who try to rhyme perfectly often end up torturing themselves into saying less than they meant to, or reversing subjects and verbs into Victorian stiffness.

So I'll often include examples of "compromise" efforts, where some lines rhyme and some don't—or where the lack of end rhymes has been made up for by effective *internal* rhymes. In such poems, the main message of the poem comes through with a minimum of artificiality and a maximum of power. Encouraging "compromise" efforts in rhyme allows students to see rhyme for what it is—a possible discipline, not a straitjacket.

This list of "categories" can go on nearly forever: "Metaphor," "Personal but Objective Imagery" and "Song Rhythms" are three more I've found helpful. The point is, different people have different internal rhythms, different ways of perceiving the world. They may find one form useful to themselves, or none at all. I offer forms as triggers, or releases, not as requirements.

By doing this, I often get back a slightly higher percentage of structured writing than I do by priming the students only with ideas. But I don't judge the "success" of the exercise on the basis of that percentage. For it seems absurd to me to expect writing in rigid forms from young spirits who are still experimenting with the putty of their potential identities.

It's enough for me simply to expose the students to various forms, because these things take time. Ten years after I read my first sonnet, I wrote a sonnet. Like the forms of our lives, literary forms ought not to be rigid universals, but slow, highly personal processes of growth.

Freak out!
As the ceiling caves in, I notice somebody
watchin.
Jesus! But no, I don't even believe.
As the bed collapses under me, he speaks
But why should I listen? They're just

(continued)

words, nothing but foam rubber.
As I sprawl on the floor, the words begin
to spiral up, up
What are they doing! They'll break through the barrier
As my body begins to dissolve, the words break through
to my ears the words! My God! That's Jesus
saying them!
As the world begins to black out, the words
ring in my ears ringing, ringing. The words
HE said—

    Die, you DIRTY BASTARD!

I like death
What a wonderful feeling,
To chop off the head of a chicken
And see it running
With its neck flopping and spurting blood
High into the air.
I like death
What a glorious feeling
Of power and masterfulness,
To hold that axe in my hand.

36. the sun with earrings

"What's that on your hat?"

I was wearing a wide-brimmed, black felt hat with a round piece of filigree silverwork on the front. Got the silver in India, and it has a design worked into it: you can see different things there—a flower, a butterfly, a man's face.

Well *I* hadn't planned it as an example, but they did. So I tossed the hat to the nearest student, and said "Okay, what do you see there?"

They passed it around, and came up with everything I've already suggested, plus a "bird."

Then someone said, "Just looks like a lot of wires to me." I couldn't find a reason to tell him that was a wrong answer. In fact, it seemed like a good idea for a poem: "Met a dude who goes around with a gob of twisted wires on his hat. Thinks it means something."

But that wasn't all. A guy offered, "It's deeper than just how it looks, right? It's a symbol." (This particular class, by the way, was composed of alleged "delinquents" and "underachievers.")

Then the girl sitting next to him said, "It looks like the sun with earrings."

I felt myself turn slightly green inside. Why didn't *I* ever think of that?

So we tried a "hat" poem: "Any sort of hat you might like to be, from any time or place. But don't tell *about* it. *Be* a hat. 'I am.' And say what color you are."

I had the papers passed to me, and read them aloud.

Then we had an awkward minute or two: I was trying to guess what else might work. Well, maybe they could talk about their town. And maybe we could learn something about *sounds* in the process.

So we made a list: "Let's make a list of short words with different sound endings, and all write it down." *They* invented the list: "Boat, die, ping, blast," etc.

"Now let's try to write a line or two about My Town. But use words from the list, and other words like them. For instance, 'My town is a groaty boat of oatmeal.' If you don't like any of the words on the list, use one you *do* like. If you don't like the words as they are, add -ing's or -ed's."

This time, instead of having all the papers passed to me, I said, "Let's see how much confusion we can make. Just pass your paper to anybody, then we'll each read a line in turn." (At first, most of the members of this particular class did not want to be caught dead reading their own "poetry" in public.) I wanted them to read aloud instead of me not only for the communal joy of hearing different human voices, but to restore to written language its life-blood, which is sound.

My town is like a mass of fleeting greeting
meeting people, all with money.

My town is like a blushy rush of mush.

✳

*My town is like a lagged dragged old hag
with a jagged bagged putrid crag.*

✳

My town is a limp lamp.

Then I tried a series of "I am something else" poems.
For instance, "What kinds of balls are there? Anything
shaped like a sphere."

They answered, "Football, baseball, golf ball, tennis,
ping-pong, basket, rubber," etc.

I kept asking. Finally someone said "Eyeball."

"Good: there's a whole new dimension. Now what
other kinds?"

"Candle: sometimes candles are ball-shaped."

"Earth. The Earth."

"Planets."

"Meatball."

"Okay. So everyone pretend he's a ball—any kind of
ball you think of—and *be* it. And try to use sound-alike
words, or maybe a color."

(The variations are endless. Try to be some particular
kind of ocean, or river, or wind, or snow, or imaginary
animal, or musical instrument. What is important is that
you get people talking about the subject before they write
—to discover just how many possibilities there are, and to

encourage each writer to be his own kind of ball or ocean or whatever, rather than a general one.)

Then someone challenged. "This is dumb. What's the point in imagining you're a ball? Huh?"

"Because it's a way to show how you feel without telling it. Look—suppose you feel really desolate—alone, without friends, and dead inside. So suppose you just write that on paper: 'I feel desolate and deserted, without friend or comfort; inside, I feel dead.'

"That's kind of flat. But suppose you go out walking, and you see this tree. It's all alone, sticking out of a cliff, or maybe on a dirty city street. Parts of it have been broken, and it's long since been unable to grow leaves.

"Suppose you *just describe* that tree, and not say anything out front about how you feel: so that someone *else*, when he reads your description, says, 'Man, that's really desolate and deserted and without comfort—you must have been feeling dead inside. And I can really get into it, too, just from the way you described it.'

"Sometimes the best way to say what you feel, or to express who you are, is to be something else, to let something else have your voice."

I was offering an analogy and my own convictions rather than proof. The "hat" and "ball" poems were too goofy: the students couldn't see, and I couldn't see, examples of how being something else could be the best way to be yourself in a poem.

But the next day they wrote to music, and I asked them again to be something else. And the students provided several examples I could have used to make the above point. For instance, a student wrote, to one of the pieces of music,

I am a particle of air; small and very minute;
I can go anywhere: Does anyone want me?

I asked questions about the particle of air.
"Well, it's not attached to anything."
"Floats free."
"Source of life."
Then I asked, "Well, suppose I cut out the part about the air, and just leave the second line: 'I can go anywhere: Does anyone want me?' "
"You just ruined it."
"It wouldn't mean as much."
"The particle of air makes the whole thing."
Then I asked, "Do you know *people* like that? Like particles of air? People who are always around, but everyone just looks right through them, though at the same time depending on them?"

The students were proving it to themselves, through their own writing: when you find something else, outside of yourself, to tie your feelings to, not only does the writing carry more communicative power; the poem comes through *more you* than it would have if you'd settled for just trying to tell how you feel.

I carried the point a step further. "Maybe it doesn't matter so much when you put yourself into a particle of air. But it does matter when you put yourself into another person: and that's what you do every time you try to create a character in a story or a play. When you're seeing a character in a movie—a character you really believe—it's impossible to think at the same time about the man who wrote the lines the character speaks. I believe that is because writing often involves a surrender of your own personality or ego to the voice of something else."

I'm green dream snow.
I'm squashed by a dog's print.
I come from the angels having a pillow fight.
JULIA NICHOLS

Snow, heaven sent, hell sent.
DEBBIE LINDSAY

I seem to be a cardboard box
But really I am silver ocean dreams

They wanted me to look at the affixation
cromolating on the lower level of paradoxal
tidings in relationship to the matrix of
being.
But really I saw LOVE.

37. the deep dark inside me

Suppose you had a third eye—an eye which could see what your regular eyes could *never* see. This eye can be anywhere you want it to be, and it can see anything you want it to. The Hindus, for instance, speak of an eye right in the middle of the forehead—an eye which sees God in everything.

What would *your* eye see? Try to write it.

> *My third eye can see the deep dark inside me.*
> *No light.*
> *No vision of what I thought there would be.*
> *What there could be.*
> *I must make more of myself.*
>
> PEARL NESTOR

Now let's go deeper with it. Much deeper. Try to forget your ordinary sense of vision completely. Throw away everything you've been taught about the proper order of words and phrases, and just write the words as they come to you. Your mind is an unknown universe: step out into a part of it you've never been to before. Let your third eye see *that*. Then write what you see as if you were making up a new language, or as if you were in a dream.

three dimensional boxes
of all sizes in every
direction. Darkness,
still, but not cold
nicks and corners
deeper and deeper
I can see no
end. Caves, rocks
cement floors,
deeper, deeper
deeper still
Black rain
soaked trees
rustling in
the wind
A river, A bridge
A broken bridge,
A bridge burning
Dark sky. No stars
and no other side

SYLVIA GREEN

She covered him silently
And left the room

This which I hold in my hand
It doesn't cost much
It does nothing
But I cherish it—
For she gave it to me.

APPLE AND PEAR

Apples are sour
Pears are sweet
If you love me
Answer my letter

38. hawaii

Like many other things, creative fire requires *friction*. Tension. And friction derives from elements so common to our lives we tend hardly to notice them unless they change or stop. Elements like weather.

All the time I was working for *Poets in the Schools* in Hawaii, I had the feeling of a thick cushion of molasses insulating my senses. The unvarying climate—where the leaves don't turn, where you hardly notice a change in season—mellows, perhaps, more than the senses.

Surely it must be a very gentle and peaceable way to live—if you're used to it. It's difficult, for instance, to think of *war* there, even with Pearl Harbor on Oahu. It's also hard to conceive of Hawaii's native and neonative cultures developing the kind of antiwhite, brown-is-beautiful, violent defiance which has grown among mainland black people over the last decade.

I at once admire and fear for the innocence of it.

Buildings and freeways
Airplanes and tourists
Then why not Maui?

This island's a sardine can
This world's an avalanche
Then why not Maui?

Searching for a meaning
Searching for an answer
Then why not Maui?

Too many detours
Too many dead ends
Then why not Maui?

It's too late now
Been in too many blind alleys
Why not Maui, you ask?
Oh, God, why make another hell?

I know the man who split time,
B.C.——A.D.
He spilled his blood for me
    and Aunt Jenny, Uncle Billy,
and YOU!
Yet you treat him like a
worn out old tire: thrown in society's
junkyards.
His name, you use to curse
your failures.
Yet—with nails in his hands
(piercing the flesh, dividing the bone
think about that)
He said I LOVE YOU.
One soon day He Shall Return—
so pick Him up and make a TURN.

JOHN RUSSELL

39. giraffes to kumquats

"Which one's best?"

I've asked classes that question hundreds of times, and with a never diminishing glee. Because the question's a put-on. I'm not implying that creative writing can't be improved. Only that there's a place you can go in your own head where no one can grade you *against others* because there is no measure.

"You can't *say* which writing's best. It's just different people coming through, each in his own way." I nearly always get that answer, without having to strain for it—except in private schools. Particularly with students at the elementary level in private schools, that question triggers an immediate competitive brawl: "You tell us." "Let's vote."

I don't like private schools. And the excessive degree of ruthless, competitive selfishness they develop in their students is only one of the reasons. Student bodies are altogether too homogeneous. Since the children have known each other, all too well, for all too many years, not only are the peer groups almost perfectly totalitarian; there is, for all practical purposes, only one peer group. No buffers. And, at many such schools, student bodies are confined to one sex.

I worked with one teacher who's taught at the high

school level in both public and private schools. He laments that the creative quality of his current private school seniors isn't up to what it was among his public school seniors. I worked in his private school—where entrance tests are rigorous, and the IQ level is very high—and in a public high school across town—an exceptionally poor school, where the measured intelligence level is below even public school averages.

By the index of creative originality, the public school writers outwrote the private school writers three to one. That's not because the private school writers are *potentially* any less creative than seventeen-year-olds anywhere else in America. It's because their environment is far too secure, and far too unvaried.

I much prefer that huge, noisy, democratic arena of healthy friction which is the public school—hoods, Navy brats, coquette primadonnas, promising whores, intellectual superstars, teenyboppers, apprentice plumbers, and long-haired mystics, all thrown in together.

It's a whole lot more like real life.

A beautiful figure, doll-like face
words of softness,
hands of gold,
golden wavy hair,
clothes of rags
not of wealth,
little house made of damp mud.
Yet so beautiful,
blue eyes always sparkle,
smile upon this doll-like face,
a face that shows sadness,
yelling,
crying,
praying,
asking Oh GOD what is a WOMAN am I one!

BERNADETTE JONES

ODE TO A BIRD

With an evil eye look
    And a scar on her cheek
Bird really thought
    She was super-chic

Masculine clothes
    And Big Black glasses
God forbid
    If you missed her classes

We'd tremble and shake
    In our torn tennis shoeses
As we'd count each other's
    Bloody Red Bruises

We turned frightened eyes
    Saw her glaring stare
She roughly yelled
    "You left a ball out there"

"Take fifty laps"
    Bird shouted with glee
"Then hurry in
    And claim your *E*"

(continued)

Out of innocent girls
She molded men
And next six weeks
She's starting over again

L & S

40. no substitute

for love

The most important feature of our schools has very little to do with imparted knowledge, but a great deal to do with social habit-training. You don't need bells, and dress regulations, and chewing gum bans, to put across a subject. But you do need them in order to impress patterns on individual behavior. Our schools are crudely Pavlovian, but relatively efficient, industries of habit. You stand a fair chance of turning out products which will fit the big machine if you pour your raw materials into the vessel not once, *but twelve years in succession*—acceptable times for the toilet; acceptable times for eating; acceptable papers of passage from one room to another; acceptable form of dress; enforced punctuality, seven times a day, 180 days a year; and any deviation from authority must occasion anxiety, guilt, and punishment.

A junior high student wrote:

> *Four walls and a ceiling*
> *Four walls and a floor*

Isn't it getting to be a bore
That's all I see day after day
But education is a must they say.

The "four walls" *are* the essential feature. And "must" is precisely the right word, not "can", or "please." Tardiness is a far greater sin than getting there on time and then looking out the window.

Grades are relatively unimportant as indices of subject mastery. What's really being graded, and stratified, is people.

If the necessities of our society happened to correspond with the real needs of human beings, then we'd have a happier country—the thing students write about five times more often than anything else, nearly always in fumbling cliches, and nearly always with the same conclusion: "Why can't it be?" But the requisites of American society and those of the individual seldom correspond. As a result, the schools teach children how to go about acquiring most of the material things they want—but at the same time, and of "necessity," the schools withhold nearly everything the people most deeply need. Thus, a lot of students feel starved, lonely, caged, spiritually impoverished. Pictures of death, desolation, and helplessness occur with excessive frequency in student writing—from all backgrounds and intelligence levels, from all across America. Examples:

Laughing, who can concentrate? Why is it I
always get the giggles at the wrong time? If
it's good to be happy why do people yell at

me for being happy? Is being serious so im-
portant that you have to push away what
you feel inside and think what THEY *want*
you to?

❋

The gulls flying over give their
raucous cries,
The cars roar by on the freeway
to nowhere,
The cows in the lake, lowing so loudly,
chew their cuds,
The lions in the trees roar
as if ready to spring,
But me, what do I do? Nothing.

DAVID COTTLE

❋

Why am I always so lonely?
I can not help it. I was born this way.
I am despised.
I am loathed.
Others run at the sight of me,
but I'm not alone. All others
will some day be like me.

I've seen so many similar pieces—caves collapsing on
themselves, funeral scenes, claustrophobic rooms and hall-
ways—that I'm hesitant to believe it comes down to isolated

expressions of isolated neuroses.

Often, these expressions of spiritual collapse lash out directly at teachers, or at the general quality of classroom education. But it would be missing the point to accuse our schools as the root of the problem: in these times, public education does not direct America's priorities—it panders to them.

The point is, if you're starving, then you're going to find a way to feed your hunger. And if you can't feed it direct experience, then you go for the next best thing: indirect experience—fantasy.

And the short quick route to fantasy is dope.

In junior highs and high schools across the country and particularly in suburbia, students have voluntarily approached us: "Sure, man, anything—uppers, downers, speed, smack—I can get you anything you want in five minutes. And good quality."

"Are you *serious?*"

"Sure. Guy out there in the halls right now. I can go right to him."

The dope scene is older than ancient China, and, to an extent, it is entirely normal and healthy. Men have always been drawn to explore the largely unknown universe of the mind, and *some* drugs are an intriguing, if shallow, tool for making the unknown more accessible. But the plague currently raging in our schools represents far more than the innocent spirit of curiosity. It derives from a sense of desperation, and of emotional poverty.

In this context—of rules, educated wants, and substituted needs—I occasionally wonder whether Dan and I represent to the students a viable way to live, or a futile,

taunting dream. For we require nothing, we impose nothing. We invite people to sit wherever they want to sit.
Whenever they ask questions beginning with "Can we" or
"Do we have to," we answer, "You're the author: *you* decide." We assert that, by the nature of creative action, no
one can be judged superior or inferior to anyone else. And
we make it stick. Each student has an unconditional chance
to be real.

But in many of the schools where Dan and I have
worked, this invitation to freedom only goes on for the
three or four days of our visit. After that, it's back to
"business."

Sometimes our classes have been interrupted by assistant principals carrying lists of names—students who cut
classes illegally to be with us. Now, if we came on like
social crusaders; if we had some extraordinary power; if
we were authentic divines; if we were famous—then I could
understand this fact of class-cutting more readily. But Dan
and I are only people. Why, in American schools, are we
most often introduced as "a special treat"? Why do we
sometimes attract an enthusiasm which approaches desperation (and sometimes from administrators and teachers,
as well as students)?

It is obvious to us—from ten years and more of trying
to make a living at it—that what we are isn't of much use to
the priorities of the American way of life. But we are, in
some way, exponents of a deprived need in the American
psyche.

I found myself laughing bitterly when, a few years ago,
the Scranton Commission exhorted the President to exercise greater "moral leadership." It was such a pitiably effete

gesture, in a way almost childishly naive, and the term "moral leadership" is so feebly remote from the core of our collective emptiness. And again, what's wrong in the schools is only a symptom of it.

A junior-high poet, for instance, finished off one of her efforts with a painful allusion to the "gutter of unwanted babies." The point is you're as likely to find unwanted babies in wealthy private homes as in public orphanages. I find them right and left in every classroom I work—in what calls itself the richest, most literate, happiest, most compassionate nation on earth.

At the root, the challenge to turn this country is personal. For "dope" is not limited to illegal chemicals. And any form of it—an expensive car, fashionable clothes, a prestigious job, a fat expense account or weekly allowance—*can* become a self-defeating illusion, and, far more important, a piss-poor substitute for love.

The remedy for all this is not to be found in sedatives, psychiatry, or corrective legislation. We are wanting a far more difficult, intimate commitment. One son, one mother, one father, one sister, one daughter, one brother, one friend: one human being at a time: either we make it on those terms, or we lose the planet.

One son, one mother, one father, one sister, one daughter, one brother, one friend: one human being at a time: either we make it on those terms, or we lose the planet.

When you're doing something you hate,
time is forcing you to comply.
When you're doing something you love,
there is no time.
So what is time?

I'm zipping along on my cycle
the wind rushing by me
everything is a blur
I'm the center of all existence

ALLEN LEVY

I walk the same street each day
But today I discovered a crack

Laughter rings deeply in a faded face.
Oh, how the birds sing.

41. i'm trying to break through

and be my self

Our classroom methods are stubbornly democratic. Each person has his own, individual form of creativity. But only occasionally is that form the written word. Hence, in selecting the student writing for this book, I was anything *but* democratic. And the results are anything but a "representative sampling" of all student work.

Mostly, I've used writing which carries a high creative charge; if you press for a definition, then I must say that all "creative charge" means is a quality in a poem which stirs me, and others who've heard it.

I've also seen a lot of writing like this:

What is beauty? I mean what
really is beauty? Is it love,
peace, joy or maybe just doing
your thing. I think it's love.

I notice two things about this sample. One, it is a sincere (and voluntary) effort. Two, it is uninspired.

Perhaps this particular person's creative medium is not words. Or perhaps it was the wrong hour of the day, or the student's mind was elsewhere, or the moon was in Pluto. Or perhaps I used the wrong stimulus; perhaps I failed to inspire.

This is Rome, not Athens. It is difficult, maybe even artificial, to try to make a creative atmosphere in an American public school. Technique alone will not open the doors. At least part of my "success" at sparking people to write can be credited to my infecting them with my own creative enthusiasm. Invisible things, like *esprit*, count at least as much as practical things, like ideas to write about.

I've explained the best guides I know to get people to stop talking like robots and start talking like themselves. And those methods do indeed reduce the amount of uninspired prattle. But I always keep in mind that a student's writing may give no clue at all to his creative aptitude; my own efforts with a paintbrush, for example, are not even as good as the poem quoted above. Besides, if most of the world's people had the temperament of the poet, the world would be in far worse shape than it is. And a good many, perhaps wiser souls already claim to have what I know very well I'm going to spend the rest of my life seeking:

MYSELF

I am myself
not no one else
Not a dog or cat
or bird or ant or a

grasshopper or a
mother girl or boy
or man or woman
I have eyes like
myself and hair
like myself and
a body like myself
I am myself
Me.

JANICE WRAY

Often, when a person outside the program sees an un-edited set of student writing, he quite naturally picks the one or two pieces out of forty with fresh, creative images and raves over them. Nothing else should be expected. People read poems because they're looking for something fresh, or uniquely funny, or perhaps enlightening.

But for an artist to carry these same exclusive standards into the classroom is a sad mistake, because it blinds him to the creative spirits of all but a handful of the students. The artist ought not to be there to play critic. And in the classroom, sincerity should count as much as genius. A student who writes five lines of what appears to be trite, but desperately sincere, philosophical chaff may well be risking more than the student who peels off twenty lines of seductive, fresh, sophisticated metaphor.

I do not mean that talented students should be sold short; I look forward to being overwhelmed by their gifted spirits. But when I first began working in the *Poets in the Schools* program, I was operating under the assumption that I would not be "successful" unless I produced reams of "brilliant" writing. Nothing should be further from the truth, for sometimes a piece is so disarmingly sincere that, inspired or not, I can't help but respect it.

> *I'm me but the people around*
> *me don't think so I'm trying*
> *to Break through and be my self*
> *But my parents and teachers won't*
> *let me they want me to*
> *be one of them But I Don't*
> *want to I'm trying to Break through*
> *and Be my self God help me please.*

FOR WENDY

at night she reaches for the warmth of my body with hers—

> when I wake up in the morning
> she is clawing at the door, reaching
> for the freedom outside

> Or sometimes she tries to run from
> the music that fills my room

she climbs upholstered facades
of hidden woofers, tweeters
  searching for the bodyless voices

(continued)

not finding them
she goes to sleep on top of one of
the speakers

She is a wrecked tarantula
　　　her black furry legs and tail sprawled everywhere
as she repeatedly washes herself
　　　　stretching her neck to clean motionless appendages

keeping her coat beautiful
　　　　　not for me
　　　　　for herself

then jumping up and catting her persian way across
　　the worn rug
　　　　meowing at the door
　　　　bracing her back on the floor
　　　　clawing at the edge of the door, trying to force
　　　　　it open

　　　　　　　there is a duplex outside my bizarrely
　　　　　　　painted subworld
　　　　　　　And a lady must have room to move

I hear a rattle and turn around to find her shaking
a long gold plastic-skinned snake
　　　　　I slap her on the head for attempting to
　　　　　sabotage the speaker and she exiles herself
　　　　　in shame

to the forgotten cobwebbed cigarette butt strewn
　　regions under my bed

(continued)

I decide to ignore her for awhile
and forget about her until she retaliates
by sticking her head up at the foot of the bed
and chewing my toes

I begin writing and she starts walking on the paper
I brush her away and she tries to rip out
        the binding of the notebook with her teeth

                I slap her on the head again and she paws
                my writing hand reproachfully

"It was bad enough," she thinks, her paws trailing
wet ink all over the paper, "when he was trucking
around with that silly grin on his face and stepping
on my tail but why does he now persist in making
imageless scrawls?"

(She cannot know I fear unscrawled images
                        more than imageless scrawls)

Or later, I move in my still-erected consciousness
    and wake her
for she has enfolded her black and silken body with
    the midnight shadows of mine

                bright green eyes fiercely flash fluorescently
                and her mouth opens in toothy surprise

my begging hand strokes for her forgiveness—for patience
for she is too free for me to ask for her love

                                MICHAEL WOLTER

42. the maggots

I generally shrug my shoulders at paranoids who can't pinpoint their persecutors. But at Z High School, there were invisible ghosts of fear circling around us all week, biding their time and just waiting for us to make one, crucial slip.

Dan McCrimmon and I got the job done in the classroom. The student writing was of a slightly higher quality than we expected, perhaps because the creative friction was greater than expected. This friction was caused by the provocative presence of two "radical revolutionary maggots" (*maggot* is the label for "freak" at Z High School), namely Dan and I. Voluntary library sessions scheduled for about eighty were running a hundred and eighty: a lot of folks just sitting around talking among themselves, listening out of the corners of their eyes. It was the last thing on our minds to chase the "idlers" out. For the real, live presence of two freaks in their school was, I think, a healthy challenge to the one-dimensional image many of the students at Z have of "longhairs." Dan and I generated a lot of peripheral human interest.

But peripheral interest is not the same as really getting into people, and for a while it looked like that was going to be impossible. Hatred usually indicates fear: the community had to find some way to cope with us. Apparently, the administrators were afraid to attack us out front—after all, this was to be a blue-ribbon federal-state program, administered from "down at the capital." The administrators' alternative was to treat Dan and I as somewhat rare and expensive zoo specimens.

So sure, we've had our classrooms invaded by cameras before, and by tape recorders, and VTR gear, and observers —but never in such huge, cold helpings. Doors of efficiently engineered fame were rapidly shutting us in from all sides. None of the teacher-observers were writing, though we warmly invited them to; much like the tightly tied knots of their own black students, the teachers were keeping frigidly to themselves, making their own outer shell around the back of the room. I kept looking for a sledgehammer to break down the walls.

On Tuesday, I found one. One of the "maggots," a gentle, deep, quiet, talented girl named Meg Wilson, brought us the following piece of work. I read it aloud in class.

"LAUGH, LAUGH, GO ON AND DROWN"
(AN EXPLANATION TO A POET)

The Poets are coming, the Poets are coming!
Students and teachers are having a ball
Planning everything they'll do
"We've got $5,000 riding on this thing,
so you kids better not mess it up."
"Monday and Wednesday and Thursday

will be our days to hear the Poets."
(from 10:57 - 11:48)
There they are through the library
windows
I see a hazy picture of two
Men standing before a huddle
of living, half-dead students and
all kinds of cameras with zoom lenses
and tripods and tape recorder wires
running all over the floor to
capture all this culture and creativity
and learning for posterity
to gawk at.
In we go, but there's something
wrong.
The teachers sit quietly cold behind
all of us, aching to have us show
our hidden depths and
for the Poets to reveal our innate
beauty
but they are dreaming, they've
censored us almost totally and covered
us up so well unders layers of
crap that it's silly to think
anyone could dig through it all
(the stinky mess)
The teachers sit stiffly at tables behind
us sprawled on the floor and we separate
them from the Poets, the Poets!
We can finally see them
and look them over

They look at us
but I know they can't see
They're far away from our trips,
and our shells of so many
years in school keep us in
plaster paralysis
All they can see is our hard
outer cast and it's not very pretty
to watch them so free
tapping sometimes with hollow
echoes on our molded minds
And from my unhappy prison
I struggle to answer them
But blurts and spurts of beautiful
thoughts are so ugly that I
spare myself the pain of listening
to my ill-formed, out of timed words
and choose instead to remain
deaf, dumb, and blind (at least
for one hour)
And no answer can travel
from me to them
So it looks like they have
all the answers when they don't
The only difference is
they know how to talk
and we stutter and mumble
from fear and dullness
Maybe they'll knock away a
chink of plaster and some of
our own music will flood out

and sing
but when the Poets leave
only whispers of messages will
lurk ghostlike in the Silence
The Teachers will hold up our
faded songs "How talented you are"
they will chirp, while under our noses
and behind our backs, they pack
in the fillers to make our
creative roughness one
smooth shiny plane again

The library fits all the teachers
and they push us and pull us
(without really knowing) into
bookcovers and woodshelves
until all that is left are the
pitiful lifeless corpses of
beautiful young bodies and minds
But the Poets sing on
and we sink ever deeper
screaming soundlessly on the deck
of the school's Titanic while
Angels and Poets watch
from above (they have grown
wings to fly)

As a result of my reading Meg Wilson's verse essay aloud and talking about it, Dan and I got through to some students we'd never have reached otherwise. Nor do I be-

lieve we alienated any teachers, except those who were
dead set against us before they ever heard of us.

Unfortunately, however, no one thought it necessary
to inform us that the community's Superintendent of
Schools, a notorious chapter-and-verse conservative, was
present during that session. You see, that particular session
featured more than Meg's verse essay. There had been
some coarse language in the previous day's student writing.
In preparing the ditto sheets for reading aloud the next day,
I instructed the typists to type only the first letter of the
objectionable words—the rest to be replaced by hyphens.
Still, the words were there. And when it came time to read
the student writing aloud, those words were spoken.

The Superintendent heard all this.

And, in the same session, an extra class had come in—
almost entirely black students. Evidently, a teacher had
taken ill, and left school in mid-day. No other staff member
in the entire school could be found to babysit, so why not
dump the class in with the hundred-odd others who had
come to hear the poets?

I might not have minded if we'd at least been told in
advance: but all we knew was that suddenly four more rows
of fixed seats had filled up with a placidly defiant knot of
black faces. (Yes, fixed seats. Over our vehement objections,
several of our sessions were held in the A-V room—a small
theater, with *a stage,* bare white walls, blacked-out windows, a blinding, buzzing abundance of fluorescents, and
the overall charm of a Kafka nightmare.)

To crack the ice for our unprepared guests, I drew
from my notebook a poem of my own about blues music
and the black experience in general. The poem includes a

number of four-letter words.

Before reading it, I explained I would not read aloud those words, for reasons we could all understand. But the Superintendent heard all this.

After that session, several of the black students, particularly the men, would say "Hey man" and "What's goin' on?" as I passed through the halls. And there must have been fifteen or twenty blacks coming in to the voluntary sessions; several wrote.

Once again, having to rise to a very difficult situation enabled us to bring forth gifts we'd otherwise never have opened. But the Superintendent heard all this.

The next evening, just before our public reading, a reporter appeared from the Z *News.* He said he'd heard we were "radical white revolutionaries preaching violence and hate."

I didn't ask him *where* he'd heard that: he wouldn't have answered, and I believe I already knew. I gave the reporter copies of publicity articles about our work, explained the purposes of the program, and told him the one revolution Dan and I support is the provocation of interior, joyful, personal growth.

The reporter then told me he'd done time in the Army with Rod McKuen, and what did I think of Rod McKuen. I told him a quarter of what I think about Rod McKuen.

The man had come looking for a big fat red herring, to drag across the very next possible edition. He came away defused. We got about twenty ho-hum lines in the morning paper.

Our final days at Z High School went very well—judging by the amount of writing, the number of people who kept hanging around, and the enthusiastic (but still un-participating) teachers who expressed their appreciation for what we were giving their students.

Another Board of Ed honcho sat in for twenty minutes, and went away praising us. And both the principal and one of the assistant principals were with us throughout our final two days. (The assistant principal persisted in hiding be-hind a carrell, picking his nose, and, presumably, listening; one of the students cracked, "Can't you get that (expletive deleted) out of here?") Both these men were present be-cause uneasy parents had called to demand that their chil-dren not be contaminated by us (all our sessions are voluntary: *no one* is required to attend—we announced that every hour). Despite all these official distractions, the stu-dents' writing, plus their interest in reading and talking about it, plus our own persistent enthusiasm, all contributed to leave the faceless ghosts of fear no point of attack.

But thinking upon the subject of what that community does to its children, I now nearly wish I *had* come with both picket signs and inflammatory literature. One of Z's mag-gots is a guy named Jim Strang—president of the student council, and ex-center on the football team.

Ex-center, because Z High School's football coach "offered" him a choice: cut your hair or quit the team (ever get an eye-full of Joe Namath's hair? Roman Gabriel's?). Jim quit the team. The resultant public bitterness is a symptom of the deep, irreparable divisions not only in the school but throughout the community.

Spirit runs high among the maggots. Strang is a talented caricaturist, and his drawings appear in a series of communal "maggot-books," to which everyone contributes what he pleases—"Zap"-style comics, poems, letters to each other. The maggots put together an act for the all-school talent show: "The Sound of Maggots," including an original song titled, "Pass Me the Rutabagas." We spent two evenings with them: one, up on "the mountain" in one of their homes, the other in a pitiably ill-equipped but lively coffeehouse.

Spirit runs high among these people, but its primary source is desperation. For the feeling of "sinking deeper," which Meg Wilson's verse essay puts across all too well, is common among them. And I wonder just how much hostility the weaker spirited among them can stand.

Dan and I had never before been given a send-off at the airport; the airport in Z is miles from town; and we've no idea how the students found out our flight number. But one, two, three at a time, they started appearing. If I felt flattered they'd come, I felt far more heartsick, knowing that basically, they had come because what Dan and I represented was so rare to them; because they'd been *driven* to come.

If my prejudices come down on their side, I feel no less the sadness of the other kids—all the potential people who've been permanently shut away in prisons of proud hate before they ever had a chance to think about growing up free.

Dan and I have seldom felt so drained. Z sucked up every drop of energy we had to give.

I am a flock of birds
Sailing in the sun
Air cools in the spaces
My bodies all glistening
Flapping our wings in unison
between my feathers
blue red green mica shine
Upward and down contracting and expanding
My many bodies flowing in flight
Little beats song soft bongo sounds
Playing Flying
Way above everything playing with myself
playing Flying
singing beating soft soft drums

Meg Wilson

I LOVE MY ERASER

Oh eraser on my pencil top
I chew on you and cannot stop
My teeth dig in until they meet
and alas you're laying by my feet
Eraser I enjoyed you so
But now you're gone like the melted snow.

ALLEN LEVY

43. in other words

you're ashamed of me——right?

Most of our daily conversation matters only to the moment: business. But sometimes the talk points behind itself, to things of permanent concern: poetry.

And sometimes the best way to show the deeper meaning in our talk is simply to record it. So try a dialogue. Leave off all the "he said"'s and "she said"'s. Just listen in on yourself, or maybe on someone else, and try to write down the things which really counted, just as they were said.

> *"Come on—I wanna dance."*
> *"Aw, let's not."*
> *"But I wanna dance. Listen, listen to the music. It's great, don't ya just love it? Let's dance."*
> *"Naw."*
> *"Why not? The music's good."*
> *"Well, just a moment—let's go get something to eat."*
> *"I'm not hungry—I wanna dance."*

"*Well—are you thirsty? Let's get something
to drink, okay?*"

"*I'm not thirsty—I wanna dance. . . . Hey
—why don't you want to dance, anyway?
You can dance good.*"

"*You look funny when you dance.*"

"*In other words you're ashamed of me—
right?*"

"*Naw—that's not it, it, it's just that, that,
aw . . .*"

"*That is what it is, isn't it? Well the hell
with you . . . Hey—how about you?—wanna
dance? Let's dance.*"

A delightful variant on this idea is to make up con-
versations between things that can't talk. Bob Jaeger, working with his fourth-graders at East Elementary School in
Littleton, Colorado, brainstormed a list of possibilities onto
the board—that is, he started with a couple of his own ideas,
then got the youngsters to add more of their own. "Make
up a conversation between a *Dr. Pepper* and a *Sprite* waiting in a pop machine; or between the stomach and a flu
bug; or between a tree and the wind; or a sidewalk and a
bunch of feet; or two toes in a hot shoe; or a bare foot and
the earth (Oh dear, look what I've stepped in)."

THE PUPPETS

There was a puppet cousin and he had to sew the string that held up his arm that broke, as he began to walk he know he would be caught so he hide in a bag and did not know who it belonged to and there was milk and some candy bars and some pop in the bag and then there was a big rattle and he was moving and could not get out she or he would not put him down and then the bag broke down he came and then he saw that he was at the puppet's room and his cousin was there he had his arm sewed back on that he had lost and then the man picking him up and put a new string on one arm and put me in a box with some others I know their names. The clown was Bongo and the other clown was Johngo but the other was shy and new so we called him Bingo and then I was home and my master was worried about me he picked me up and put me in bed and so my friend went home and I fell asleep and I had a happy day and played as cinderella in a play I had fun and I got married and I had a beautiful gown and I lived happy as can be. Hi. Have a happy life.

BARBARA WINKLER

GHETTO BLUES

Subway stations, prison halls
Cold stamp rations, juvie walls
The upper rust of dope and hurt
The trashy streets all full of dirt
This is the ghetto you better believe
And ain't it a pity I can't leave.

LORETHA HALEY

44. not to teach,

to awaken

I have not presented my recipes-for-sparking-writing in any sequential order in this book. But I do in the classroom.

If I started out, for instance, by playing some music and saying, "Just write about anything you feel like," that's precisely what I'd get back—a splatter of trite abstractions.

We need a certain number of arbitrary, somewhat rigid vessels to pour our feelings into. And evoking poetry means, to me, provoking people into discovering something they did not know, rather than allowing them to settle for what they do know.

So I begin with simpler, more restrictive exercises— maybe "likes," or rhythm exercises, or colors, or dialogues— to invite students to try some tools. *Then* the free-association exercises—and again, *only after priming with examples of other student writing*.

Also, any exercise will occasionally go flat. I've tried an idea ten times, and harvested ten good sets of writing. Same idea, same approach. But the eleventh time, zilch. It depends on the particular class, the part of town, the hour of the day, the weather, and who was up too late the night before. All the more reason to offer options.

Further, I've been obliged by circumstance to develop methods which can inspire students to write (a) communally, and (b) in five days or less. That's an exquisite challenge, and it's a valid way to write. Valid because (a) each of us is—in spite of the incessant talk about "alienation"— part of a very large community. I believe each of us ought to be minimally responsible for sharing our creations with others, and for making our creations minimally intelligible to others. As for (b), sometimes short-term pressure yields better results than long-term discourse.

Of course, most serious creative writing is not done communally; it is done solitarily. And it more often takes five years or more than it does five days or less. So the very most I've been able to do is plant a few time bombs and hope they eventually explode; or give a push, and sometimes a well-placed kick, to people who are already well along the way; or to affirm creative talent wherever it surfaces, whether or not it happens to be *writing* talent.

All my classroom techniques are triggers or seeds. And the writing itself should testify to that. Most of what I coaxed out of the students is from that original, upswelling birthquake of raw energy—unlike those pseudoprofessional, at times heavily coached pieces of writing which win contests.

Nor have I included any programs for thorough study in the disciplines of poetry. I deeply value my own early training in both grammar and writing technique. But *Poets in the Schools,* by its very nature, is not intended to replace or to compete with the long-term learning projects which are the rightful labors of dedicated, full-time teachers.

A few critics of the program contend that it spreads itself too thin: too many poets, in too many schools, for pointlessly short stays. When a guest poet, who wants to work with the same students for four or five days, is carted around from school to school only for one-shot readings, the result may indeed be frustrating to the poet. But even then, the criticism is unfair.

As most of those in *Poets in the Schools* will tell you, we have nothing in particular to teach. At most, we seek to awaken. And once someone's awake, or wants to be awake, then that's that: the rest is up to him.

Anyway, I believe that the most real and permanent things in life are often the most momentary. A single inspired smile, or the sudden light of discovery on a human face, is more immortal than any great piece of stone or canvas or paper.

And for those things, five days is plenty.

WEARING MY REALITY TO SCHOOL

Reality is a green stocking cap,
planted firmly on my head.
A voice raised from on high,
"Young lady would you please remove your
    hat in the building!"
I removed it.
A smile of satisfaction from the mighty;
out of sight, around a corner,
on goes the hat,
my dear green hat,
my reality,
"You with the hat come into my office!!!"
Rules against hats in the building,
The mighty on high says,
He will suspend me,
for wearing my reality to school.

TIA BERG

45. biting the hand
that feeds

One thing has particularly distressed me about *Poets in the Schools* ever since my introduction to it. The program involves—I suppose it can only afford to involve—artists who happen to be "socially acceptable." I clearly recall working in one state where those with mustaches or beards were hardly allowed to work at all. A few of them were invited to the initial planning conference, and were allowed ten minutes each to audition before an assembly of teachers and administrators. But when it came to choosing, the choosers were local administrators. When I asked the state director of *Poets in the Schools* why the hairier artists weren't getting offers, she replied that of course the decision had to be left in the hands of participating schools. Incidentally, I got the clear impression that by asking such a question, I had pretty well scrapped my chances for working that state in the future.

If she thought I was implying she was gutless, she was right.

The Summer 1973 issue of *West Coast Poetry Review* was completely taken up with articles by writers who have worked in the *Poets in the Schools* program, and included excerpts from this book. One of the essays in the *Review* was by Bill Ransom.

I appreciated the wealth of information in Mr. Ransom's article, the obvious care with which he put it together, and his deep compassion for the students. One paragraph in Mr. Ransom's essay especially attracted my attention:

Many administrators in the school system share the opinions of the public concerning the behavior, or misbehavior, of artists. We have all seen TV shows that prey on the stereotype of the artist as swishy, headstrong, fluctuating in and out of reality, devoid of common sense, incompetent and useless to the community at large. Consequently, we often expect that to administrate a program consisting primarily of artists would be to suffer through tantrums, tardiness, irresponsibility, and shameless morality suits. Administrators, like the public itself, have to be exposed to artists in order to be convinced that artists, too, are human, that they do not eat their young or anyone else's, that they may even be skilled mechanics or carpenters or mothers or fathers. Indeed, many administrators are surprised to discover that artists CAN function within proscribed timetables, and are ecstatic when they find that some artists even ENJOY working within regular schedules.

But many artists *are* headstrong. They *do* fluctuate in and out of reality (how can you be an artist and *not* do that?). And though they are seldom devoid of common sense, they may have little expertise in the diplomatic proprieties which are tacitly expected of artists in the program. Artists are not prone to public tantrums, but many of them are not hesitant to state their beliefs.

If a student brings in an exceptional piece of work between classes, the artist may very likely be "tardy" to the following class. And though most artists are not prone to go out looking for "shameless morality suits," the morality they observe may not have everything in common with the morality of *Poets in the Schools* administrators. They do not eat anyone's young, but few of them are skilled mechanics or carpenters. They are artists. And though they CAN function within "proscribed timetables," they sometimes find themselves, and the students, in conflict with the school's regular schedule. I fail to make any connection between the presence or absence of *any* of these qualities and Mr. Ransom's apparent desire to demonstrate that "artists, too, are *human.*"

I don't happen to have a beard or mustache. But I know a lot of folks who have both those and more, and who—irrespective of their merit as artists and irrespective of their ability to turn students on—are therefore refused work in the program.

With the possible exception of Matthew Arnold, I find it difficult to think of many major writers at work before 1900 who would be welcome in a classroom. And after 1900, the list gets pretty short after T. S. Eliot and Edgar Guest and maybe Rod McKuen.

A lot of effective, genuine people are doing important work in this program, which has indeed served to break down some of the cultural barriers between artists and the rest of society. But it needs to be recognized that none of us would be permitted access to classrooms unless we fit a very specific, well-mannered, social profile. To that extent, the program, like the society which funds and administrates it, is not all it could be.

I remember sitting one day in a state director's office, and his telling me, "You're one of the Beautiful People, and that's really what we're looking for." Though I didn't get up and urinate on his desk, I seriously considered it.

This place took me and hit me
A blow so fast and hard
And I crouched down with my tail between my legs.
Then I followed it. I heeled. I tried to get along
And it kept me chained behind in its back yard.
I was trained, no longer free,
as the way I used to be
before I came and lost all I once had.
And then you came along
And you sang with me your song
Which was the key to the chains around my head.
You showed me things I used to know
My memory flashed like stars
And I'm breaking through like sunlight through the clouds.
Though you are leaving
I can find my way somehow
But thank you. To be free, I am so proud.

BECKY MOORE

46. child,

fly blind, fly blind

The building's striped all candy pink and white, to resemble an old big-top. And inside is the all-time, high-time, casino of casinos: they call it *Circus Circus*. And it's in the all-time, high-time, city of American Cities: they call it Las Vegas.

But they shouldn't have stopped at twice. They should have called it *Circus Circus Circus*. For like the circus itself, *Circus Circus* is a symbol of life. And it has three magical levels.

The second, or middle level, opens outward off a huge, elliptical balcony-walkway. It's the arcade, for the kids "from seven to seventy," as they say.

There you can see the dirty peep show: "Adults only. X-rated. See the live naked dancing girl. She wiggles, she's gorgeous, she's exciting. She's got it and she loves to show it."

Or you can throw darts at balloons, and win a doll. An IBM computer will punch out your star-chart. You can blow up a photograph to a two-foot-by-three-foot poster of *yourself*! There's a shooting gallery and a handwriting analyst. At the "Magic Mansion," you can buy your own tricks. Every fourteen seconds, an electronic recording beckons you in: "You CAN fool all of the people all of the time. You can even fool your WIFE. It's MAGIC."

Abraham Lincoln might shudder, but after all: it sells.

Mid-level is where you leave the youngsters. They're not allowed, you see, on the main (lower) level. But they can look down onto the gaming floor (just as in a slaughterhouse, you can look down onto the kill floor).

Rows and rows of slot machines. Blackjack and poker tables, craps, a wheel of fortune. Half-naked, beautiful women wait at your elbow, to make change, to bring you a cocktail or a hamburger, to empty your ashtray. You won't feel a thing, till you've blown your last nickel.

Hark! On a mike at one end of the balcony: a real live old-time *ringmaster*. "Laydee-e-e-eez and Genndullmun, your attention please; all eyes to the highest point in the arena."

The highest point. Look! There's a *man* perched on a tiny platform sixty feet above the kill floor.

Far below, inside a ring of craps tables, the floor opens, like the doors into hell.

And what do we see? Volcanic fires? No—a tiny mattress of foam rubber, on top of a somewhat more efficient pneumatic cushion.

The Wurlitzer organ finds suspense pitch. The slightest deviation, and the daredevil's an instant corpse. Now don't close your eyes: yes, Matilda, he's really going to dive.

And there he goes—falling, falling, falling, like a slow-motion dream. Thwap! You can hear the sudden hiss of air.

And the old Wurlitzer squeals with joy, as the man rises from his foam-rubber deathbed, smiling and bowing.

As if this were not enough, *Circus Circus* has a long, slotted rail built into the ceiling, with a *bicycle* attached to it. You can't see the man on the bicycle very well, though, because he's dressed in black and the spotlights avoid him. But you *can* see the gilded cage he's pedaling around the track, and the cage holds four—count 'em, *four*—bikinied go-go girls, shaking their hips as if they were in heat, and shooting long, squeaky, phallic balloons at you through the bars. All the while, yet another beautiful girl on the balcony sings "Love Makes the World Go Round."

"Love Makes the World Go Round." My Zen funny-bone took a triple spiral fracture.

But the best act on the monorail is the dapper don who pedals the bicycle *in* the spotlight, *upside down*. And he's holding a woman. By his *teeth*. And she does trapeze tricks, all the way around, and all the way is at least 350 yards.

No net. The popcorn catches in your throat. You keep thinking he can't bear it a second longer; he's going to let go, and the beautiful Hilda will plunge to her death on a craps table.

And it suddenly breaks through to your vacationing mind: the people up there are REAL.

Circus Circus can do violence to your mind. For instance, how can you think of the people at the baccarat table, throwing out their twenties, their hundreds—risking nothing—and in the same instant, think of that man keeping 130 pounds of human being from death solely by his teeth?

How can you do it? Well you just *do*, that's all. Because they're all there, under one roof. Just like life.

And let's not forget the invisible people in the control booth. And the architect, who was paid off long ago and doesn't come around much any more. And the owner, who fulfilled a boyhood dream. After all, it's not every day you can walk off the street and straight into the *Divina Commedia*.

One of the high trapeze acts features a *six-year-old child!* And he does part of the act BLIND. They tie a black cloth sack over his head, like they used to put on people before they chopped off their heads. And then the child swings out there on the high trapeze, lets go, somersaults, and waits for the guy on the other trapeze (his father) to catch him.

BE AS A CHILD. FLY BLIND. DON'T WORRY. TRUST ME. I'LL CATCH YOU. CHILD, FLY BLIND, FLY BLIND. Be as dust at the feet of the Master. Child, fly blind, fly blind.

I left the *Circus-Circus*, and I left humbled. I walked to the parking lot, slithered into the vomit-pink Ford Pinto the Nevada Council of the Arts had hired for me, and galloped out into the desert.

There, late in the afternoon, I came upon Paiute cliff ruins, circa 800 A.D. The Paiutes left some pictographs, scratched into the rocks.

More recent contributions include "Bob + Elsie," "Fred Fucks With Freda," etc. Also a cinder-block crapper, concrete picnic tables, a parks-department marker, and very numerous shards from broken beer and wine bottles.

R-r-r-rip! I tried to believe there's really no qualitative difference between Paiute pot-shards and twentieth-century bottle fragments. But it didn't work very well, and I couldn't help remembering the two-hundred-odd artificial horses under the hood of the Ford Pinto, waiting to trample a century to dust—and the hundreds of hydrogen megatons, sealed into shiny metal pills, waiting to be swallowed by our just and honorable politicians, waiting to be released by their stomach acids, waiting to splatter the guts of a very small planet over a tiny corner of the cosmos.

There was one tree there, and a bird sang. I wondered if there were birds like that a thousand years ago.

I wonder what the Paiute children learned. Actually, all children in all the world at all times have only one thing to learn. But it is a hard thing. Maybe it is too hard, and that is why many old and wise people say we are doomed.

NBC News once telecast a report from the Hopi reservation at Old Oraibi, Arizona. The mud walls of Old Oraibi have stood for 600 years longer than this muscular infant we call America.

The white men are strip-mining the soil of the Hopi. But the men of the tribe say the white men are taking out more than coal: Old Oraibi is a sacred place; the mouths of machines are eating on the heart of Mother Earth. The metal worms are eating in the place where all things are joined.

The Hopi say that the vision of spiritual masters is a necessity in the high councils of the world. Accordingly, the Hopi invited the President of the United States to sit in their lodges.

The President does not come. How could he? How could we accept such a leader? We who have *advanced* so far beyond primitive superstitions, we who see so quickly through the embarrassing hallucinations by which ignorance explains itself. We who have developed "the courage of despair" to cope with the purposeless stars and the scientists whose findings are *true* because they are based on *fact*. How could we accept a leader who went humbly before primitives, and asked for their wisdom and guidance? Surely we would find him infirm.

Wandering the Paiute ruins, I wondered what Paiute children felt when they first discovered the stars. They had no reflector telescopes. They did not know relativity theories and quantum physics. They had no electron microscopes, not even electric lights. They did not even *know* that the earth is round.

But I bet they had some poetry. I bet they sang. I bet they *knew* what it is that all children either conquer or forfeit to history.

It was quiet out there by the unimproved road, just at the feet of what, a mere million years ago, were underwater mountains. It was real quiet.

The bird sang again. Yes, there must have been birds like that, even that long ago.

I didn't feel creepy, but I felt alone. I stooped for a handful of sand, and squeezed it through my fingers. For a while, I stood by a big cactus and listened to the wind blow music through the spines.

But then the sun went behind the mountain, and I thought, "Shit. What if the car breaks down out here? You don't even have a coat with you. No food. Long walk, huh?"

So I climbed back in the puke-pink Pinto. The radio

was on, quietly, and there was a lot of static. I was dislocated. I honestly *expected* to hear that radio play a live, Paiute war chant.

I drove across the desert, back onto the highway, and over the last rise. I really didn't expect to see anything, except maybe the edge of the world. I for sure didn't expect to see Las Vegas, Nevada, a long thin line of neon cut like a bloody eyelid across the dusk. It looked like a spaceport.

Maybe the Paiutes had a science-fiction writer. If he was really a good one, he could have foreseen Las Vegas. And if we had any really good ones *now*, we would be as unbelieving of their tales as the Paiutes would have been of the story of Las Vegas. We couldn't *afford* to believe such writers, of course, because if we did, we would have to judge ourselves "illiterate" and "primitive," no less so than the Paiutes are by our standards.

And even our Plato, our Copernicus, our Edison, Ford, Freud, Einstein—what is any of them, but a little child flying blind and not knowing it? How long before we begin to comprehend the extent of our own ignorance, and fathom the hallucinations of "fact" by which we explain our ignorance to ourselves? . . . we who are so clumsy and ill-prepared before even the crudest moments of mortal wonder.

How long, before we strive to reawaken the wise child within us all, the ancient child which hears the voice of our deepest desire: "Let go. Don't worry. I'll catch you. Child, fly blind, fly blind."

acknowledgments

MY THANKS TO the students, teachers and administrators at:

Bonanza Elementary School
Las Vegas, Nevada

Caliente Elementary School
Caliente, Nevada

Casady School
Oklahoma City, Oklahoma

Central Junior High School
Anchorage, Alaska

Cheltenham Elem. School
Denver, Colorado

Clark High School
Las Vegas, Nevada

Clark Junior High School
Anchorage, Alaska

Chugiak Junior-Senior High School
Chugiak, Alaska

Deadwood Elementary School
Deadwood, South Dakota

Dimond High School
Anchorage, Alaska

East Ely Grade School
East Ely, Nevada

Ely Grade School
Ely, Nevada

Farrington High School
Honolulu, Hawaii

Ferron Elementary School
Las Vegas, Nevada

George Washington High School
Denver, Colorado

Herron Elementary School
Las Vegas, Nevada

Holland Hall School
Tulsa, Oklahoma

Huntsville High School
Huntsville, Alabama

Ilima Junior High School
Ewa Beach, Hawaii

Incline High School
Incline Village, Nevada

Iolani School
Honolulu, Hawaii

Isaac Newton Junior High School
Littleton, Colorado

Lead High School
Lead, South Dakota

Lena Juniper Elementary School
Sparks, Nevada

Lincoln High School
Tacoma, Washington

Lovelock Elementary School
Lovelock, Nevada

Lovelock High School
Lovelock, Nevada

Matt Kelly Sixth Grade Center
Las Vegas, Nevada

Mears Junior High School
Anchorage, Alaska

Moore Elementary School
Denver, Colorado

Mt. Tahoma High School
Tacoma, Washington

Nevada Girls Training Center
Caliente, Nevada

North High School
Denver, Colorado

Pohakea Elementary School
Ewa Beach, Hawaii

Putnam City West High School
Oklahoma City, Oklahoma

Reno High School
Reno, Nevada

Romig Junior High School
Anchorage, Alaska

Sheridan Junior High School
Minneapolis, Minnesota

South High School
Fargo, North Dakota

South High School
Minneapolis, Minnesota

South St. Paul High School
St. Paul, Minnesota

Sparks Jr. High School
Sparks, Nevada

St. Mary's Academy
Littleton, Colorado

St. Paul Open School
St. Paul, Minnesota

Stadium High School
Tacoma, Washington

Traner Junior High School
Reno, Nevada

Valley High School
Las Vegas, Nevada

Weatherly Heights Elementary School
Huntsville, Alabama

Wendler Junior High School
Anchorage, Alaska

West High School
Denver, Colorado

Wilson High School
Tacoma, Washington

Also, my thanks to:

Laura Richards, for "Little John Bottlejohn," in *Tirra Lirra,* published by Little, Brown and Company.

George Braziller, Inc., for permission to reprint from *The One Real Poem Is Life,* by Douglas Anderson. Copyright © 1973.

West Coast Poetry Review, for permission to reprint from William Ransom's "Artists in the Schools" (*WCPR* #8), and from my own articles, "I've Decided That When I Grow Up I'm Going to Be a Kid" (*WCPR* #8) and "Biting the Hand That Feeds" (*WCPR* #10).

And my eternal gratitude to F. Bird—for the "Wee Folk" tale, and for loving, positive criticism of the revisions of this book and of my life.

index of titles and first lines

index of titles and first lines